A CASE FOR A FEDERAL INDIA

A Study on Comparative Federalism

SIDDHARTH SRIVASTAVA

INDIA • SINGAPORE • MALAYSIA

Notion Press Media Pvt Ltd

No. 50, Chettiyar Agaram Main Road,
Vanagaram, Chennai, Tamil Nadu – 600 095

First Published by Notion Press 2021
Copyright © Siddharth Srivastava 2021
All Rights Reserved

ISBN
Paperback 978-1-68538-940-6
Hardcase 978-1-68563-942-6

Contents

Acknowledgements

First and foremost, my sincerest gratitude to my parents and my elder brother, without whose guidance and support, I may be a headless chicken running around finding my place in the world.

I must mention that writing this book would not have been a possibility without a first-rate researcher to guide me through the labyrinth of authorities, archives and databases across four nations through various research portals, unbeknownst to my technologically challenged self. Therefore, I acknowledge the tremendous assistance from Ms. Nikita Sinha, Legal Associate at ABN Amro, Amsterdam, who arduously spent hours providing me with ready access books, articles, manuscripts and case laws from various nations across the world. I am fairly certain that her diligence and resourcefulness have added more to this book than she realises. It is pertinent to mention that Nikita's help would not have been possible without the support of Leiden Law School's library which houses an enormous volume of authorities.

My gratitude to Hon'ble Mr. Justice R. C. Lahoti, Former Chief Justice of India for his legal sermons and lectures which tremendously helped me develop an understanding of comparative constitutional law. A constitutional scholar himself, my stint at his esteemed office enabled me to think beyond the contours of the observations and judgements of the Hon'ble Supreme Court of India and ignited an interest towards comparative constitutionalism.

I must convey my indebtedness to Hon'ble Mr. Justice Rajive Bhalla, Former Judge, Punjab and Haryana High Court. I would write "Justice (Retd.)" instead of 'Former' while addressing his lordship but he always refutes stating "a judge always remains a judge, he never retires". Each day in the office he would disquisition his juniors on court craft and reading of the law. I have learnt tremendously at his office under his tutelage, along with his sons Shubham and Yajur, who have prodigiously guided me in my very nascent career.

My sincerest gratitude to Mr. Ashok Kumar Singh, Senior Advocate, Supreme Court of India. I have learnt a great deal about academic writing from Mr. Singh. His knowledge of law of arbitration is second to none and I owe much to him for imparting his knowledge to his juniors. I distinctly remember revising a research paper atleast twenty times under his tutelage. His eye for detail and perfectionist nature is what young lawyers like me strive to accomplish.

I shall forever be indebted to Prof. Ved Kumari, Vice Chancellor, NLU Odisha and Former Dean, Faculty of Law, University of Delhi. One of the finest professors in legal academia, I owe much to her lectures at University of Delhi.

My sincerest gratitude to Mr. Praveen Mahajan, Managing Partner at Equi Law Partners, one of the finest trial lawyers I have ever witnessed. I have learnt enormously from my stint at his chamber and I state this without reservation - his reading of the law and court craft surpasses most in the legal profession.

My indebtedness to Mr. Arpit Batra, Spl. Public Prosecutor for Income Tax Department. I owe my development as a legal professional in the early stages of my career largely to him. A fine criminal lawyer, most of my internships including my very first job at the Office of Hon'ble Mr. Justice R. C. Lahoti, are owed to his investment in me. For that, I am forever indebted to him.

My gratitude to Dr. Amrisha Pandey, Asst. Professor at Gujarat Maritime University for her invaluable lessons on academic writing. Her guidance has been invaluable in my research and academic endeavours.

Not a word in this book would have been possible without the efforts of the aforementioned persons. For this, I am eternally grateful to them.

Introduction

Federalism is a structure which provides a certain degree of autonomy to the States while simultaneously creating a unified central government in charge of national affairs. It is therefore a two-tier structure i.e. it has a double government, one for the Union as a whole and one for each State. Each government derives its powers from the Constitution of the Federation, which in some cases allows the States to have their own respective Constitutions, as in the U.S.A. Therefore, a federation is a union of several independent States coming together to form a unified nation which mutually benefits all such States, thereby permitting them to present a unified stand against any external threats and promoting collective economic prowess. The Union guarantees each State certain rights, protections and freedoms to handle its own affairs. This is the basis of a federal government.

A federation, however, is not a foolproof system and suffers from various fallacies, discrepancies and imperfections or flaws. Since the inception of the principle of federalism, several disputes have arisen between the States vis-à-vis the Union and between two or more States with regards to the distribution of powers, which at times have even led to civil wars, if not fall of federal governments (see Southern States' revolt against Federal Govt. in U.S.A.[1]). The Federal Courts have had to adjudicate countless number of such disputes and lay down interpretations of the Constitutions which benefits the Union as a whole and keeps the freedoms and rights of the States intact.

Since 1787 when the first federation of the world came into existence i.e. U.S.A., several other nations have adopted the federal structure including Australia, India, Canada, Switzerland among others. However, one peculiar thing to be noted in the subsequent federal structures is that they have appropriately modified their versions of federalism and adopted several safeguards in their respective Constitutions, learning from the

---

1   Hubbard, Charles (2000). The Burden of Confederate Diplomacy. Knoxville: University of Tennessee Press. p. 55. ISBN 1-57233-092-9; *Tikkanen, Amy (June 17, 2020). "American Civil War". Encyclopedia Britannica*

experiences of other nations. For example, the Constitution of U.S.A. does not enumerate all the subjects in their Legislative Lists, that is to say, it only enumerates the subjects on which the Union can legislate and leaves the rest to States, which has resulted in several conflicts between the Union and States pertaining to transgression of each other's legislative spheres. Subsequently, the respective Constitutions of Canada and of India have tried to make the Legislative Lists as exhaustive as possible through an attempt to exhaustively enumerate almost all subjects which could be legislated upon by dividing them into three Lists.

Therefore, almost all the federal Constitutions of the world are different from each other in one respect or the other. The problem which has therefore arisen is that the Constitutions which deviate from the Constitution of U.S.A., considered to be a purely federal Constitution, have been characterised either as quasi-federal or watered-down federalism by judges and academicians alike. This has resulted in a centrist trend wherein the courts have judicially interpreted the Constitutions to be leaning more towards the Centre than the States. Such interpretation erodes or waters down the rights of the States which had been guaranteed by the Constitutions and provides a set back to the federal structure. Since the Indian Constitution has been consistently characterised as quasi-federal or more unitary, the federal government has been indirectly empowered to act as the supreme government of the land, at times even foregoing the constitutional limitations and interfering with the administration of the States, contrary to the constitutional mandate. Instances of such are many, as these situations have taken place in almost all federal nations including the U.S.A., Australia and Canada.

In light of the preceding paragraph wherein we observed that federal Constitutions have deviated from the American Constitution in one way or another, thereby being characterised as quasi-federal, it is pertinent to mention that even the American Constitution, which came into existence about two centuries ago, has been considerably watered down or altered in order to effectively deal with the modern-day problems. For instance, the American federation presently provides for emergency powers which were absent about two centuries ago. Therefore, it cannot be said that the Constitution of U.S.A. is a purely Federal Constitution. In the author's opinion, almost all the Federal Constitution have been substantially altered to cater to the needs and demands of the 21st century, however, in principle, all the Constitutions are still the same and serve the same purpose but through slightly different means and modes. Such means and modes have been veiled under the garb of different principles however, once the veil of such principles/constitutional provisions is lifted, it is evident that each Constitution serves the same purpose. Therefore, instead of watering down a federal structure or naming a structure quasi- federal, it is advised that all these structures be addressed as federal structures and any modifications brought to such structures must make it a separate kind of federalism instead of doing away with the principle of federalism itself, thereby keeping the federal structure intact. For instance, *Austin* propounded the term 'cooperative federalism' to indicate a kind of federalism which requires cooperation between States and federal governments.[2]

Therefore, the author seeks to examine the federal structure of the Indian Constitution and capitulate that the Indian federalism is no different from that of other major Federations across the world, thereby concluding that Indian federation is not quasi-federal but federal in nature. In the first Chapter, the author seeks to examine the fundamental features of federalism which shall be present in a federation. Once the author analyses and discovers the crucial features of a federation, the author seeks to examine each of these principles in the light of Indian federation in the subsequent chapters. The author seeks to compare the Indian federation with that of U.S.A., Australia and Canada, which are considered to be federal nations. In conclusion, the author seeks to show that Indian federalism is not different to that of other federations and cannot be referred to as 'quasi-federal or watered-down federalism or unitary'. The form of the federations may be different to one another however, substantially these federations are the same.

---

[2] Granville Austin, The Indian Constitution: Cornerstone of a Nation

CHAPTER 1

Political Structures

Every Constitution in the world can be categorized as either Unitary or Federal. Historically, most of the governments were unitary. From the era of kingdoms to feudalism to early modern States, all the powers were vested in one central figure in a nation. This central figure could either be a monarch or a central government which dominated the affairs of a nation and all the powers were vested in this sovereign figure. As opposed to this, in the late 18th century, a new form of government called federalism came into existence, beginning with the United States of America. With the advent of colonialism and modern warfare, several independent States decided to form an alliance wherein these States could stand together as one nation, combine their prowess to protect themselves against external threats, promote collective economic strength and at the same time retain their powers of governance within their boundaries. Such a structure came disguised as a blessing, a win-win situation for everyone concerned. Hence came into existence the concept of Federalism.

Unitarianism

A brief introduction to the unitary structure will aid the reader in understanding the fundamental differences between the unitary and federal structures. It is essential to understand the term 'unitary' in its literal sense before a legal examination. According to the Oxford Dictionary, 'unitary' is defined as 'of or pertaining to, characterized by, based upon, or directed towards unity'.[3] A 'unitarian', as per the Oxford Dictionary, is a person 'advocating, promoting, or directed towards national unity, union, or centralization in government and administration'.[4] Therefore, as a necessary corollary, a unitarian is a person advocating centralization of government within a nation state. In a political sense, 'unitary' may indicate a form of government which displays attributes of a unified government or a government wherein all the powers are centralised.

---

3   'Unitary', Oxford Dictionary of Law (7th edn, OUP 2013)
4   'Unitarianism', Oxford Dictionary of Law (7th edn, OUP 2013)

Legally, a unitary Constitution is one wherein the set of powers, whether judicial, legislative or executive, are vested or predominantly exercised by the central government in a nation without any constitutional limitation on such powers. A.V. Dicey, in his landmark work, Law of the Constitution (10th Edn.)[5], defined Unitarianism as:

"Unitarianism means the concentration of the strength of the State in the hands of one visible sovereign power."

Therefore, in a Unitary State, the powers vests in one government i.e. the central government and all powers exercised by any other administrative body are subsidiary or delegated powers. Therefore, a single government is supreme in a nation and exercises all such powers it can legally exercise.

As Dicey has formulated:

"Under a unitary government, the sovereign power clearly and visibly, so to speak, resides in some one body, e.g. the King, Parliament, or the like which is supreme throughout the whole of the country. All other authorities whatever power they may possess, can claim nothing but delegated powers; they have no appearance of sovereignty & they are not in any sense part of the sovereign power."[6]

A major example of this type of government is England. The central government acts as the sovereign authority and it subordinates such powers to local governments and authorities as it may deem fit. In a Unitary State, the central government has absolute authority and its actions cannot be called into question in any court of law on the ground that it has transgressed the jurisdiction of local authorities. Therefore, the judicial review does not concern itself with the distribution of powers between the centre and subordinates. These local authorities have only such powers as delegated by the central government and any act done under a power not granted to it is ultra vires and void.

Alen and Strong[7] have laid down two essential conditions for a Unitary State - a central government or authority which must be supreme and absence of subsidiary sovereign bodies. Alen and Strong argue that the

---

5   A.V. Dicey, Law of the Constitution, 10th Edn.
6   A.V Dicey: General Characteristics of English Constitutionalism: Six Unpublished Lectures, p. 74
7   C.F. Strong, Modern Political Constitutions, 6th Edn. (London) 1963.

central government shall be supreme and sovereign i.e. its powers shall not be exercised by other authorities as a matter of right but only through delegation by the former. The central government is therefore the sovereign body and no other body in the country can exercise such sovereignty. In England, popularly known as a Parliamentary sovereignty[8], the Parliament enjoys sovereignty and not the Constitution (as in U.S.A.) or the people (as in India).

In short, a Unitary State is one where the central government is the supreme or sovereign power in the nation and exercises all such powers itself or through delegation to subordinate authorities whose authority is limited to the powers granted to it by the central government. Subordinate authorities are formed only for the smooth and efficient functioning of the government and not to grant special rights to the people living under the jurisdiction of such authorities.

Federalism

The other end of the spectrum is occupied by Federalism. It is an entirely contrasting concept vis-a-vis Unitarianism. Unitarianism and Federalism occupy the two extremes of the horizon, one favouring the centre and the other favouring the States. But what exactly do we understand by Federalism? Isn't the supreme power exercised by the central government in every country? The latter is precisely the question which gives birth to Federalism. It is a structure where the sovereign power is not exercised by the Centre but rather, it is shared between the Centre and the States, each drawing its power from the Constitution. Prof. Neumann[9] distinguished between the two structures in the following words:

"Federalism is a form of distributing power. Power in a constitutional sense, may be regarded as the ability to make decisions and to see that they are carried out. If, therefore, the component parts of a State have no power of policy decision in any field but are confined to carrying out central government directives through the medium of an institutional fabric of Federal form, it is not a Federal but a Unitary State."

It is pertinent to mention that there is no agreed definition of federalism. The reason which can be attributed to this lack of agreement

---

8   'What is the Role of Parliament', Parliamentary Archives, United Kingdom

9   Neumann, European and Comparative Government (1960), pp. 679 et. Seq.

is the dynamic nature of federalism. Of course, the orthodox, pre-modern authors[10] consider the true concept of federalism to be that of United States of America and in their opinion, any deviation from American federalism cannot be called federalism. Most modern academicians including the author believes that Federalism is a highly dynamic and ever-changing concept which cannot be confined to a water-tight box. The boundary of such a box shall always be blurry, if not transcended time to time. Even in America, as shall be seen through the course of this book, federalism has changed substantially from its original version which came into existence about two centuries ago.

Historically, the word 'federal' is derived from the Latin word *foedus* which means covenant. *Davis*, considering the Latin origin of the word federal (foedus), wrote *"Based on the idea of covenant, which is synonymous with the ideas of promise, commitment, undertaking, or obligation, vowing,… we come upon a vital bonding device of civilization… involving the idea of cooperation, reciprocity, mutuality, and.. the recognition of entities".*[11] Thus, a federation, according to *Davis*, may be considered as a synthesis of ideas of promise, commitment and obligations to one another, to bond into a collective civilization involving cooperation, recognition and mutual respect for one another. Many authors have tried to define federalism. *Dicey* describes a federation as a structure which seeks union and not unity.[12] He laid down two conditions for creation of a federation i.e. (a) the body of States forming a federation are 'so closely connected by locality, by history, by race, or the like, as to be capable of bearing, in the eyes of their inhabitants an impress of common nationality' and (b) such inhabitants must desire a union and not unity.[13] He argues that a federal State intends to *"reconcile national unity and power with the maintenance of 'State rights'".* In the years that followed, *Prof. Wheare* defined federalism as a *'method of dividing powers so that the general and regional governments are, each within a sphere, coordinate and independent'.*[14] The *Encyclopedia Britannica*

---

10 Wheare, Modern Constitution (1966); Federal Government (1963); M.P. Jain, Indian Constitutional Law, Vol. 1, 5th Edn., (2003)

11 Robert Schutze, Political Philosophy of Federalism, Max Planck Encyclopedia of Comparative Constitutional Law (2016)

12 Dicey, Law of the Constitution (10th Edn), p. 141

13 A.V. Dicey, An Introduction to the Study of Law of the Constitution 141 (10th Edn. 1959)

14 Wheare K.C., Federal Government, Oxford University Press, London, 1964

described a federation as a system where, *"the States agree to delegate to a supreme federal government certain powers or functions inherent in themselves in their sovereign or separate capacity…So far as concerns the residue of powers unallotted to the central or federal authority, the separate States retain unimpaired their individual sovereignty, and the citizens of a federation consequently owe a double allegiance – one to the State and one to the federal government"*.[15]

Along with the academic definitions, it is essential to acquaint the reader with the varied definitions adopted by courts in federal nations. Federalism is, according to the Supreme Court of India, *"a concept which unites separate States into a Union without sacrificing their own fundamental political integrity. Separate States therefore, desire to unite so that all the member States may share in formulation of the basic policies applicable to all and participate in the execution of decisions made in pursuance of such basic policies. Thus, the essence of a federation is the existence of the Union and the States and the distribution of powers between them. Federalism therefore essentially implies demarcation of powers in a federal compact."*[16] Lord Hardane[17], while commenting on the Canadian federation described federalism as *"In a loose sense, the word 'Federal' may be used, as it is there (in Canada) used, to describe any arrangement under which self-contained States agree to delegate their powers to a common government with a view to frame and entirely new Constitutions even of the States themselves. But the natural and literal interpretation of the word confines its application to cases in which these States, while agreeing on a measure of delegation, yet in the main continue to preserve their original Constitutions."*

According to the author, a federation occupies the middle ground between complete State autonomy and a Unitary State. In a federation, two or more States come together to form a Union or rather, a loose form of alliance wherein a national government is formed at the centre while each State is permitted to enact its own government, with such division of powers as may be prescribed by the Constitution. It follows as a necessary corollary that a written Constitution is essential for establishment of a federation. The Constitution dictates the distribution of powers between the national and State governments and each government owes its existence

---

15   'Federation', Encyclopedia Britannica.

16   A. M. Ahmadi, J. S.R. Bommai vs Union of India (1994) 3 SCC 1 Para 14

17   A.G. for Australia vs. Colonial Sugar Refining Co. (1914) AC 237 (252-254)

to the Constitution. Therefore, federalism concerns itself with the division of powers between the Centre and the States, subject to the constitutional limitations wherein the spheres of legislative, executive and judicial powers of each are coordinate and independent of each other. The States enjoy some autonomy and are granted wide legislative and executive powers.

Despite several attempts to define federalism, the dynamism of this concept defeats any definition which tries to circumscribe federalism. As can be seen, *Dicey* and *Prof. Wheare* occupy the old school wherein they give a strict definition to federalism and disagreeing with any definition which deviates from American federalism. Their views have been strongly challenged by many courts and academia alike, considering the ever-changing dynamics of political structures in federal nations. For instance, the United States of America has conceded more power to the centre than was envisaged originally by the drafters of the Constitution through various constitutional amendments and judgements.

Contrary to *Dicey* and *Wheare*, *Prof. Neumann* and *Reagan*[18] liberally interpret Federalism. The Historian *Edward A. Freeman*, in his book '*History of Federal Government*'[19] argued that Federalism is to be interpreted liberally and it cannot be confined to a water-tight compartment. According to *Freeman*, "*the name Federal Government may be applied to any union of component members where the degree of union between the members surpasses that of mere alliance, however intimate, and where the degree of independence possessed by each member surpasses anything which can fairly come under the head of mere municipal freedom.*"

Similarly, *Prof. Wagner*[20] argues that whether a State is federal or unitary is one of degree and the answer will depend on how many federal features it possesses. Wagner argued that whether a nation is federal or not has to be decided by the number of federal features it possesses in contrast to the unitary features and in case the former outweigh the latter, the Constitution can be described as federal. *Livingston*[21] has rightly asserted that federalism is more of a functional than an institutional concept and any theory which asserts that there are certain inflexible characteristics without which a

---

18   Reagan, The New Federalism (1972), p. 1.
19   Freeman, History of Federal Government, pp. 2-3.
20   Prof. W.T. Wagner, Federal States and their Judiciary, p.25
21   Livingston, Federation and Constitutional Change 1956, pp. 6-7

political system cannot be federal ignores the fact *"that institutions are not the same things in different social and cultural environments".* Similarly, Friedrich[22] argued that federalism should not be seen *'only as a static pattern or design but defined in dynamic terms. Federal relations are fluctuating relations in the very nature of things.'*

The concept of federalism, therefore, cannot be static in the modern day and age. It is a highly dynamic concept which cannot be circumscribed into water-tight specific features which must be present in a federal nation. Accepting this dynamic nature of Federalism, *Davis* described it as *'not one single idea but a whole intricate and varied network of interrelated ideas and concepts – of contract, of partnership, of equity, of trusts, of sovereignty, of Constitution, of State, of international law'.*[23] Similarly, *Granville Austin,* in his remarkable work on Indian Constitution[24], described federalism liberally as *'an idea and a set of practices, the variety of which depends upon the goals of the citizenry and its leaders, the consequent definition of the term and the conditions present in the would-be federation'.* According to his definition, each nation can ascribe a different definition to federalism as no two federations can be the same. Even *Prof. Wheare* conceded that in order to classify a constitution as federal, a predominance of federal principal and not religious adherence to it is required.[25]

It is this dynamic nature of the federalism which the author seeks to explore through this book and conclude that the Constitution of India is indeed federal in nature. Federalism cannot be limited to the federal structure of the United States of America, but it should be a flexible concept where certain deviations from features of traditional federalism exist, keeping in view the peculiar position and government of each nation. Considering this argument of dynamic nature of federalism, the author seeks to analyse whether the Constitution of India is federal or not.

---

22   Carl J. Friedrich, Trends of Federalism in Theory and Practice, 7, 23, 173 (1968).

23   S. R. Davis, The Federal Principle: A Journey through Time in Quest of a Meaning 5 (1978)

24   G. Austin, Working a Democratic Constitution, The Indian Experience 555 (1999)

25   Wheare K.C., Federal Government, Oxford University Press, London, 1964, pg. 14

CHAPTER 2

Features of Federalism

Since the objective of this work is to analyse the federal nature of the Indian Constitution, it is essential to study it in light of features of federalism. Federalism has certain features or fundamentals which are present in every federal nation in one form or the other. Since a predominance of federal features and not religious adherence to it is the norm[26], it is essential to chart out the characteristics which can be termed as federal or pro-federation and determine if the federal characteristics outweigh the unitary ones. This chapter seeks to examine the fundamental features of federalism which must be present in order to classify a system as federal.

The features of federalism are equally debatable and contentious as is the definition of federalism. In the preceding paragraphs, it was submitted that according to *Prof. Wagner*[27], whether a State is federal or unitary is one of degree and the answer will depend on how many federal features it possesses. He argued that if the federal features outweigh the unitary features, the Constitution can be characterized as federal. However, a problem which then arises is, what are these federal features? The author must concede the answer to this question remains elusive and highly contentious.

Several jurists and practitioners have attempted to lay down the features of federalism. According to *Dicey*[28], to begin with, the test for a federal Constitution is two-fold – a distribution of powers between the Union and the States; such distribution of powers is legally justiciable in order to enable the judiciary to intervene in case a dispute arises between them. Dicey therefore, relied on the division of powers and its justiciability as the criteria for federalism. The author believes this test to be flawed because in both unitary and federal structures, powers are indeed divided between the Centre and the States. Even in Unitary States, there exists a division of powers however, the central government exercises sovereign powers whereas the unnecessary powers are vested in the State governments. This

---

26   Wheare K.C., Federal Government, Oxford University Press, London, 1964, pg. 14

27   Prof. W.T. Wagner, Federal States and their Judiciary, p.25

28   Dicey, Law of the Constitution, 10th Edn, p. 164

brings the principle of federalism on par with unitarianism. Therefore, there needs to be some more features which shall be added to this test.

Prof. Neumann considers the real division of power between the States and the Union which operates as a constitutional limitation upon both is the true test of Federalism.[29] *Prof.* Neumann has therefore relied on the constitutional division of powers between the Union and the States. This is broadly the most important feature of federalism. However, there are several factors to be taken into account while applying this test, such as nature of the distributed powers, center's control over the States, emergency powers, powers pertaining to unilateral amendment of the Constitution etc.

According to *Dr. D. D. Basu*[30], the Indian constitutional scholar and author, the features of federalism can be summed up as follows: distribution of powers; dual government; no unilateral change; written Constitution; and authority of courts. *Geoffrey Sawer*[31], an Australian scholar, laid down certain conditions that must be met for establishing a Federal State. These conditions are – an independent country with a central government empowered to govern the country; the country shall be divided into separate geographical States having their own respective governments; the power to govern is distributed between central and State governments; such a distribution of powers is set out in the Constitution rigidly and it cannot be amended by the central government or any State; the Constitution provides for dispute resolution in case of conflict between the centre and the States; the distribution of powers is enforced and interpreted by the judiciary. He mentioned that the judiciary is empowered by the Constitution to pronounce binding verdicts concerning the validity of legislations or exercise of powers by the government or disputes between the Centre and the States.

Similarly, *A. Lijphart*[32] identified the following as features of federalism - a written Constitution laying down the division of power and guaranteeing that the legislative powers of central or State governments cannot be taken away; a bicameral legislature wherein one chamber represents the people as a whole and another which comprises of representatives of the States;

---

29   Neumann, European and Comparative Government (1960) pp. 679 et. seq.

30   D. D. Basu, Comparative Federalism, 2nd Edn. (2007), p. 23-32.

31   Geoffrey Sawer, Modern Federalism (Watts and Co. London 1969)

32   Lijphart, Arend. "Non-Majoritarian Democracy: A Comparison of Federal and Consociational Theories." *Publius*, vol. 15, no. 2, 1985, pp. 3–15. *JSTOR*, www.jstor.org/stable/3329961. Accessed 30 June 2020.

Over-representation of the smaller component units in the federal chamber of the bicameral legislature; the States have a right to be involved in the process of amendment of the federal Constitution but can change their own Constitution unilaterally; State governments in federations have a larger share of power as compared to their counterparts in Unitary States.

Withal, in light of the discussion in the preceding paragraphs, the author believes it prudent to classify these features in six (6) categories, with other sub-issues being a part of these categories. In the following paragraphs, the author discusses the features which are considered to be essential for federalism.

First, one of the basic features of federalism, according to the author, is the federal sentiment imbibed in the political structure. There shall be a sentiment of federalism i.e. there shall be an intention to form and run the government as federal. This sentiment is the result of two conflicting ideas - desire for national unity and maintenance of autonomy of each State. As *Dicey* correctly puts it, "A Federal State is a political contrivance intended to reconcile national unity and power with the maintenance of 'State rights'".[33] The federal sentiment is derived from the history leading to formation of the federation, provisions of the Constitution, constituent assembly debates, spirit of Constitution, judicial interpretation etc. The federal sentiment is translated into a written Constitution which lays down the pillars of the federation. Therefore, the enactment of a written Constitution is also a necessity for federalism.

Second, it has been frequently argued that a federation can be formed only if two or more independent States decide to unite for geographical, political, economic, racial or other reasons to form a nation. Therefore, there must be an agreement between independent States to form a Union. However, this is not an absolute rule as it is subject to certain modifications. To cite an example, the Australian Constitution has been adjudged as federal however, the States in Australia are not independent but autonomous as they were under the imperial rule. Another modification, as has been accepted by many authors, states that a federation may be formed by other modes such as a treaty or through transforming a unitary State into federal (see Canada). In addition to this, it is prudent to analyse the territory to

---

33   Dicey, Law of the Constitution, 10th Edn, p. 141-143

which the federation extends including membership of the federation, reorganization of States and acquisition of new States.

Third, despite the fact that States form a federation by surrendering some of their powers to the central government, they retain some of the rights and powers which allow them to remain autonomous. As *Dicey* stated, a federation attempts to reconcile national unity along with preservation of States' rights. These 'States' rights' form a crucial part of a federation. If the States have bare minimal rights, the State is more unitary than federal as it tends to give federal government immense power over the States, degrading States to mere administrative units. In federations, States are guaranteed rights through a written Constitution which cannot be abrogated by the federal government. These rights allow States to retain autonomous powers in their respective regions.

Fourth, considering that the basic purpose of the formation of a federation is preservation of the autonomy of the States along with national unity, there are certain situations where national unity takes precedence over the autonomy of the States. External aggression or war can be considered a good example for the same. During a situation of war, the federal government may have to take away the autonomy of the State to divert funds, engage State law enforcement personnel, suspend civil rights etc. In such situations, the federal government assumes complete control over the nation including States. However, such powers of the federal government shall not be abused. There have been instances in many federal nations wherein the federal government misused its emergency powers to take control of the State governments to further their political objectives. Therefore, it is essential to ascertain the existence of emergency powers, the extent to which the federal government can override the powers of the State government, the duration of such overriding and under what conditions can such powers be exercised.

Fifth, as a necessary corollary to the preceding paragraph, the powers of the federal government and the State government are expressly laid down in the written Constitution. The Constitution divides the legislative powers of the governments under separate Lists known as Legislative Lists (See Schedule VII, Constitution of India). The States can legislate only on the subjects included in the State List, and on some occasions, even in Concurrent List. Similarly, the federal government can legislate on

Federal List however, there are instances wherein the Federal government can override the States' power to legislate on State List but only as per the procedure laid down in the Constitution. In the absence of such Lists, there would be utter chaos in the federation as each government would attempt to transgress the legislative powers of the other. It is therefore necessary to have a distribution of powers in a Federal State.

Lastly, it has often been observed that in Unitary States or federations with unitary leanings, the matters assigned to the State governments are subordinate or unimportant. It is essential to ascertain the validity of this proposition in the Indian context. Further, most traditional federations grant a State citizenship, in addition to the citizenship of the federation. Therefore, it is crucial to understand this feature and its purpose in context of our target federations.

Therefore, broadly, the features of federalism can be summed up as follows:

1. Federal Sentiment
2. Formation of Federation and Territory
3. States' Rights
4. Legislative Lists or Distribution of Powers
5. Emergency Powers
6. Importance of Matters Assigned to States and State Citizenship

These features, as briefly discussed earlier, are the parts of a nation which affect the federal structure. As Prof. Wagner suggested, if on analysis of these features it is concluded that the federal features of a Constitution outweigh the unitary, the Constitution can be characterised as federal. Therefore, in the subsequent chapters, the author will explore these essential features of federalism in the four federations - U.S.A., Canada, Australia and India with a view to conclude that India possesses the necessary ingredients for federalism, similar to the aforementioned federations. Each chapter shall examine the above mentioned issues with regard to each of these federations and consequently attempt a comparative study vis-à-vis India. In conclusion, the author will show that India is indeed a federation and not quasi-federal considering that it possesses each of the federal features present in other federations.

CHAPTER 3

Federalism in India

The purpose of this book to analyse the dominance of federalism or lack thereof in Indian Constitution in light of the principles laid down in the preceding paragraphs. Therefore, it is essential to introduce the reader to the federalism in India, as it stands. This chapter discusses the views of jurists and decisions of the Hon'ble Supreme Court of India on federal characteristics of the Constitution of India. The author intends to highlight the lack of study which went into the federal question in India wherein most of the aforementioned features were not discussed or deliberated upon. As we observed in the preceding chapter, federalism is a much more complex structure and requires a detailed study of its features to ascertain whether a nation is federal or not. Such a study, however, was not undertaken by the Hon'ble Supreme Court of India before characterising the Constitution as quasi-federal.

India, from its inception, was destined to become a federation considering that several provinces and princely States came together to form the nation that is India. Owing to the cultural, linguistic and religious diversity in India, a federal structure was the only appropriate choice considering the varied interests of the highly heterogenous society, rendering a unitary structure unworkable. With a federal structure, each province or princely State was guaranteed certain rights, as enumerated in the Constitution of India. We shall see the history leading to a federal India in the next chapter. The discussion in this chapter shall be limited to characterisation of the Constitution as federal or quasi-federal.

Dr. B.R. Ambedkar described the Constitution as 'federal though it is designed to become unitary in the times of war or disruptions, whether internal or external'.[34] The Objectives Resolution adopted by the Constituent Assembly on 22 January 1947 stated that the Union shall only have the powers of Foreign Affairs, Communication and Defence and the residuary powers shall be left to the States, partly due to the demands of Muslim

---

34   D. D. Basu, Comparative Federalism, 2nd Edn. (2007), p. 116.

League as well. This represented a loose federation or a confederation. However, once the Indian Independence Act was passed and the creation of Pakistan and present-day Bangladesh seemed inevitable, the Constituent Assembly decided to adopt a different structure. The members of the constituent assembly, according to Austin[35], came to a consensus that the form of structure shall be reconsidered. The Second Report of the Union Powers Committee observed:

"Now that the partition is a settled fact, we are unanimously of the view that it would be injurious to the interests of the country to provide for a weak central authority which would be incapable of ensuring peace, of coordinating vital matters of common concern and of speaking effectively for the whole country in the international sphere."

The Assembly thus decided to adopt a structure with a relatively stronger centre with the residuary powers vested in the Union, contrary to Objectives Resolution. The riots which ensued from the partition and the external threat from Pakistan, Bangladesh and Chinese frontiers demanded a stronger central government. The Objectives Resolution was therefore upended and the recommendations of the *Union Powers Committee* were accepted.[36] Thereafter, the Constitution of India was drafted bearing in mind the need for a strong centre. As *Sarkaria Commission Report*[37] pointed out:

"The primary lesson of India's history is that, in this vast country, only that polity or system can endure and protect its unity, integrity and sovereignty against external aggression and internal disruption, which ensures a strong centre with paramount powers, accommodating, at the same time, its traditional diversities. This lesson of history did not go unnoticed by the framers of the Constitution. Being aware that, notwithstanding the common cultural heritage without political cohesion, the country would disintegrate under the pressure of fissiparous forces they accorded the highest priority to the ensurance of the unity and integrity of the country."

Therefore, considering the various factors influencing the political structure of India, the framers of our Constitution decided to form a federal Constitution with a strong centre. Unsettled borders, aggressive neighbours, abject poverty, strong religious sentiments, anti-national groups and

---

35 Austin, Indian Constitution (1966), pp. 190ff
36 I CAD, 57
37 Sarkaria Commission Report, p. 7

diversity of culture, language and religions forced the hand of the drafters of our Constitution to adopt a structure which caters to the needs of every community and at the same time ensuring a strong unified nation to tackle external problems. It is however pertinent to mention that the Constitution of India does not mention the word 'Federal' but only mentions that India is a 'Union of States'.[38]

Owing to the strong centre, *Prof. Wheare* wrote that the Constitution of India is 'quasi-federal' and not purely federal.[39] Similarly, *Austin*[40] has described it as 'cooperative federalism' whereas *Jennings*[41] classified it as a federation with a strong centralizing tendency. On the other hand, there are several scholars who have described the Indian Constitution as federal.[42] The reader may notice that the jurists who classified the Indian Constitution as quasi-federal or not federal were of traditionalist school. The jurists abiding by the school of modern federalism concluded that the Indian federation is actually federal in nature. The rationale behind this is that in the years following the enactment of traditional Constitutions, even the traditional federations have centralised their structures owing to the various global events which demanded a centralisation of resources and a collective response. We shall see the centralisation of federal nations in the following chapters.

Despite all these attempts to study federalism in India, it is essential to discuss the findings of the Hon'ble Supreme Court of India as these have a direct bearing on the Constitution and actions of the governments. This chapter discusses the position of the Indian courts which have time and again characterised the Constitution as not federal or quasi-federal. Of course, the author disagrees with the present position as it is contrary to the modern-day concept of federalism. Hereinafter, the author shall discuss the judgements of the Hon'ble Supreme Court of India which have characterised the Indian Constitution as either not federal or quasi-federal. It is pertinent to mention that the critique of the observations of the courts in India is

---

38 Art. 1, Constitution of India

39 Wheare, Federal Government 27-8 (1964): 48 All LJ 21

40 The Indian Constitution – The Cornerstone of a Nation, 187.

41 Ivor Jennings, Some Characteristics of the Indian Constitution, p. 1

42 Alexandrowicz, C. H., Constitutional developments in India, Bombay: Oxford University Press, 1957; Nicholas, Australian Constitution, (1952), pp. 144; Alan Gledhill, The Republic of India, London: Stevens and Sons, Ltd.1951; M.P. Jain, Indian Constitutional Law, Vol. 1, 5th Edn., (2003)

discussed in Chapter 12. The following judgements, among others, have been earmarked for this discussion:

1. State of West Bengal vs. Union of India 1963 AIR 1241
2. Kesavananda Bharti vs. State of Kerala (1973) 4 SCC 225
3. Shamsher vs. State of Punjab 1974 AIR 2192
4. State of Rajasthan vs. Union of India 1977 AIR 1361
5. Pradeep Jain vs. Union of India 1984 AIR1420
6. S. R. Bommai vs. Union of India (1994) 3 SCC 1
7. Ganga Ram Moolchandani vs. State of Rajasthan (2001) 6 SCC 89

There had been several decisions prior to the *West Bengal* case, however, it was the first case which analysed the federal features at length. Following the *West Bengal* case, came *Kesavananda Bharti*, often dubbed as the most important case in the constitutional history of India. In *Kesavananda Bharti*, the Hon'ble Supreme Court discussed the federal character only to a limited extent i.e. pertaining to the government's amending power of the Constitution. However, remarkably enough, the Supreme Court declared federalism as a basic feature of the Constitution of India thereby ensuring that the federal character cannot be removed from the Constitution by the government. The subsequent judgements however, altered the view of the Supreme Court with regards to federalism. For instance, in *Shamsher vs. State of Punjab*, the Supreme Court held that the Indian structure is quasi-federal. Similarly, in *State of Rajasthan vs. Union of India* and *Pradeep Jain*, the Supreme held that the extent of federalism in India is largely watered down. These judgements paved the way for subsequent characterisation of India as a quasi-federal nation. In *S.R. Bommai's* case which involved a very important landmark discussion involving the internal emergency powers of the government, the Hon'ble Supreme Court characterised the States as quasi-federal vis-à-vis the Union, thereby declaring that the Union stands at a higher pedestal than the States. The more recent judgement of *Ganga Ram Moolchandani* attempted to reverse the position of the earlier judgements by declaring that the Indian Constitution is federal in form and marked by characteristics of traditional federations. The discussion in this judgement is highly unsatisfactory wherein casual observations have been made that India is indeed federal without considering any authorities like its earlier counterparts.

To begin with, in *West Bengal vs. Union of India*, the apex court characterized the Indian Constitution as 'true to any traditional pattern of federation'. In this case, the court adhered to the traditional view of federalism and ignored the peculiar provisions of the Constitution which do not conform to the standards of pure federalism. After the *West Bengal* case, the judgment in *Keshavananda Bharti* was delivered in 1973. In this case, the apex court held that federalism is a part of the basic structure of the Constitution and it cannot be done away with through constitutional amendments. It observed "our Constitution is federal in character, and not unitary." However, in *Shamsher vs. State of Punjab*, Krishna Iyer, J. watered down federalism in India and described it as 'an Indo-Anglian version of the Westminster model with quasi-federal adaptations'. After the decision in *Shamsher*, the Supreme Court adhered to the proposition that Indian Constitution is not purely federal but rather quasi-federal or a watered-down version of federalism.

Subsequently, in *State of Rajasthan vs. Union of India*, Beg, C.J. relied in the findings of *Prof. Wheare* which characterized the Indian Constitution as 'more unitary than federal'. Beg, C.J. wrote observed *"In a sense, therefore, the Indian Union is federal. But, the extent of federalism in it is largely watered down by the needs of progress and development of a country, which has to be nationally integrated, politically and economically coordinated and socially, intellectually and spiritually lifted."* Similarly, in *State of Karnataka vs. Union of India*, Beg, C.J. wrote that our Constitution has strong unitary features in it despite the federal structure. In *Pradeep Jain*, the apex court observed *"moreover, it must be remembered that India is not a federal State in the traditional sense of that term."*

However, once the verdict was delivered in *S.R. Bommai vs. Union of India*, the question of Federalism was decided. Ahmadi, J. accepted *Prof. Wheare's* argument and described the Constitution as 'quasi-federal', being a mixture of federal and unitary features but leaning more towards the latter. He observed *"Thus in the United States, the sovereign States enjoy their own separate existence which cannot be impaired; indestructible States having constituted an indestructible Union. In India, on the contrary, Parliament can by law form a new State, alter the size of an existing State, alter the name of an existing State, etc., and even curtail the power, both executive and legislative, by amending the Constitution. That is why the Constitution of*

India is differently described, more appropriately as 'quasi-federal' because it is a mixture of the federal and unitary elements, leaning- more towards the latter but then what is there in a name, what is important to bear in mind is the thrust and implications of the various provisions of the Constitution bearing on the controversy in regard to scope and ambit of the Presidential power under Article 356 and related provisions."

The position laid down in *S.R. Bommai* still holds ground with regards to federalism in India. However, the discussions in these judgements pertaining to federal character of India is highly unsatisfactory due to an absence of an in-depth study of the features of federalism and their presence in the Constitution. As we shall see in the following chapters, the position of federalism in India is quite similar to the ones in America and Australia i.e. the traditional federations. One may say that the Indian Constitution does not conform to federalism as propounded in the 18th century, however, one may observe that even the American and Australian federations do not conform to the traditional view of federalism. Over a course of two centuries, even the traditional federations have developed centralising tendencies and therefore are very much similar to federalism in India. In light of these observations, the author writes a critique of the Indian position as explained by the courts, characterising the Constitution as quasi-federal in chapter 12.

CHAPTER 4

Federal Sentiment

The federal sentiment refers to the intention of drafters of the Constitution and the constituent assembly to form a federation as opposed to the Unitary State. The word 'federation' may not be mentioned in the Constitution itself, but the spirit of federalism can be ascertained from the structure of the government, intention of lawmakers and the provisions of the Constitution which indicate a federal bend. Therefore, it is essential to find the spirit of federalism in a nation for ascertaining whether it is federal or unitary.

This chapter explores and analyses the history of federal nations and the intention of their lawmakers to enact a federal Constitution. The author will delve into the constitutional history of target jurisdictions with an attempt to show that the founding fathers of their Constitutions intended to adopt federalism. To this effect, these countries enacted a federal written Constitution. For this purpose, the respective Constitutions of United States of America, Australia and Canada will be analysed to ascertain the federal sentiment which existed in the minds of the drafters of the Constitution. Consequently, the author will analyse the Constitution of India through its constitutional history, intention of the members of the constituent assembly and subsequent developments through court cases and amendments to ascertain the existence of a federal sentiment and conclude that India was intended to be a federation. The author will eventually conclude that the federal sentiment existed in each of the federal nations and their respective Constitutions were drafted along the lines of federalism.

Before we proceed to the discussion, the author seeks to introduce a rather curious observation. Is it a mere coincidence that the first federations came into existence in former colonies of the British Empire? If we have a look at the federal nations across the world, we will discover that earliest federations among these nations were indeed former colonies of the British Empire i.e. United States of America, Australia, Canada and India. The author submits herein that it is not a mere coincidence but rather a development which burgeoned from the political structure of the British Empire and its colonies across the world, wherein the empire headed the governments of the colonies through the British Parliament, but local governance of people was largely left to the colonies themselves. This observation was rightly addressed by *Andrew McLaughlin*[43]. The author seeks to briefly explore the observation.

The British Empire was run by the authority of the crown. The crown was in charge of military and navy, foreign affairs, war and peace and communications. The rest of the functions were largely left to the governments of the colonies. For instance, local policing, municipal functions, education etc. were legislated upon by the local legislatures established by the authority of the crown but run independently. The British Parliament did not legislate upon these internal functions of the colonies. This pattern is quite similar to a federal structure of our target federations. In fact, if the British Empire remained united as it was in the 18th and 19th century, maybe the same structure would have been followed by the empire resulting in a federal empire. This is precisely the reason why, albeit latently, colonies felt that federalism was the appropriate structure since most of the legislators from colonial era were used to such a structure. These circumstances indicate that the sentiment of federalism existed among the people of federal nations even before the principle of federalism was propounded.

In the light of these, let us see how the federal sentiment was present in our target nations. The discussion followed hereafter will exhibit that the founding fathers of each of the federal nations intended the nation to be a federation. It is, however, pertinent to mention that the author will briefly discuss the existence of a federal sentiment among the founding fathers of federal nations without delving into the elaborate history of how the Constitutions of these nations came into existence, considering that this book is intended to be legal.

United States of America

The concept of federalism vegetated from the political structure of the government of U.S.A. in the early days of its independence. In the year 1776, the Declaration of Independence was adopted by the people of the country. Prior to the establishment of America as a Nation State, the former colonies (present day 'States' of the United States of America) established

---

43   McLaughlin, Andrew C., 'The Background of American Federalism', The American Political Science Review, Vol. 12, No. 2 (May, 1918), pp. 215-240.

their respective independent State governments and discarded the colonial charters which governed them under the colonial rule. In order to bring the States together to form a Union, the founding fathers of the nation decided to create a confederation in America instead of a federation, thereby permitting States to largely retain their independence. Hence, the Articles of Confederation were adopted and approved by the Congress which established a State-centric government.[44] The central government was granted powers limited to declaring war, treaty making, maintenance of army and navy. The residuary powers were exercised by the States. It is pertinent for the reader to note here that the intention of the founders of America had been to give States enormous powers vis-à-vis the Union, hence the adoption of confederation.

The Articles of Confederation however, provided for a substantially weak government at the centre and proved to be largely ineffective. The Articles did not allow the government to collect taxes, regulate trade or give directions to the States. Thus, it was witnessed that most States worked only for their own development with no concern for the collective and the central government was powerless to interfere. Owing to this, the government was not able to raise funds and resultantly failed to pay the national debt incurred during the American Revolution. In fact, some States even began issuing their own currency which led to an economic crisis. As a consequence, there arose a demand for reconsidering the Articles of Confederation.[45] Thus began an inclination towards a federal government.

Therefore, the Constitutional Convention of 1787 was convened to analyse and study the shortcomings of Articles of Confederation. This involved a detail study of the principle of federalism and their incorporation into the Constitution of America so as to maintain the equilibrium of power

---

44 Jensen, Merrill (1940). *The Articles of Confederation: An Interpretation of the Social-Constitutional History of the American Revolution, 1774–1781. ISBN 9780299002039.*; Jensen, Merrill (1943). *"The Idea of a National Government During the American Revolution". Political Science Quarterly.* **58** *(3): 356–379;* Jensen, Merrill (1950). *The New Nation: A History of the United States During the Confederation, 1781–1789. ISBN 9780930350154.*; Bouton, Terry (2012). "The Trials of the Confederation". In Gray, Edward G.; Kamensky, Jane (eds.). The Oxford Handbook of the American Revolution. pp. 370-387. ISBN 9780199746705.

45 See Boyd, Eugene, 'American Federalism, 1776 to 1997: Significant Events', January 6, 1997; History of Federalism in United States, Brewminate – A History of federalism in the United States

between the Centre and the States while at the same time granting the central government enough powers to effectively manage national affairs. It is pertinent to mention that a constitutional convention in America is equivalent to a constituent assembly in India. In the light of this inclination towards federalism, the Constitution of the United States of America was drafted.

During the Convention, the groups in favour of federalism and against it were often at loggerheads. To support the idea of federalism, 'The Federalist', a series of 85 essays written by James Maddison, John Lay and Alexander Hamilton were published with a philosophical argument favouring federalism.[46] On the other hand, people against federalism, seldom called anti-federalists, protested against the adoption of a federal Constitution and demanded a system of governance which would protect the States from the whimsical and tyrannical powers granted to the national government. However the group in support of federalism came to power, gaining nationwide support. As a result, the basic foundations of American federalism were laid down by Federalists including George Washington, Alexander Hamilton and John Adams.[47] The structure, provisions and limitations of federalism were debated at length in the Convention. It sought to give more powers to the central government '...*in order to form a more perfect Union..*' including the power to levy taxes and control over commerce, with an intention to move towards federalism.[48] The founding fathers realised that the idea of having powerful States was counter-productive to the federation and may eventually lead to self-destruction in the long run.

The debates in the Convention therefore were largely centered around establishing a federal government. The new Constitution was thus drafted with an intention to create a federal structure. The only matters left to

---

46 The Federalist: a Collection of Essays, Written in Favour of the New Constitution, as Agreed upon by the Federal Convention, September 17, 1787, in two volumes (1st ed.). New York: J. & A. McLean. 1788.; Harvey Flaumenhaft, "Hamilton's Administrative Republic and the American Presidency," in The Presidency in the Constitutional Order, ed. Joseph M. Bessette and Jeffrey K. Tulis (Baton Rouge and London: Louisiana State University Press, 1981), 65–114.

47 Encyclopædia Britannica (2007). Founding Fathers: The Essential Guide to the Men Who Made America. John Wiley & Sons. ISBN 978-0-470-11792-7.

48 Creating the United States, Formation of Political Parties, Digital Library of Congress, United States of America

discuss were the structure of federalism vis-à-vis the division of powers between States and Central government. The Constitution attempted to protect the interests of the States from the potential tyranny of the federal government by providing for two chambers in the legislature – the House of Representatives and the Senate, along with wide State representation. Furthermore, the Constitution went a step ahead towards strengthening of the central government by inclusion of Article VI which provides for supremacy of federal laws over the State laws in case of conflict.

Thus, a federal government was established at the centre. It must be noted here that the intention to create a federal nation existed from the time Articles of Confederation came under review. The Federalists strongly advocated for the federal form of government, wherein the States' rights can be preserved while empowering the central government with stronger powers to govern national affairs such as taxation, regulation of trade etc. For several years, the debate between federalists and anti-federalists continued however, the inclination towards federalism was established with the passing of Sherman Anti-Trust Act in 1890, marking the era of supremacy of the central government. The great depression of 1920's further added to the demands for a stronger national government. Thereafter, it has been clear that America is purely a Federal State. The federal structure had been laid down in the form of a written Constitution. Withal, the intention of the forefathers of the United States of America was to establish a federal government, as has been highlighted in the preceding paragraphs.

Australia

The inception of Australian federation was rather peculiar, as compared to United States of America and Canada. The formation of the Australian nations was not triggered by any pressing need for protection against external aggression or cultural or linguistic differences or collective prowess to defeat colonialism. The federation of Australia was formed for economic and administrative reasons, after extensive and patient discussions on the structure of the nation. Australia largely modelled their structure on similar lines as that of United States of America.

Australia, in the 19th century, comprised of six States - New South Wales, South Australia, Tasmania, Victoria, Western Australia and Queensland, which operated as distinct self-governing colonies of the British Empire.

These colonies, considering their self-governing nature, had their own laws, tariffs, railways, commercial regulations, trade barriers etc. which resulted in hindering the growth of the Australian sub-continent as a whole. These produced several problems and differences among the people and colonial governments.[49] As an attempt to reconcile these differences, discussions were held to find common ground and establish a new order for governance, as a consequence of which, the idea of a unified Australia was first mooted.

As early as 1880, the Australian Natives Association[50], an association of white Australian natives, committed itself to federalism and laid the organisational and financial groundwork for federal leagues in the country which lobbied in favour of a unified federal Australia. Consequently, the Federal Council of Australasia was established in 1885[51] to resolve the inter-colonial issues such as trade barriers, defence, tariffs etc. and attempt to reconcile the differences, eventually culminating in a demand for a unified nation. Therefore, the idea of federalism was ingrained in the minds of the founding fathers of the nation even prior to the beginning of constitutional conventions.

As Sir Henry Parkes called for 'a great national government for all Australians'[52] in October 1889, the States conducted a series of conventions to decide the structure of a unified Australia and develop a framework for the Constitution. As opposed to America and Canada, the Australian States were not concerned with external aggression, cultural or linguistic differences among the people for accepting a federal nation, but rather with economic considerations. The States were concerned about matters such as economic growth including removal of tariff barriers for intra-country trade, immigration, obtaining investment capital with a collective prowess and greater strategic presence in the global market.[53] These considerations were suitable for a decentralized structure of governance which would

---

49　Defining Moments – Federation, National Museum Australia.

50　Blackton, Charles S., Australian Nationality and Nativism: The Australian Natives' Association, 1885-1901, *The Journal of Modern History*, vol. 30, no. 1, 1958, pp. 37, 46.

51　Deaking, Alfred, The Federal Council of Australasia, 1895, University of Sydney Library, 2000

52　"Sir Henry Parkes's Tenterfield Oration, 1889". ABC Online. 14 February 2007. Retrieved 23 October 2018.

53　W.G. McMinn, Nationalism and Federalism in Australia (Oxford: Oxford University Press, 1994)

ensure a unified country and self-governance of States at the same time. As a result, it was decided that the federal structure would the most suitable for serving the respective interests of States. Therefore, the founding fathers of the Constitution, considering that the unified Australia was founded under different circumstances than its federal counterparts, intended a minimally centralised Union.[54] Hence, unlike other federations, there was absence of opposition to the idea of federalism. Most of the States and their representatives accepted federalism and found it to be a perfect match for their aspirations.

Thus, the Constitution of Australia was drafted keeping in mind the federal structure which had been adopted by the founding fathers. Once the structure and framework for the Constitution was finalised, the draft Bill was sent to the colonies to be voted by the electorate. By 1899, the founding fathers succeeded in obtaining the majority's approval in all the participating States. The Constitution was then laid before the Imperial Parliament in Britain which passed it into a law. Hence, the Commonwealth of Australia Constitution Act 1900 was enacted, resulting into the formation of Federation of Australia.[55] As the reader will notice, the founding fathers of the federation of Australia, even prior to their official discussions on the Constitution, decided that a federal structure is the most appropriate structure for their governance. As a result, the written Constitution was drafted with a federal sentiment.

Canada

The Canadian federalism came into existence from the peculiar diversity of cultures and languages which existed in Canada prior to its independence. Upper Canada was dominated by English speaking Canadians whereas Lower Canada was dominated by French speaking Canadians, each region having its own Parliament. Apart from these, there were other miniscule habitations spread across the country. As a necessary corollary of diversity, the people and their representatives from each part were often at loggerheads with their counterparts. There were several instances of rebellions or infighting among the two groups. However, the British government was

54 Nicholas Aroney, The Constitution of a Federal Commonwealth: the making and meaning of the Australian Constitution (New York: Cambridge University Press, 2009) 276

55 J. A. La Nauze, The Making of the Australian Constitution (Carlton: Melbourne University Press, 1972)

determined to form a unified government as the existence of two provincial government resulted in huge administrative inefficiencies and therefore, these were a burden on the thriving British Empire. As a result, the British Parliament attempted to unify the people of Canada through the enactment of the British North America Act, 1940 also known as the Act of Union, 1840 which resulted into abolition of separate Parliaments of Upper and Lower Canada and establishing a new political entity – Province of Canada.

Owing to the diversity in the country, the British Parliament which enjoyed sovereignty over the Province of Canada as its colony, deemed it fit to form a structure which protects the diverse interests of varied people living in the country and at the same time ensures British paramountcy. The structure of the Canada was thus, built upon the Constitution of the British Empire, as discussed earlier. The British Empire was empowered to deal with defence, communications and foreign affairs whereas the colonies were made self-governing bodies for domestic affairs. Therefore, in order to secure the interests of the English as well as French speaking people and maintaining British paramountcy at the same time, it was decided to create a nation where the interests of the States are secured by vesting major powers of governance with them.

However, as Canada approached the eve of independence from Britain, the founding fathers of the nation convened conferences to discuss the structure of the government to be formed for an independent Canada. Therefore, a conference was convened in Charlottetown in September 1864 to create a confederation unified under the name of Canada. The Charlottetown conference laid down the framework for a confederal Canada which was elaborately discussed in a subsequent conference held in 1864 in Quebec.

However, the idea of a confederation was discarded at the Quebec Conference. Two alternatives emerged – a Unitary State or a Federation.[56] This remained the chief reason for a conflict in the conference. One of the groups argued in favour of a Unitary State considering that a purely federal structure was failing in United States of America having resulted in a civil war, as seen in the preceding paragraphs. Another reason for apprehension against the federal structure was the rising tensions between America and

---

56   Buckner, Phillip A. (7 February 2006). "Québec Conference". *Historica Canada.*

Britain which called for a stronger central government to ensure the war efforts are not compromised, if a situation arises.

The other group however argued in favour of a federal government under the trepidation that their cultural and linguistic identities will be lost under a Unitary State. This group asserted its support for a Federal State under the assumption that the political party enjoying majority in the centre, whether English or French, would intend to benefit their own community at the expense of the other. Therefore, they argued in favour of stronger provincial governments vis-à-vis the central government.

Eventually, upon culmination of the conference, it was decided that a federation shall be formed and the powers shall be divided between the provincial governments and the federal government.[57] Owing to the diversity, the conference adopted a stronger federal government at the centre to ensure that neither of the regions are at a disadvantage, granting them equal representation and powers in the Constitution.[58] In pursuance of this, Seventy-Two (72) Resolutions were adopted at the Quebec Conference which laid down the federal framework of Canada. These Resolution significantly influenced the British North America Act, 1967 which brought major amendments to the Canadian federation. Thus, the founding fathers decided to adopt a federal structure of governance in Canada and agreed to draft a federal written Constitution.[59] The founding fathers of Canada, learning from the American example, amended their federal structure

---

57 Bruchesi, Jean (1956). Canada. Toronto, Ontario: Ryerson Press.; Colquhoun, A. H. (1964). The Fathers of the Confederation. Toronto, Ontario: University of Toronto Press.; Creighton, Donald (2012). Canada's First Century, 1867-1967. Toronto: Oxford.

58 Driedger, Elma A. (1976). The Consolidation of the North America Acts. Ottawa: Department of Justice.; Finlay, John L (1991). Pre Confederation Canada. Scarborough, Ontario: Prentice-Hall.; Francis, R.D. (2013). Origins. Toronto, Ontario: Nelson Education.

59 Krikorian, Jacqueline (2017). Roads to Confederation. The Making of Canada, 1867. Toronto, Ontario: University of Toronto Press.; Laforest, Guy (2015). The Constitution that Shaped Us. Montreal, Quebec: McGill-Queen's University Press.; Moore, Christopher (2015). Three Weeks in Quebec City. New York, New York: Allen Lane.; Trotter, Reginald George (1971). Canadian Federation. New York, New York: Russel & Russel.; Waite, P. B. (1972). Confederation, 1854-1867. Toronto, Ontario: Holt, Rinehart and Winston of Canada.; Warner, Donald (1960). The Idea of the Continental Union. Lexington, Kentucky: University of Kentucky Press.

thereby creating a stronger centre, in accordance with the peculiar needs of their nation. The Canadian structure thus involved elements of both, the British unitary system (stronger centre) and American federalism.[60]

Therefore, in Canada, just as in America, the founding fathers intended to create a federal Constitution owing to the peculiar needs and diversity in the country. Therefore, the federal sentiment was present in the Canadian Constitution from the very beginning. Since the purpose of the study in this chapter is to ascertain the federal sentiment in the formation of the Canadian Constitution, the preceding paragraphs show the circumstances which influenced the adoption of a federal structure and that the founding fathers possessed the federal sentiment while drafting the Constitution. Hence, federalism prevailed in Canada.

India

The framers of the Constitution of India learnt a great deal from the experiences of other English-speaking federations such as U.S.A., Canada and Australia.[61] The experiences of these federations provided ample knowledge and guidance to the framers to assess the advantages and disadvantages of a federal structure and frame the Constitution appropriately. Further, another reason for adoption of a federal structure is the comfort of constituent assembly members with a federal structure considering that the British Empire operated as a loose federation. The Empire, as discussed earlier, handled the defence, foreign relations and communications while leaving the rest for the colonies. Considering that the constituent assembly members were well acquainted with such a structure, federalism seemed to be a comfortable option.

According to the constitutional scholar *H. M. Seervai*, a federal solution to the political problem in India was envisaged, though a distant prospect, as early as 1918 through the Montague Chelmsford Reforms (1918) and Simon Commission (1929).[62] However, the adoption of a federal structure was not given much consideration as the rising freedom struggle in India forced the British to maintain a strong centre to ensure their paramountcy over the gem of their empire. Even the princely States favoured a federal India under

---

60   Buckner, Phillip A. (7 February 2006). "Québec Conference". *Historica Canada.*
61   Jain, M.P., Indian Federalism: A Background Paper
62   Gwyer and Appadorai, Speeches and Documents on the Indian Constitution, Vol. 1, pp. 213-214

the British Empire as it allowed them to retain their autocratic powers. The rulers of these princely States had been assured protection from external aggression or internal disorders by the Empire through various treaties and covenants. The loyalty of these princely States to the Empire under a federal system allowed the British to counter the political struggle and gain support of these States.[63] It can however be seen that considering the diversity in race, religion and language in India, a federal solution seemed to be the right one to all concerned parties.

As a result, the Government of India Act 1935 upon which the Constitution of India heavily relies, adopted the federal structure upon its enactment. The federal structure seemed to be a workable solution as the leaders of a unified India preferred a loose federation considering the varied diversity of race and religions. Prior to the partition of India in June 1947, the Constituent Assembly had agreed to a loose federal structure wherein it was announced through the Objectives Resolution that the Union shall have only three powers i.e. Defence, Foreign Affairs and Communications whereas the States shall be autonomous units having residuary powers.[64]

Therefore, the Republic of India was intended to be federal[65] during the Constituent Assembly debates though the nature of the federation was largely in question. As the debates progressed, there was a general consensus among the members that, considering the external aggressions against India as well as the vastness of the country and its heterogenous elements, a purely unitary structure was neither desirable nor practicable.[66] Further, as *Prof. Sawyer* quoted *"the sub-continent of India was another area which by reason of size, population, regional (including linguistic) differences and communication problems presented an obvious federal situation, if not the possibility of several distinct nations"*.[67] Therefore, a federation was considered to be an acceptable idea.[68] This idea of federalism was prevalent throughout the assembly debates though some centralising elements were added to the federal structure.[69]

---

63 Seervai, H. M., Constitutional Law of India, 4th Ed. Volume 1, Universal Law Publishing, pp. 286-287
64 Basu, D. D. Commentary on the Constitution of India
65 See Government of India Act, 1935
66 See Constituent Assembly Debates
67 Sawyer, Modern Federalism (1969)
68 Basu, D. D., Comparative Federalism, Lexis Nexis, India 2007, pp. 116
69 XI CAD, 57-58; II CDA, 300

However, with the dawn of partition and the ensuing atrocious massacre and riots, the members of the Constituent Assembly called for a reconsideration of the federal principle.[70] It seemed that the idea of a loose federation was not workable considering the change of circumstances and widespread chaos resulting from partition. As the Second Report of the Union Powers Committee[71] observed:

"Now that the partition is a settled fact, we are unanimously of the view that it would be injurious to the interests of the country to provide for a weak central authority which would be incapable of ensuring peace, of coordinating vital matters of common concern and of speaking effectively for the whole country in the international sphere."

Thereafter, the assembly began to reconsider the federal features and opted for a federal government with a strong centre. Even in the years succeeding the adoption of the Constitution of India, the courts have time and again emphasised that the Constitution is federal in principle. Federalism in India is a matter of principle, not of administrative convenience.[72] Beg, C.J. observed that the Indian Constitution is, in a sense, federal and has appearance of a federal structure.[73] In fact, federalism has been considered to be a part of the basic structure of the Indian Constitution.[74]

Nonetheless, the principle of federalism prevailed through the Constitution. Considering that the object of this chapter is to trace the federal sentiment, the author focused on the presence of an intent to form a federal Constitution, regardless of a strong or weak centre. As shown in the preceding paragraphs, the founding fathers of the Republic of India intended from the very beginning to adopt a federal structure, considering the various circumstances at play in the nation on the eve of independence and the days that followed. In light of the extreme cultural, religious and linguistic diversity in India, the federal solution seemed to the perfect fit for the nation. The Constitution of India was thus drafted with a federal sentiment.

---

70   Austin, G., Indian Constitution (1966) pp. 190
71   2nd Report, Union Powers Committee, 05.07.1947, 1st Ser., pp. 70-71: IV CAD, p. 60
72   Jain, M.P., Indian Constitutional Law, 7th Edn. Lexis Nexis 2016 pp. 749
73   State of Rajasthan vs. Union of India AIR 1977 SC 1382: (1997) 3 SCC 592
74   S. R. Bommai vs. Union of India AIR 1994 SC 1918: (1994) 3 SCC 1

Conclusion

As seen in the preceding paragraphs, a federal sentiment was prevalent in the federations which came to be characterised as federal. The author attempted to trace the circumstances under which the federations came into existence and such circumstances necessitated a need for a federation, as opposed to a Unitary State. Some federations were concerned with diversity of race, languages and religions whereas the others were concerned about economic factors. However, all these were characterised by one common element, the founding fathers had a federal sentiment while deciding upon a structure for their respective nations. This federal sentiment was present in all these federations and as a result, these nations became federal.

In the United States of America, considered to be the first federal nation in the world, federation was seen as an upgrade to a confederation. The latter provided for a substantially weak central government without powers to collect, tax, regulate trade or give directions to States. As a result, the central government was bereft of funds to carry on its functioning and failed to repay the debt incurred during the American Revolution. Further, the States were given unbridled powers to regulate their affairs, eventually resulting into disputes with other States. These factors collectively called for a reconsideration of the confederation which resulted in the formation of a federation. The Constitutional Convention, dominated by leaders preferring a federation over a Unitary State, decided that the federal structure would be the most appropriate choice. Another factor which increased the federal bend was the domination of Federalist Party. As a result, the Constitution was drafted with a federal sentiment and hence, predominantly federal.

In Australia, unlike America or Canada, federalism was adopted with economic considerations instead of racial, linguistic or religious differences. The six States, erstwhile colonies of the British Empire, came together to discuss the prospects of a unified Australia due to the constant conflicts between these regions relating to trade barriers, inter-state travel, immigration, tariffs etc. As an attempt to reconcile these differences, the idea of federalism was mooted as early as 1880. Most of the States and their delegates were convinced that federalism was the right option for their governance. Considering that the people were not as diverse as aforementioned federations, there was an absence of widespread opposition to federalism. The States were happy to forego the powers of defence, foreign relations and communications to the federal government and retain their autonomy. Therefore, even prior to the constitutional conventions, the idea of federalism was ingrained among the States. As a result, the Constitution was drafted with a federal sentiment running through its very veins.

In Canada, circumstances were quite different from those in America. The Canadian people were divided due to their linguistic differences. The English and French speaking people were divided into different States and thus, demanded a loose federation to protect their respective interests and retain autonomy. This notion of retaining autonomy pressed the demand for a federation. However, learning from the American model wherein a weak central government had collapsed, the Canadians called for a federal structure with a strong centre. Another factor which strengthened the demand for a strong centre was the possibility of external aggression due to the growing tensions between America and Britain. Thus, the federal sentiment prevailed in the framers of the Constitution of Canada, owing to its peculiar circumstances. As a result, the Constitution was drafted with a federal sentiment.

India, being one of the newfangled nations to have adopted federalism, learnt a great deal from the experiences of America, Canada and Australia. Considering the extremely diverse population divided by linguistics, race and religions, India required a structure which could provide ample protection to the interests of all the people and ensure national integrity at the same time. As a result, federalism seemed to be the only option which could help achieve the consent of all parties concerned. However, India did not adopt a purely federal structure. Learning from the other federations and extraneous circumstances present during the partition, a federal structure with a strong centre seemed to be the ideal choice. As seen in the preceding paragraphs, the federal sentiment ran through the discussions of the Constituent Assembly. Even prior to the eve of Independence, the Britishers had sought to establish a federal structure in India as early as 1918, albeit for their own colonial purposes. This reflected in the Government of India Act, 1935 which introduced a federal system for the first time. The Constitution of India borrowed heavily from the said Act, as a necessary corollary of which, the federal principle was also inculcated. As a result, the Constitution of India was drafted with an intent to form a federal structure.

As seen in the preceding paragraphs, in each of our target federations, there ran a federal sentiment throughout their respective constitutional assemblies. The founding fathers of these nations intended to form a federal structure in these nations, albeit for different reasons. But the common thread which ran through all of them was the federal sentiment i.e. an intention to form a federal nation. A federal sentiment is a crucial aspect for a nation to be characterised as federal. India, as seen earlier, was intended to be a federation, as did other federations. The leaders were well acquainted with federalism and the colonial powers intended to form a federation in India as well. Therefore, India, from the very beginning was intended to be federal. The issue which was debated upon in the assembly was the type of federalism i.e. with a weak or strong centre. Hence, a federal sentiment was present among the constituent assembly members. Thus, India became a federation albeit with a strong centre.

CHAPTER 5

Formation of Federation and its Territory

Another crucial aspect of federalism is the mode of formation of the federation. It has been frequently argued that a federation can be formed only if two or more independent States decide to unite for geographical, political, racial or other reasons to form a nation. In other words, the traditional mode of formation of a federation involves several independent or autonomous States coming together to form a Union through a voluntary agreement[75], without giving up their independent existence or autonomy, with the common purpose of defence or economic prowess or efficient administration depending upon the situation. The federations of U.S.A., Australia and Switzerland were formed through this mode. However, with the formation of Canada, another mode of formation became popular wherein the existing nation is transformed into a federation through dividing the territory into provinces and granting autonomy to such provinces, thereby adopting a federal structure. As the constitutional scholar *D. D. Basu* writes, whether the mode of federation is centrifugal or centripetal, one common feature is that these units enjoy autonomy, whatever be the nomenclature.[76]

According to the author, there are five issues which need to be considered in this chapter having a direct bearing on the federalism in a nation. These pertain to - mode of formation of the federation; procedure for reorganisation of States; admission of new States; mode of acquisition of new territories; and powers granted or restrictions imposed on newly admitted States. Withal, these issues govern the formation of the federation and rights of States with regards to their respective territories.

This Chapter will discuss the mode of formation of the federation in each of the target jurisdictions i.e. U.S.A., Canada, Australia and India along with the aforementioned ancillary issues. The author will conclude that the

---

75 Cf. A.G. for Commonwealth vs. Colonial Sugar Refining Co. (1914) AC 237 (252-54)

76 Basu, D. D., Comparative Federalism, Lexis Nexis, India 2007, pp. 148

mode of formation of the federation and issues pertaining to regulation of territory in India are similar to the ones in other federations, thereby exhibiting that the Indian position is similar to the ones in traditional federations.

United States of America

A federation is formed when several States find it advantageous to come together for geographical, political, economic or racial reasons, to combine themselves and form a common or national government, while retaining their independence and autonomy at the same time. The States do not intend to give their independence away, if they indeed do so, it would result in a Unitary State. These States desire a Union but do not desire unity.[77] In light of these, fifty (50) component States came together to form the United States of America as constituent members of the Union rather than administrative units.[78] Originally however, there were thirteen (13) States which formed the federation of United States.

First, considering that there were only 13 States which formed a federal Union initially, several States became a part of the federation after the enactment of the Constitution. Therefore, it is necessary to understand the mode of admission of new States into the Union. America has liberally admitted new States into the Union as 37 new States have been admitted or created after coming in force of the Constitution, either through admission or reorganization of existing States. Article IV, Section 3(1) of the Constitution of United States of America enables the Union to admit new States. It states, *"new States may be admitted by the Congress into this Union..."*. However, no procedure or conditions for admission of States have been provided in the Constitution although, jurists have attempted to lay down some guidelines[79]. As a result, the Congress exercises complete discretion over imposing any condition for admission although, once a State has been admitted, it is not necessary for such State to obey such conditions[80] considering that the Constitution applies to all States equally[81]. Thus, all members of the American federation, be it original members or

---

77   Dicey, 10th Edn., pp. 141-43

78   Basu, D. D., Comparative Federalism, Lexis Nexis, India 2007, pp. 33

79   Cf. West, American Government, 1946, p. 290; Ogg & Ray, Essentials of American Government, (1965), pp. 45-46.

80   Coyle vs. Smith (1911) 221 US 559

81   "America is a Union of equal States", ibid.

ones admitted subsequently, enjoy all the powers entrusted to the original States under the Constitution.[82]

Second, another dimension which concerns the mode of formation of the federation is the power to adjust or reorganize the territory of existing States. In U.S.A., the States are considered to be 'indestructible'[83] i.e. it is not permitted for the national government to alter the boundaries of the States, as they existed at the time of their admission, without the consent of the respective States, according to Art. IV, Sec. 3(1) of the Constitution. However, the States and the Union may mutually agree to make such alterations. The said Article provides:

"New States may be admitted by the Congress into this Union; but no new State shall be formed or erected within the jurisdiction of any other State, nor any State be formed by the junction of two or more States, or parts of States, without the consent of the Legislatures of the States concerned, as well as of Congress."[84]

Through this common consent mechanism, there have been readjustments and reorganization of States in the past. Some leading examples include Tennessee from North Carolina[85], Kentucky from Virginia[86], Maine from Massachusetts[87], West Virginia from Virginia[88] and Vermont from New York[89].

---

82 Pollard vs. Hagan (1845) 3 How 212 (223)

83 Texas vs. White (1868) 7 Wall 700 (720)

84 Art. IV, Sec. 3(1) of the Constitution

85 Hugh T. Lefler and Albert R. Newsome, *North Carolina: The History of a Southern State* (3rd ed., 1973); William S. Powell, *North Carolina through Four Centuries* (1989); Scott, Joseph and Smith, Daniel. "A map of the Tennessee government, formerly part of North Carolina, taken chiefly from surveys by Gen. D. Smith & others." [Philadelphia]: [M. Carey]. circa 1794.

86 Kentucky: Secretary of State – Land Office – Kentucky County Formations; "How Kentucky Became a State". *Puerto Rico 51st*. August 8, 2014. Retrieved February 21, 2020.

87 "Maine's Path to Statehood". *PR51st.com*. Retrieved May 31, 2017;

88 "Proclamation 100 – Admitting West Virginia Into the Union", John T. Woolley and Gerhard Peters, The American Presidency Project *"Archived copy"*. Santa Barbara, CA. April 20, 1863; Lincoln and West Virginia Statehood* By J. Duane Squires Volume 24, Number 4 (July 1963) *"Archived copy"*. *Archived from the original on 2010-06-27.*

89 Slade, William, Jr., Compiler. *Vermont State Papers: Being a Collection of Records and Documents Connected with the Assumption and Establishment of Government by the People of Vermont, Together with the Journal of the Council of Safety, the First*

Third, as concerns the mode of acquisition, the American Constitution does not provide for acquisition of a new territory by the federation. The mode of acquisition is executed as per the Rules of International Law[90] including Purchase, Cession, War, Treaty and Annexation.

Fourth, the territory acquired by the United States is not *ipso facto* placed on the same pedestal as other States. The Constitution only applies to such States to whom the Congress expressly directs its application.[91] Therefore, unless the admission of a State is accompanied by a formal Congressional declaration[92], the territory does not become a part of the United States. In other words, even after the admission of a State by the federation, the Congress needs to expressly approve its admission in order to bring it on par with the other States of the federation.

In conclusion, the American federation was formed through an agreement between thirteen (13) independent States to come together and form a common nation. The American Constitution also provides for admission of new States, as a result of which, around 37 new States were admitted into the federation. Territories may be acquired by the federal government through the rules of international law. Once admitted, all such States enjoy equal rights under the American Constitution. However, the power to readjust or reorganize the boundaries of the existing States is limited. Such a reorganization can be effected only with the consent of the States, accompanied by an approval by the Congress. Lastly, the States can only become a part of the federation after a formal Congressional declaration of the same.

Australia

Initially, Australia was formed by five (5) States namely – New South Wales, Victoria, South Australia, Queensland and Tasmania. These were the original States which existed when the federation of Australia was formed. Subsequently, Western Australia joined the aforementioned five

Constitution, the Early Journals of the General Assembly, and the Laws from the Year 1779 to 1786, Inclusive.; Middlebury, Vermont; 1823. Pp. 13–19.; Van Zandt, Franklin K.; *Boundaries of the United States and the Several States*; Geological Survey Professional Paper 909. Washington, D.C.; Government Printing Office; 1976. The standard compilation for its subject.. P.63.

90   American Ins. Co. vs. Canter (1828) 1 Pet 528; Jones vs. U.S., (1890) 137 US 202

91   Downes vs. Bidwell (1901) 182 US 194

92   Balzac vs. People of Porto Rico (1922) 258 US 298

States in the federation. Therefore, Australia was formed with the coming together of several States, similar to America. However, the reasons for such a Union were different i.e. the Australian States were more concerned about the economic welfare and administrative efficiency than defence or freedom from colonial powers. This mode of formation of the federation is considered to be the original mode of formation.

Second, as concerns the admission of new States, the Constitution of Australia expressly provides for admission of new States in the federation, much alike America. Chapter 6 (New States) of the Australian Constitution provides:

"121. New States may be admitted or established

The Parliament may admit to the Commonwealth or establish new States, and may upon such admission or establishment make or impose such terms and conditions, including the extent of representation in either House of the Parliament, as it thinks fit."

As the reader may see, these provisions enable the government to admit new States into the federation. However, it is necessary to notice a stark difference from the American mode of admission of new States. In Australia, the government has been empowered to impose any terms or conditions it may deem fit for admission of the new States, including its representation in the Parliament. As a result, the States will have to adhere to these terms and conditions even after their admission unlike America, wherein a State stands on an equal footing vis-à-vis other States in the federation upon admission. Further, the Constitution of Australia itself provides for certain rights which are only conferred upon the original States.[93] These rights cannot be availed by the States admitted after the Constitution came into existence, even though they may be a part of the federation. This power to admit new States with conditions, however, has never been utilized by the federation.

Third, unlike America, the Constitution of Australia expressly provides for the modes of acquisition of territories i.e. the Australian Constitution specifically lays down as to how new territories may be acquired. Sec. 122[94] of the Australian Constitution provides:

---

93 W. Australia vs. Commonwealth (1975) 134 CLR 201 (257)
94 Chapter VI, Constitution of Australia

"122. Government of territories

The Parliament may make laws for the government of any territory surrendered by any State to and accepted by the Commonwealth, or of any territory placed by the Queen under the authority of and accepted by the Commonwealth, or otherwise acquired by the Commonwealth, and may allow the representation of such territory in either House of the Parliament to the extent and on the terms which it thinks fit."

As per this provision, the Parliament is empowered to deal with three kinds of territories which fall outside the territories of the existing States. These are 'territory surrendered by any State and accepted by Commonwealth'; 'territory placed by the Queen under the authority of the Commonwealth'; and 'territories otherwise acquired by the Commonwealth'. Among these, the 'territories otherwise acquired by the Commonwealth' includes the territories acquired under the rules of Public International Law including but not limited to cessation, treaty, war, annexation etc.

Fourth, the Constitution of Australia expressly empowers the government to alter the boundaries of the States. The Parliament can alter the territories of an existing State or form a new State by carving out from territories of existing States. This power to alter the boundaries of the States or forming a new State is similar to that of America however, in addition to obtaining consent of States for alteration of boundaries, the Constitution of Australia prescribes another mandatory condition for such alteration.

"123. Alteration of limits of States

The Parliament of the Commonwealth may, with the consent of the Parliament of a State, and the approval of the majority of the electors of the State voting upon the question, increase, diminish, or otherwise alter the limits of the State, upon such terms and conditions as may be agreed on, and may, with the like consent, make provision respecting the effect and operation of any increase or diminution or alteration of territory in relation to any State affected.

124. Formation of new States

A new State may be formed by separation of territory from a State, but only with the consent of the Parliament thereof, and a new State may be formed by the Union of two or more States or parts of States, but only with the consent of the Parliaments of the States affected."

In Australia therefore, mere consent of the legislature of the State will not suffice but the majority of eligible voters in that State must approve such an alteration of boundaries. Further, it is pertinent to mention that the alteration of the boundary of a State cannot be made even with an amendment of the Constitution without the approval of the voters of the concerned State. In this regard, it is necessary to see last paragraph of s. 128 of Constitution which enforces this proposition:

"No alteration diminishing the proportionate representation of any State in either House of the Parliament, or the minimum number of representatives of a State in the House of Representatives, or increasing, diminishing, or otherwise altering the limits of the State, or in any manner affecting the provisions of the Constitution in relation thereto, shall become law unless the majority of the electors voting in that State approve the proposed law."

As a result, no amendment to the Constitution can result in alteration of the boundaries without the consent of the voters. Therefore, in principle, the Parliament of Australia is empowered to create new States by carving out portions from old States or through altering the boundaries of the existing States, only with the consent of the majority of eligible voters in the concerned State. However, there exists a peculiar provision which allows the State to surrender its territory to the Commonwealth.[95] This surrender of territory does not require the approval of the voters of the State.[96]

Fifth, s. 122 empowers the Parliament to make laws for the governance of the acquired territories. Such power is plenary, that is to say, it is absolute in nature and not bound by the constitutional limitations imposed on the government such as distribution of powers between federal and State governments.[97] Unless such a territory is admitted as a 'State' of the federation, it is merely a dependency[98] and the Parliament is authorized to exercise plenary powers over it. This provision is starkly different from that

---

95 Sec. 111, Chapter V, Constitution of Australia
96 Paterson vs. O'Brien (1978) 138 CLR 276 (280-281)
97 Buchanan vs. Commonwealth (1913) 16 CLR 315; Wynes Legislative and Executive Powers, 1956 pp. 152-160
98 Australian National Airways vs. Commonwealth (1945) 71 CLR 29 (79)

of American Constitution wherein, upon admission, every State is equal has rights under the Constitution.

In conclusion, the Australian federation, like American, was formed through an agreement between five (5) independent States, with a sixth State joining thereafter to form a common nation. The Australian Constitution prescribes that new States can be admitted into the federation. However, unlike the American federation, the Parliament is empowered to impose terms and conditions on the new States which shall remain in place even after they are formally admitted whereas in America, after admission, all States are equal before the Constitution. In fact, in Australia, original States enjoy special rights under the Constitution. Another contrast to the American federation is that while altering the territories of the existing States, mere consent of the concerned State legislature will not suffice but majority of the eligible voters of the State must approve such an alteration. Lastly, unless a territory is admitted as a 'State', the Parliament enjoys plenary or absolute power over its governance without any constitutional limitations.

Canada

In contrast to the American and Australian federations, the Canadian federation was not formed through coming together of several States but rather by breaking down a single country into several autonomous States. The mode of formation of a federation cannot be restricted to the conventional mode of several States coming together to form a common nation, but also includes breaking up of a Unitary State into a several units and forming a Federal State. There has been a general consensus among the academicians and jurists that Canada should be admitted into the family of federations.[99] Therefore, it must be acknowledged that a federation may be formed by a mode other than by way of treaty or agreement between independent States.

---

99 Sawyer, Modern Federalism (1969) pp. 30, 127, 179, 186; Wynes, Legislative, Executive and Judicial Powers (1970), p. 2; Kennedy, Constitution of Canada; Garner, Political Science and Government (1951), p. 321; Lipson, Great Issues in Politics (1981), p. 296; Gettel, Political Science (1967), p. 229; Friedmann, Constitutional Government (1950), p. 210; Carter & Herz, Major Foreign Powers, (1972), p. 658; Dawson, Government of Canada (1970), p.76; Newmann, European and Comparative Government (1960), p. 678; De Smith, Constitutional Law, (1973), p. 33; Rep. of the Royal Commission of Inquiry on Constitutional Problems (Quebec, 1956) Vol. II pp. 97-131.

The provinces of Canada did not possess any separate existence under the British Empire in Canada. The British, while withdrawing from Canada after its independence, decided to divide the country into provinces and form a common central government while simultaneously granting autonomy to these provinces. *Lord Haldane* observed that Canada is a federation only *in a loose sense relying on the pre-federation status of the units and the mode of formation.* However, this was rebutted by *Lord Watson*[100], with *Lord Haldane*[101] himself accepting the rebuttal soon after. *Lord Watson*[102] held that the result of British North America Act, 1867 was that the British Crown's authority was divided between the federal government and the provinces such that they were bound by the limitations imposed by the Constitution, each representing the Crown and neither was subordinate or a delegate of the other. Affirming this view, *Lord Haldane* in *Bonanza case*[103] observed:

"...the Lieutenant – Governor...is as much the representative of Her Majesty for all purposes of provincial government as the Governor General himself is for all purposes of Dominion Government."

Thus, Canada, regardless of the mode of formation, is considered to be a federation. The Canadian mode of formation reaffirms the view that a federation need not be formed through an agreement or treaty between independent States but rather can be formed through breaking up of a Unitary State and converting it into a federation. This mode is suitable for nations with very diverse people, such as Canada wherein the nation was divided between English speaking and French speaking provinces, so as to ensure that the rights of the people are preserved and protected. As a result, the Canadian federation was converted from a Unitary State to a federation. The three States which initially formed the federation were Canada (including Quebec and Ontario), Nova Scotia and New Brunswick. Subsequently six (6) new State were added to the federation. These are Manitoba, British Columbia, Prince Edward Island, Saskatchewan, Alberta and Newfoundland.

---

100 Liquidators of Maritime Bank vs. Receiver General of New Brunswick (1892) AC 437 (441-443)
101 Bonanza Creek Co. vs. The King (1916) 1 AC 566
102 See Maritime Bank
103 See Bonanza

Second, as concerns the mode of admission of new States, the Constitution of Canada expressly provides for the admission of new States. S. 146 of the Act provides:

"It shall be lawful for the Queen, by and with the Advice of Her Majesty's Most Honourable Privy Council, on Addresses from the Houses of the Parliament of Canada, and from the Houses of the respective Legislatures of the Colonies or Provinces of Newfoundland, Prince Edward Island, and British Columbia, to admit those Colonies or Provinces, or any of them, into the Union, and on Address from the Houses of the Parliament of Canada to admit Rupert's Land and the North-western Territory, or either of them, into the Union, on such Terms and Conditions in each Case as are in the Addresses expressed and as the Queen thinks fit to approve, subject to the Provisions of this Act;..."

This provision allows the government to admit new colonies into the Canadian federation. As the reader may see, s. 146 states the name of each province which shall be a part of Canada thereinafter. However, any province whose name is not mentioned in s. 146 cannot be admitted to the federation. In author's view, admission of any other State would require a constitutional amendment of s. 146 itself. In the absence of such an amendment, the Constitution does not expressly permit the admission of new States. This provision is on the opposite side of the spectrum, America and Australia being on the other side considering that both the latter nations permit admission of new States without constitutional amendments.

Third, the Constitution of Canada does not provide for the mode of acquisition of new territories. As a result, much like the American federation, the acquisition of territories is done in accordance with the modes of acquisition as per the established rules of Public International Law including Purchase, Cession, War, Treaty and Annexation.

Fourth, the Parliament of Canada is empowered to alter or reorganize the territories of States or create new States by altering territories of other States, albeit not unilaterally. Sec. 43 of the Constitution of Canada provides for the alteration or reorganisation of the territories of the States. Sec. 43 States:

"43. Amendment of provisions relating to some but not all provinces

An amendment to the Constitution of Canada in relation to any provision that applies to one or more, but not all, provinces, including

a. any alteration to boundaries between provinces, and

b. any amendment to any provision that relates to the use of the English or the French language within a province,

may be made by proclamation issued by the Governor General under the Great Seal of Canada only where so authorized by resolutions of the Senate and House of Commons and of the legislative assembly of each province to which the amendment applies."

For altering or reorganising the territories of States, the assent of both Houses of the Parliament along with the resolution approving the same passed by the legislative assemblies of each State whose territory is proposed to be altered, is required. Without these approvals, such an alteration cannot be performed. Therefore, the Canadian system of alteration of territory is the same as American system. It does not require approval of the majority of the voters in the affected State, unlike Australia.

Fifth, the State admitted to the federation though admitted as a new State, may not be offered full legislative powers assigned to the original States as per the British North America Act, 1867.[104] The Constitution of Canada therefore does not guarantee equality to all the States in the federation. This position is similar to the Australian position wherein the newly admitted States do not possess same powers or rights as do the original States. However, in America, all States admitted into the federation are equal before the Constitution.

In conclusion, the Canadian federation was formed in a starkly different manner from that of conventional federations such as America and Australia. The Canadian federation was formed by breaking up a Unitary State into several provinces thereby forming a federation. It was not formed through any agreement or treaty between the States. Many modern writers and jurists, as discussed earlier, have accepted the view that such a mode of formation can be adopted to form a federation. Therefore, the Canadian federation was formed by three (3) States in the beginning, later joined by another six (6) States. The Constitution of Canada expressly allows admission of new States however, such an admission requires a

104 A.G. for Saskatchewan vs. Canadian Pacific Ry., (1953) 2 All ER 970 (972-74) (PC)

constitutional amendment permitting such an admission, dissimilar to America and Australia which do not require a constitutional amendment. Such new States may be acquired as per the rules acquisition of territories, recognized under International Law. The Constitution of Canada, like America, permits alteration of territories of a State with an express approval from the concerned State's legislature. Lastly, similar to Australia, the newly admitted States do not enjoy same legislative powers and rights as do the original States of the federation.

India

As seen in the preceding paragraphs, there are two modes of formation of a federation – forming a common nation through agreement between independent States or converting a Unitary State into a federation by breaking it down into several provinces. In author's view, India is a mixture of both these modes of formation. The provinces which were within the territory allotted to India at the time of independence were assimilated automatically into the newly formed Union. However, nearly half of the territory of India was under the domain of princely States, which called for an agreement with these States to assimilate them into the Union.

Prior to its independence from the British in 1947, India was a Unitary State comprising of several provinces and princely States. On the eve of independence, India was divided into three different nations – India, Pakistan and Bangladesh (erstwhile East Pakistan).[105] As a result, these provinces were divided among the three nations. The princely States however, were given an option to either join India or not.[106] Considering that there were about 565 princely States in India (covering around 40% of the area; 23% of the population)[107], an agreement with these States to retain their allegiance to India was necessary for national security, maintenance of internal peace and retaining a larger geographical area. Therefore, the government commenced a drive headed by Shri Sardar Vallabhai Patel to

---

105 The Oxford History of the British Empire: Historiography, edited by R. W. Winks. Oxford: Oxford University Press. ISBN 978-0-19-820566-1. OCLC 1036799442.

106 Ishtiaq Ahmed (1998). *State, Nation and Ethnicity in Contemporary South Asia.* London & New York. p. 99; Ravi Kumar Pillai Kandamath (2016) Yaqoob Khan Bangash. A Princely Affair: The Accession and Integration of the *Princely States of Pakistan, 1947-1955, Asian Affairs, 47:2, 316-319,*

107 *Datar, Arvind P. (18 November 2013). "Who betrayed Sardar Patel?". The Hindu.*

enter into agreements with these States ensuring their allegiance to India.[108] These discussions, often forceful[109], eventually led to these princely States becoming a part of the Republic of India. Hence, the provinces or States were assimilated themselves, however, the government had to sign agreements with the princely States to retain them in the Union.

As can be seen from the preceding paragraphs, the government indeed entered into agreements, whether express or implied with these princely States to induct them into the Union. In fact, a compensation was paid to these princely States as consideration for their consent. This compensation is popularly known as 'Privy Purses', which were abolished by the government in 1971.[110] The readers may recall this as the famous 'Privy Purses' case[111], studied by students and practitioners alike. Further, the princely States were allowed some autonomy for local governance through the Instrument of Accession while the power to govern national affairs including defence, external affairs and communications belonged to the government of India.[112] It is therefore submitted that the Indian Union was formed partly through converting the Unitary State into federal along with several States entering into an agreement to become a part of India with an intention to form a federal Union wherein these States shall retain some autonomy. Thus, the Union of India is a mixture of American and Australian mode of formation on one hand and Canadian mode on the other.

Second, coming to the mode of admission of new States, Article 2 of the Constitution of India provides:

---

108 *Furber, Holden (1951), "The Unification of India, 1947–1951", Pacific Affairs, Pacific Affairs, University of British Columbia, **24** (4): 352–371, doi:10.2307/2753451, JSTOR 2753451*

109 *Bajwa, Kuldip Singh (2003), Jammu and Kashmir War, 1947–1948: Political and Military Perspective, New Delhi: Hari-Anand Publications Limited, ISBN 9788124109236; Aparna Pande (16 March 2011), Explaining Pakistan's Foreign Policy: Escaping India, Taylor & Francis. pp. 31–. ISBN 978-1-136-81893-6; Jalal, Ayesha (2014), The Struggle for Pakistan: A Muslim Homeland and Global Politics, Harvard University Press, p. 72, ISBN 978-0-674-74499-8; Samad, Yunas (2014). "Understanding the insurgency in Balochistan". Commonwealth & Comparative Politics. **52** (2): 293 320. doi:10.1080/14662043.2014.894280. S2CID 144156399.:*

110 26th Amendment to the Constitution of India, 1971.

111 1971 AIR 530; 1971 SCR (3) 9

112 White Paper on Indian States (1950)/ Part IV/ Instrument of Accession, Ministry of States, Government of India

"Parliament may by law admit into the Union, or establish, new States on such terms and conditions as it thinks fit."

The Parliament is therefore allowed to admit new States into the Union of India. This article is similar to that in the Australian Constitution[113] which provides that new States can be admitted by a law of the Parliament including imposition of such terms and conditions as it may deem fit. By the virtue of this provision, several States such as Nagaland, Himachal Pradesh, Meghalaya, Manipur, Sikkim, Tripura etc. have been admitted into the Union.

Third, the position in India regarding alteration or reorganisation of boundaries of States is the exact anti-thesis of that in America, Canada and Australia. The Union Parliament is empowered to reorganize the boundary of a State, alter the boundary or eliminate a State altogether without the consent of such a State. This proposition follows from the Apex Court's observation in *State of West Bengal vs. Union of India*[114] that the Parliament is invested with the authority to alter boundaries of any State and to diminish its area so as to even destroy the boundaries of State with all its powers and authority. Similarly, Art. 3 of the Constitution empowers the government to make such alterations unilaterally:

"3. Formation of new States and alteration of areas, boundaries or names of existing States: Parliament may by law

> *(a) form a new State by separation of territory from any State or by uniting two or more States or parts of States or by uniting any territory to a part of any State;*
>
> *(b) increase the area of any State;*
>
> *(c) diminish the area of any State;*
>
> *(d) alter the boundaries of any State;*
>
> *(e) alter the name of any State;"*

These powers are however followed by a stipulation that such a Bill affecting the boundaries or names of the States shall be referred by the President to the legislature of the concerned State for expressing their views, albeit within a specific time. Any failure to respond within the specified

---

113 Sec. 121, Constitution of Australia
114 AIR 1963 SC 1241

time shall be considered a waiver of the State's right to express its views. This stipulation is contained in the proviso to Article 3:

"Provided that no Bill for the purpose shall be introduced in either House of Parliament except on the recommendation of the President and unless, where the proposal contained in the Bill affects the area, boundaries or name of any of the States, the Bill has been referred by the President to the Legislature of that State for expressing its views thereon within such period as may be specified in the reference or within such further period as the President may allow and the period so specified or allowed has expired."

As a result, the Constitution expressly empowers the Parliament to alter or reorganize boundaries of any or every State without the authorisation or approval of the concerned States' legislatures. However, such a situation never happens in practice. In practice, most of the alterations or reorganisation of States have been undertaken due to the pressure from the legislators of a State or the population therein. In the words of *Sh. H. M. Seervai*[115], the renowned constitutional scholar:

"..in practice, it is not the Union which has redrawn the map of India; on the contrary, the hands of a reluctant Union has been forced by extra-constitutional agitation in the States, since most of them wanted to be regrouped on a linguistic basis."

If we look at the States formed after the Constitution came into force, one would realise that almost all of these States were formed through widespread demand and agitations of the people of those States. Andhra Pradesh, the first State to be formed on a linguistic basis after independence[116], was the result of a State-wide movement wherein thousands of supporters demanded the State of Andhra to be carved out from the erstwhile State of Madras. Similarly, the State of Telangana was carved out from the State of Andhra Pradesh in 2014,[117] following the massive protests and demand

---

115 Seervai, H. M., Constitutional Law of India, 4th Edn., Universal Law Publishing, pp. 290

116 "SRC submits report". *The Hindu*. Chennai, India. 1 October 2005.

117 "Pro-Telangana AP govt employees threaten agitation". *The Economic Times*. 10 February 2012; Telangana Students Suicides Increase in Hyderabad http://www.politicsdaily.com/2010/02/25/telangana-protests-student-suicides-increase-in-hyderabad-durin/

for Telangana, to which the government acceded.[118] Similarly, other States including the State of Jharkhand[119], State of Uttarakhand[120], State of Chhattisgarh[121], State of Nagaland[122] etc. were created as a result of protests from the people of the State itself with the Union being reluctant to such formation. Therefore, even though in form, the provision for alteration and reorganisation of States' boundaries can be undertaken unilaterally by the Union, in substance such a practice has never taken place in India. It has always been the States who forced the Union to create a new State or alter boundaries.

Further, in case such alterations are made without the consent of the State, the political parties in power at the centre will lose the support of an entire State. From a political standpoint, such a move to unilaterally alter the boundary of a State without its consent may bring disrepute and disapproval which could result in adverse results for the ruling party from the people of the State. Similarly, the Parliament has representatives of all the States in each House who are elected to ensure that the interests of their respective States are accounted for in every decision that is taken. If any such decision is taken against their interests, such members ensure that the word of disapproval reaches the government. To cite an example, the Smt. Harsimrat Kaur Badal resigned as a Union Minister due to the central government's alleged violation of rights of the farmers in State of Punjab.[123] In fact, in practice, the opposition parties usually join the protests from such members against unilateral alterations to pressurise the central government to not undertake such alterations. Withal, there are several practical limitations imposed on the Union government which discourages it from unilaterally altering or reorganizing the boundaries of the States. Hence, if the reader looks at the substance and not the form of

---

118 Telangana bill passed in Lok Sabha; Congress, BJP come together in favour of new State". Hindustan Times.

119 History of Jharkhand, Jharkhand History". *traveljharkhand.com*; "Tributes pour in for Justice Shahdeo", The Pioneer, 10 January 2018.

120 Kumar, P. (2000). The Uttarakhand Movement: Construction of a Regional Identity. New Delhi: Kanishka Publishers.

121 Prithak Chattisgarh, 4 July 2010

122 Inoue, Kyoko, Integration of the North East: The State Formation Process, IDE JETRO Publication.

123 Harsimrat Kaur Badal resigns as Union Minister protesting over farm bills, Live Mint, September 17, 2020

alteration of boundaries, it is clear that the Union cannot unilaterally alter such boundaries, which is in conformity to the federal principle.

Fourth, the Constitution does not expressly provide of mode of admission or acquisition of new States. The States need not be pre-existing independent States but can be formed through converting a Union Territory into a State[124], reorganisation of boundaries of existing States[125] to create a new State, acquisition of foreign territory[126] or admission of a new independent State[127] into the Union. In addition to these, the Union of India may acquire new territories as per the rules of international law[128] such as cession, purchase, treaty, war, annexation etc., similar to the American position.

Lastly, once a territory is acquired by the Indian government, such a territory is not automatically designated as a State or the Union Territory unless such a territory has been duly acquired as per public international law. Till such acquisition takes place, the Foreign Jurisdiction Act, 1947 applies to such territories. The Act empowers the government to exercise such jurisdiction as it deems fit and possesses power to make appropriate orders in such territory.

Summing up the aforementioned paragraphs, federal India was formed through a mixture of both modes of formation – through agreement between independent States, i.e. the princely States and breaking a Unitary State into several provinces, thereby converting it into a federation. Thus, India is a mixture of American and Australian mode of formation on one hand and Canada on the other. Indian federation provides for admission of new States expressly through the Constitution itself with power to impose such terms and conditions as it deems fit, similar to Australia and Canada. The federation can acquire another State through converting a Union Territory into a State, reorganisation of boundaries of existing States to create a new State, acquisition of foreign territory, admission of a new independent State or as per the rules of international law. Further, even though the Constitution empowers the Parliament to unilaterally alter or

---

124 The State of Himachal Pradesh Act, 1970; The North Eastern Areas (Reorganisation) Act, 1971
125 State of Nagaland Act, 1962
126 Re, Berubari Union, AIR 1960 SC 845
127 See admission of State of Sikkim
128 Masthan Sahib vs. Chief Commissioner AIR 1963 SC 533

reorganise the boundaries of the States, in practice it is the States which expressly force the Parliament to alter such boundaries. The author has argued that all the instances of alteration of boundaries of States in India have been undertaken due to immense pressure and demands from the State itself. As a result, the federal principle is upheld. Lastly, newly admitted territories are not automatically inducted into the Union and till such time they are not inducted, the government governs such territories according to the Foreign Jurisdiction Act, 1947.

Conclusion

As seen in the preceding paragraphs, there are two modes of formation of a federation. The first mode of formation, employed in Australia and America, involves an agreement between independent States to form a common nation while retaining their autonomy. Both these nations were formed by coming together of independent States, be it for political, geographical, strategic or economic reasons, to form a common nation. The second mode of formation, through which Canada came into existence as a federation, involved breaking up a Unitary State into several autonomous provinces thereby converting it into a federation.

India is a mixture of the two modes of formation i.e. through agreement and through conversion. India was a Unitary State under the British Empire, comprising of several States which were neither independent nor autonomous. In addition to these States, there were over five hundred (500) princely States ruled by monarchs. Therefore, to come into existence as a federation comprising of all of these territories, the founding fathers of India divided the Unitary State into several provinces based on linguistic, cultural and economic factors along with a view to ensure administrative efficiency. In addition to this, the Union needed to enter into agreements with these princely States to induct them into the federation. As a result, India was formed through converting a Unitary State into several provinces and entering into agreement with other independent States to assimilate them into the federation. As discussed earlier, the principle of federalism permits a federation to be formed through either of these two modes of formation. Therefore, India was formed in accordance with the acceptable modes of formation of a federation.

In addition to the mode of formation, the author discussed four ancillary issues – i. admission of new States in the federation; ii. Mode of acquisition of territories; iii. reorganization of territories or boundaries of States; iv. Powers of newly admitted territories. The assessment of these issues in light of the federal principle is necessary to ascertain whether a nation is federal or unitary.

First, as concerns the admission of new States into the federation, both American and Australian Constitutions expressly empower the federal government to admit new States into the federation along with imposition of terms and conditions however, there is a difference between their respective modes of admission. While American government can impose terms and conditions for admission, the States are not bound by these once fully admitted i.e. upon admission all States are equal under the Constitution. On the other hand, Australian government can impose any condition on the States which shall remain even after their admission i.e. the newly admitted States do not have the same rights and protections available to original States of the federation. It is pertinent to mention that both these nations do not require constitutional amendments to admit new States. However, the Canadian Constitution requires amendments to the Constitution in order to admit new States upon imposition of such terms and conditions as it deems fit, akin to Australian federation. The mode of admission in India is similar to that of America and Australia wherein the Constitution expressly allows admission of new States without amendments to the Constitution and upon imposition of such terms and conditions it deems fit. Therefore, the mode of admission of new States in India is similar to federations of America and Australia.

Second, the author discussed the modes of acquisition of new territories by a federation. In America, the Constitution does not expressly provide for mode of acquisition and thus, such acquisitions are executed as per the rules of public international law including Purchase, Cession, War, Treaty and Annexation. Similarly, the respective Constitutions of Australia, Canada and India permit the federation to acquire territories as per the rules of international law. In addition to these, the Australian government can acquire territories through surrender by existing States or territory placed under the government by the Queen. As a result, the mode of acquisition of territories by India is similar to that of traditional federations.

Third, the mode of alteration or reorganisation of boundaries of States forms a crucial part of the federal principle. In America, the States are considered to be indestructible and therefore, the federal government cannot unilaterally alter their boundaries. However, if the States whose boundaries are proposed to be altered consent to the same, the alteration can be executed. The Canadian Constitution provides for a similar provision. For such an alteration in Canada, the assent of the both Houses of the Parliament along with the resolution approving the same passed by the legislative assembly of each State whose territory is proposed to be altered, is required. The Australian Constitution goes one step further, it mandates that mere consent of the legislature of the State will not suffice but the majority of eligible voters in that State must approve such an alteration of boundaries. Therefore, in addition to assent by the legislature of concerned States and Parliament, an approval by majority of voters is required.

India has a provision dissimilar to our target federations in form such that the central government can unilaterally alter the boundaries of the States without their consent. However, in substance, such an alteration or reorganisation is effected by States themselves and not the federal government. If we look at the States formed through adjustment of boundaries of existing States after the Constitution came into force, one would realise that all of these States were formed through widespread demand and agitations of the people within those States themselves. Even though the provision for alteration and reorganisation of States' boundaries can be undertaken unilaterally by the Union in form, in substance such a practice has never taken place in India. It has always been the States who forced the Union to create a new State or alter boundaries. Further, due to political reasons, the ruling party in the central government refrains from unilaterally taking such decisions as they risk losing support of the people of the concerned State. Therefore, unless a demand comes from the State itself, the federal government does not make changes to the boundaries of States. As a result, the alteration or reorganisation of boundaries of States can only be effected by the consent of the States, similar to the provisions of federations of America, Australia and Canada.

Fourth, the territories acquired by the federations are not automatically declared as States of the federation. In America, a Congressional declaration or Parliamentary approval is required to admit a territory as a State. Without such an approval, even if the territory is admitted, it does not come on par with other States. In Australia, unless a territory is admitted as a 'State', it remains a dependency of the federation and Parliament exercises plenary powers over its governance. Similar to Australia, territories acquired by Canada may not be given powers equivalent to the original States and may be subject to interference by the federal government. In India, similar to Australia and Canada, the federal government can exercise powers over the States unless they are fully admitted as a 'State' of the Union. Till such time, the Foreign Jurisdiction Act, 1947 applies to such territories. As a result, the position in India is similar to that of other federations.

As seen in the preceding paragraphs, the position in India pertaining to the mode of formation and territory of the Union is similar to that of America, Australia and Canada. The author discussed the mode of formation of the federation, admission of new States in the federation, mode of acquisition of territories, reorganization of territories or boundaries of States and powers of newly admitted territories. There are minute differences, if any, but in substance, the provisions in India are similar to the aforementioned federations, serving the same purpose albeit through slightly different means. Hence, as regards the mode of formation and territory of a federation, India is on par with other federations of the world.

CHAPTER 6

States' Rights vis-à-vis the Union

While formation of a federation demands surrender of rights and powers by the States in favour of the federation, the States are granted some rights vis-à-vis the federation which allows them to protect and retain their autonomy, constitutional status and govern themselves. As *Dicey* stated, a federation attempts to reconcile national unity with preservation of States' rights. These "States' rights" form a crucial part of a federation. If the States are assigned barely minimal rights, they portray a more unitary structure than federal. Therefore, it is essential that the States retain some powers and rights so that they are not degraded to mere administrative units. These rights allowing limited autonomy to the States cannot be abrogated by the federal government.

As a result, it is essential to analyse the rights of the States against the federation and the extent to which the federation can abrogate such rights. In this context, the author shall be analysing eight (8) issues which are essential for the protection of the rights of the States.

First, there shall be participation of States in the amendment of the Constitution. The bedrock of a federation is the arrangement in accordance with which the States have surrendered their autonomy and powers, albeit partly. This arrangement shall be kept intact otherwise the entire federal structure may collapse. For ensuring the comity of a federal structure, the process of amending the Constitution shall be rigid. In other words, it must be ensured that the federal government cannot unilaterally amend the Constitution to the detriment of the States. If it were so allowed, the federation will not continue for long. *Dicey* demands that such amendments shall require consent of all the States[129] however, in practice, consent of all States may be impracticable and will result in extreme rigidity which may result in policy paralysis and hinder the development of a nation. As a result, most federations require consent of a certain number of States for such amendments. The purpose of such a provision is to ensure that no

---

129 Dicey, 10th Edn, p. 147

decision which may be detrimental to the States can be taken without their consent.

Second, the Constitution must provide provisions for protection of States against extinction. Since the States surrender their powers of defence to the Union upon entering the federation, the Union has a duty to defend the States. This duty has a dual context. First, it is essential that the States do not have unilateral power to secede or withdraw from the Union. Usually, the Constitution itself provides for mechanism of secession from the Union however, in practice, almost all federations are indestructible. Second, the Union has an obligation to protect the States and its organs from internal or external aggression. Here, there may be a need to protect the States from aggression by other nations or from internal disturbances which may require deployment of armed forces for maintenance of law and order.

Third, the Union exercises control over the agreements and treaties with foreign countries. The States surrender their power pertaining to foreign affairs to the Union considering that it would be unreasonable and counter-productive if States are allowed to deal with foreign countries. Similarly, the Union exercises control over the agreements which the States may have amongst themselves to the detriment of the other remaining States. This provision ensures that some States cannot create a monopoly over, say, trade of certain materials or goods to the exclusion of other States. A Union must therefore have adequate powers to restrict the States from dealing with foreign countries directly and from entering into agreements with other States of the federation to the detriment of remaining States.

Fourth, for smooth functioning of a federation, it is essential that the federal laws retain supremacy when contrary to the State laws. Such an arrangement not only prevents a chaotic situation resulting from contradictory legislations of the Union and the States, but it is also essential for keeping the federation intact.[130] However, it is pertinent to mention that the federal law shall have been competently enacted to enjoy supremacy over the State law. Such a situation usually arises in the context of legislative powers enumerated in the Concurrent List or subject matters upon which the federation and the States are both empowered to legislate. To cite an example, it may be necessary for the Union to ensure that forest cover, mentioned in Concurrent List, shall be increased throughout the country

130 Cf. Fed. Saw Mill vs. James Moore, (1908) 8 CLR 465 (530)

in observance of the international obligations.[131] In such situations, it is essential that the law enacted by the Union shall prevail over the law enacted by the State, which may prescribe a lesser forest cover, to the extent of repugnancy in the latter.

Fifth, another conspicuous feature of federalism is that many federations permit the States to enact their own Constitutions for their governance. United States of America and Australia are examples of federations wherein States have their own respective Constitutions. Similarly, Switzerland and Malaysia allow States to have their own Constitutions as well. The Constitutions of the States allow a substantial deal of autonomy to the States and reduces the interference of the Union in their affairs. Additionally, it allows the States to protect the rights of their residents and ensure their welfare. These State Constitutions are however subject to limitations provided in the Constitution of the country so that they are not contrary to the federal principle.

Sixth, federal control over the State legislations has often created difficulties in federations. Some federations such as America and Australia do not permit federal control over State legislations. However, such control is exercised indirectly, as we shall see in the following paragraphs. On the other hand, Canada and India permit federal control over State legislations to the extent that the federation may veto the State legislation in some situations. Technically, the federations should ensure that the federal government is not allowed to interfere with State legislations. Federal interference may result in impeding the State autonomy thereby undermining the federal principle. However, such interference is justified in some situations to ensure unity, uniformity, national security and deter legislations detrimental to the interests of other States.

Seventh, similar to the federal control over State legislations, federal control over State administration has created impediments as well. As per the principle of federalism providing for dual governments - each independent and distinct in its own sphere of governance, federal control over State administration is not permitted. However, after a period of two centuries since the inception of the first federation, each federation gradually realised

___

131 See India's Nationally Determined Contributions (NDCs), submitted under the United Nations Framework Convention on Climate Change (UNFCCC); "Govt launches pilot project to increase forestcover in 5 States", Live Mint, 17 June 2019

the importance of such interference in certain situations. Such control is essential considering that States have limited finances and no control over the defence forces which may be required for maintenance of law and order. In fact, during elections, federal governments often depute their personnel to the State governments due to lack of manpower of the latter.

Eighth, there shall be a machinery available for settlement of disputes between the federation and States or between two or more States. On many an occasion, the federal governments in most federations have attempted to impede on the States' respective spheres of governance. In such cases, the federal courts have provided much needed relief to the States and ensured that the federal government operates within the contours of the Constitution. Hence, it is essential to have a dispute settlement forum for differences between the Union and the States.

These issues cumulatively aid the assessment of the autonomy afforded to the States in a federation. Purely federal structures such as America and Australia provide for these provisions in their respective Constitutions. With this discussion, the author will attempt to conclude that such rights accorded to the States in target federations are similar to that in India. The author will analyse these eight issues with respect to each of the target federations, thereafter, comparing each of the federations with India. The aforementioned issues shall be dealt with briefly, without going into the intricacies involved therein. The mere existence of these features is sufficient for our purposes.

United States of America

First, unilateral amendments to the American Constitution by the federal government are not permitted. State participation in constitutional amendments is mandatory. To this effect, Article V of the American Constitution states:

"Article V

The Congress, whenever two thirds of both Houses shall deem it necessary, shall propose amendments to this Constitution, or, on the application of the legislatures of two thirds of the several States, shall call a convention for proposing amendments, which, in either case, shall be valid to all intents and purposes, as part of this Constitution, when ratified by the legislatures of three fourths of the several States, or by conventions in three fourths thereof, as the one or the other mode of ratification may be proposed by the Congress;"

As the reader may see, a constitutional amendment can only be valid if ratified by three-fourths of the States of the federation. In addition to this safeguard, the Congress can only convene a convention for proposing amendments if two-thirds of both Houses of the Federal Parliament assent to it. Considering that the States are represented in these Houses through their elected members, the States have a discretion to vote in favour or against the convention. No amendment moved in contravention of this Article shall be valid.[132] Therefore, the American Constitution provides for a two tier protection against unilateral amendments of the Constitution. First, both Houses of Federal Parliament have to convene and assent to amendment with two-third majority and second, three-fourth of the States shall ratify the amendment. Withal, even if 14 out of 50 States of the federation disagree with the amendment, the amendment shall stand defeated.

Second, there must be protection of States against extinction. This protection comprises of two aspects, as discussed in the preceding paragraphs. The first aspect concerns the right of States to withdraw or secede from the federation thereby resulting in their extinction. It is essential that such secession or withdrawal is not permitted in order to ensure unity and continuity in a federation. As a result, in the American federation, the States are indestructible.[133] The States can neither be removed from the map through adjustment of boundaries (as discussed in the preceding chapter) nor can they be allowed to withdraw or secede from the federation.

The American Constitution is silent on the right to secede from the federation. Thus, this proposition was decided by the Federal Supreme Court in the case of *Texas v. White*[134], due to its absence from the Constitution. Before Texas was formally admitted into the Union, the State brought a suit before the Federal Supreme Court to enforce a federal bond against debtor. The latter took the defence that since Texas was not a State of the Union, the Supreme Court lacked jurisdiction to entertain the suit under Article III S. 2(1). The majority of the court rejected this plea, holding that Texas never ceased to be a member of the Union by her unilateral ordinance of secession.

---

132 Hawke vs. Smith (1920) 253 US 221; C.C.L. pp. 117-118.
133 Texas v. White (1868) 7 Wall 700 (720)
134 ibid

Once admitted into the federal Union there's no place for revocation except through revolution or through consent of States. Therefore, the States cannot unilaterally secede from the Union.

The second aspect concerns the protection of States from external aggression or internal disturbances such that these do not result in extinction of the States. Since the States surrender their powers of defence to the federation, the federation has a duty to ensure the protection of such States. In this respect, Article IV (4) of the American Constitution provides:

"The United States shall guarantee to every State in this Union a republican form of government, and shall protect each of them against invasion; and on application of the legislature, or of the executive (when the legislature cannot be convened) against domestic violence."

According to this provision, the federation has a constitutional duty to protect the States from external aggression and against internal disturbance such as armed rebellions, riots etc. Such a duty of the federal government is absolutely necessary to protect the States considering that they are completely powerless in matters of defence.

Third, Article I, S. 10(1), (3) of the American Constitution provides that States cannot enter into any 'treaty, alliance or confederation' or any other agreement with another State or foreign power without the consent of the Congress. As a result of this provision, the States of the federation are prohibited from entering into any such agreements with either the other member States[135] or with foreign States[136].

Fourth, as discussed earlier, it is essential for a federation to smoothly function that in case of a conflict between the federal and the State law, the federal law shall prevail. If not so, it may result in a chaotic situation wherein the States will commence legislating contrary to federal laws to suit their own needs and demands. As a result, Article VI, S. (2) provides:

"This Constitution, and the laws of the United States which shall be made in pursuance thereof shall be the Supreme law of the land; anything in the Constitution or laws of any State to the contrary notwithstanding."

---

135 Williams v. Bruffy (1878) 96 US 176 (183)
136 Holmes v. Jennison (1840) 14 Pet 540

According to this provision, whenever the federal legislature legislates on a particular subject matter either expressly or impliedly, the State laws which are contrary to such federal law shall yield to the federal law. However, such a provision is only attracted if the federal law is constitutionally valid.[137] This provision ensures federal supremacy, being essential for survival of a federation and empowers the federation to maintain uniformity in situations which demand so.

Fifth, the American federalism permits the States to enact their own respective Constitutions. However, these Constitutions cannot be contrary to the federal Constitution. These Constitutions are subject to two limitations. First, if a State adopts a Constitution which does not provide for a 'republican form of government' or subverts such a government, the federal government is empowered to undertake action against such State to restore order.[138] Second, in case there is a conflict between the State and federal Constitution, the latter shall prevail.[139] As a result, the States are empowered to enact their own Constitutions provided that such Constitutions are not antithetical to the federal Constitution.

Sixth, since a federal Constitution enshrines the principle of dual government, both the governments are independent in their respective spheres and neither government can impede on the legislative powers of the other.[140] Therefore, the federal government cannot exercise any control or veto over the law passed by a State legislature, provided that the State legislature is legally empowered to enact such law. The Governor, head of a State, is empowered to veto a bill passed by State legislature[141], akin to President's veto on a federal bill. However, neither the Governor can veto a federal bill nor can the President veto a State Bill[142].

Seventh, akin to federal control over State legislation, federal control over State administration is not permitted in a federal structure.[143] The

---

137 Gulf R. Co. v. Hoffiey (1895) 158 US 89; Prigg v. Pennsylvania (1824) 16 Pet 536 (618)
138 Article IV, S. 4, Constitution of America
139 Article VI, S. 2, Constitution of America
140 Rahrer, In re, (1891) 140 US 545
141 Stedman, State and Local Governments (1976), p. 131.
142 Article I, S. 7(2), American Constitution; Wheare, Legislatures (1962), pp. 3, 163; Fincher, Government of the U.S. (1976), p. 191.
143 Collector v. Day (1871) 11 Wall 113

State's employees are tasked with administration of the State whereas the federal employees execute federal laws without interference from the other.[144] Therefore, in America, the Governor of a State is directly elected by the people of the State to the complete exclusion of federal interference.[145]

In light of the preceding paragraphs concerning federal control over State legislations and administration, it is pertinent to mention that most modern-day federations provide for federal control over State legislation and administration, either directly or indirectly. Over the years, the American government realised that there are certain matters which albeit are under the State administration, they have an impact on national welfare. Therefore, it will be against the interests of the nation to leave such matters to the prerogative of the States considering their highly limited financial resources. In such situations, the federal government exercises power over the State administration through grants-in-aid.[146] This power to provide grants is derived from the 'general welfare' clause in the Constitution.[147]

These grants are usually provided subject to certain conditions imposed by the federal government. Through these conditions, the federal government exercises considerable control over the State legislature and government. Such conditions aid the federal government in introducing uniformity in actions of the States which are necessary for national welfare. Further, it helps the Union in providing financial aid to underdeveloped States. Thus, the federation requires the States to fulfil the conditions in order to receive grants and maintain supervision over the States. These grants may not only involve federal supervision but also require States to enact legislations as a qualifying condition for the grant.[148] Though it may be argued that such exercise of control by federation over States is a violation of the federal

---

144 McCulloch v. Maryland (1819) 4 Wh 316

145 Stedman, State and Local Governments (1976), p. 131.

146 D. D. Basu, Comparative Federalism, 2nd Edn. (2007), p. 54

147 Article I, S. 8(1)

148 Fullilove v. Klutznick, (1980) 448 US 448 (459); Lace vs. Nichols (1974) 414 US 563 (568); Cf. King v. Smith (1968) 392 US 309 (324); Pennhurst State School v. Halderman (1980) 451 US 1 (16); Nicholas Henry, Governing at the Grassroots (1980) pp. 294

principle[149], the Federal Supreme Court has upheld such a system.[150] As a result, though the federal government cannot exercise powers over State legislatures or administration, in practice the federal government indeed exercises such control by way of conditional grants.

Eighth, on many an occasion, the three organs of a government – executive, legislature and judiciary may exceed its domain and enter that of another organ. In such cases, it is essential for a special forum to adjudicate the disputes in order to avoid anarchy and complete chaos. In America, Article III, S. 2(1) provides that the jurisdiction to entertain and adjudicate disputes between the Union and the States and between the States *inter se* shall vest exclusively in the Federal Supreme Court. Therefore, any such dispute is adjudicated by the Federal Supreme Court whose decisions are binding on all parties concerned.

In conclusion, the eight aforementioned features of federalism are present in the American federation. The author concludes that the American Constitution does not permit unilateral amendment of the Constitution without the assent of the States. Secondly, the federation has a duty to protect the States from extinction, either internal or external. Third, the federation has exclusive authority to enter into agreements or treaties with foreign countries. Fourth, the federal supremacy shall be maintained in a federation i.e. the federal law shall prevail over the State law in instance of contradiction. Fifth, the States are permitted to enact their own respective Constitutions provided they adhere to the constitutional limitations imposed on such Constitutions. Further, the federal government can neither directly exercise control over State legislation nor can the former exercise control over State administration. However, as discussed in the preceding paragraphs, the federal government indirectly exercises control over State administration and legislation through conditional grants. Lastly, there shall be a dispute settlement mechanism in case a dispute arises between the Union and the States or between the States inter se. For this purpose,

---

149 Cf. National League of Cities v. Usery (1976) 426 US 833; Lane County v. Oregon (1869) 7 Wall 71; Stedman, State and Local Governments (1976), p. 46; Griffith, Impasse of Democracy, (1939), p. 195; Woodrow Wilson, Constitutional Government, (1908) pp. 183-84.
150 Fullilove v. Klutznick, (1980) 448 US 448; Buckley v. Valeo (1976) 424 US 1 (90-91); Helvering v. Davis (1937) 301 US 619.

the American Constitution provides for the Federal Supreme Court which possesses exclusive jurisdiction to decide such disputes.

The aforementioned paragraphs cast light on the essential features of federalism pertaining to States' rights vis-à-vis the Union in America which is often employed as a benchmark for federalism. In light of this, the other federations shall be analysed by the author.

Australia

First, the Constitution of Australia does not permit unilateral amendments of the Constitution without the participation of the States, similar to the American position. However, the Australian system adds another safeguard i.e. the consent of the electors of a State in addition to the approval of the legislature of the concerned State. The Constitution provides that any such amendment shall be passed with an absolute majority in both Houses of the Commonwealth Parliament. Once passed by the Parliament, the Bill is submitted to a referendum. At the referendum, the Bill must be approved by a double majority i.e. a national majority of electors in States and a majority of electors in majority of States (at least four out of six).[151] This double majority makes constitutional amendments nearly impossible, such that only eight (8) out of forty-four (44) proposed amendments have been passed till date. In case the amendment is passed by the legislatures and electors alike, the Governor General shall assent to the amendment. Therefore, the constitutional amendment in Australia is much more complex and arduous than the American system, designed perfectly to safeguard the interests of the States. The reader may note that though such a system protects the States' rights, it may bring immense administrative inefficiency and policy paralysis considering that any constitutional amendment is nearly impossible and may require enormous funding to garner support in the entire country.

Second, as discussed earlier, the protection against extinction comprises of two aspects – protection against aggression, whether internal or external, and right to secede from the Union. Section 119 of the Australian Constitution provides:

---

151 S. 128, Constitution of Australia

"119. The Commonwealth shall protect every State against invasion and on the application of the Executive Government of the State against domestic violence."

Therefore, similar to the American position, the federal government has a duty to protect the States, not only from the external aggression by a foreign State or non-State actors but also from internal disturbances. Since the States renounce their powers of defence in favour of the federal government, it is implicit that the federation protects the States.

As regards secession from the federation, the Preamble to the Australian Constitution declares the Union as 'one indissoluble Federal Commonwealth'. As a result, the States do not have a right to secede from the Union. This denial of a right to secede was established through a precedent in 1934 when the State of Western Australia requested the British Parliament to sanction a secession however, it was held that the State does not have a right to request such a secession even though it was supported by the State legislature along with a plebiscite of the residents of the State.[152] The secession of a State, however, can be effected if all the States of the federation consent to such secession along with the consent of the federal government. Therefore, the provision in Australia is similar to the American position to the extent that the States are not permitted to secede. However, unlike America, the States in Australia can secede if all the States and federal government consent to such secession.

Third, since the States renounce their powers pertaining to foreign affairs in favour of the Union, the States cannot enter into any treaty or agreement with foreign States. The treaty-making power and engaging in foreign affairs vests in the federal government[153], to the complete exclusion of the States.

Fourth, as discussed earlier, in case of a conflict between the federal and the State law, the federal law shall prevail. Such a proposition is essential for a federation to smoothly function and maintain uniformity in matters of national importance. To this effect, section 109 of Australian Constitution provides:

---

152 Rep. of the Joint Committee of Parliament on the Petition of Western Australia, (1935)

153 R vs. Burgess, (1936) 55 CLR 608 (641, 686)

"109. When a law of a State is inconsistent with a law of Commonwealth, the later shall prevail, and the former shall, to the extent of the inconsistency, be invalid."

The Australian Constitution, similar to American, ensures federal supremacy with a constitutional provision itself. The desire for federal supremacy in the Australian Constitution is amplified by the fact that the powers enumerated in s. 51 are concurrent, as the word 'exclusive' is not mentioned in s. 51, as is in s. 52. It is pertinent to mention that s. 51 lays down the legislative powers of the federal government whereas s. 52 lays down the 'exclusive' powers of the federal government. This creates a conflicting situation as both, the State and federal legislatures, are empowered to legislate on the subjects mentioned in s. 51. As a result, it is essential that a supremacy clause is provided in the Constitution. In Australia, s. 109 provides for the supremacy clause. The supremacy is further strengthened by the 'Covering Clause V'[154] which lays down the doctrine of federal supremacy by providing that the federal laws shall be binding on the States notwithstanding anything in the laws of the States. Therefore, the doctrine of paramountcy exists in the favour of the federal government in cases of conflicting laws of the States and the federation.[155]

Fifth, the Australian Constitution, akin to American Constitution, permits the States to enact their own Constitutions. Section 106 of the Australian Constitution provides that the State Constitution shall be subject to the federal Constitution, thereby implying that any provision in the former inconsistent with the latter shall be void. As a result, this provision ensures federal supremacy so far as the respective Constitutions of the States and the federation are concerned.

Sixth, similar to American, the Australian Constitution enshrines the principle of dual government i.e. both the governments are independent in their respective spheres and neither government can impede on the legislative powers of the other.[156] Therefore, the federal government cannot exercise any control or veto over the law passed by a State legislature provided that the State legislature is legally empowered to enact such law. The Governor of

---

154 Covering Clauses in the Australian Constitution can only be amended by the Imperial Parliament and not by the Australian Parliament. As a result, anything provided in the Covering Clauses is highly arduous to amend.
155 Spratt vs. Hermes (1965) 114 CLR 226
156 Rahrer, In re, (1891) 140 US 545

a State cannot veto a Federal Bill, likewise the President cannot veto a State Bill. However, the Crown may disallow a State legislation.[157] Therefore, quite contrary to the federal principle, the powers to disallow a State legislation have been given to the Crown i.e. the British government which may be influenced by the opinion of the Federal Parliament. Therefore, the Federal Parliament may indirectly veto a State legislation.

Seventh, similar to America, the federal control over State administration is not permitted. Both, the State and federal governments work in their own spheres of administration. As a necessary corollary, the State Governor is elected by the State, acts on the advice of the Ministers of the State and exercises the functions of the crown in relation to a State.[158] To this effect, the federal government and State governments have their separate civil services.

However, as seen with the American system, most modern-day federations provide for federal control over State legislations and administration, either directly or indirectly. Following the American model, the intrusion of federal government into State legislation and administration in Australia has taken place through conditional grants[159] having been upheld as valid, though the States are not bound to accept such grants.[160] Further, the financial powers of the federal government to spend on 'Commonwealth purposes' has been substantially expanded by the courts. This power is not only limited to the legislative powers of the federal government but also extends to the subjects reserved for legislative powers of the State such as roads, housing, education etc., provided that it is acted upon for purposes of national importance.[161] In fact, the courts have allowed the federal government to provide direct subsidies to residents of the States without the State acting as an intermediary so that the inefficient or unwilling State machinery cannot compromise the interests of the citizens.[162] In practice, the States are more than willing to obey the directions of the federal government in order to receive such

---

157 Section 58, Constitution of Australia
158 Horwitz vs. Connor (1908) 6 CLR 38; Williams vs. A.G., (1913) 16 CLR 404
159 Victoria vs. Commonwealth (1975) 134 CLR 338
160 S. Australia vs. Commonwealth (1942) 65 CLR 373; Victoria vs. Commonwealth (1975) 134 CLR 338
161 Victoria vs. Commonwealth (1975) 134 CLR 338
162 Fajgenbaum & Hanks, Australian Constitutional Law, (1980)

grants. Further, the courts have expanded the scope of 'defence' power[163] of the federation holding that the federation can employ the States' employees to the exclusion of the States as a war measure.[164]

Therefore, similar to the American position, despite the presence of dual governments not permitted to interfere with each other, the federal government with the aid of judiciary has created mechanisms to frequently intrude into State governments' spheres of legislation and administration for purposes of national importance. Though technically the governments are not permitted to do so, in practice, the federal government often enters the administrative domain of the States.

Eighth, as discussed earlier, a system of dispute resolution is essential for disputes between the federation and State governments or between two or more State governments. Art. 75 of Australian Constitution which provides for dispute resolution between the aforementioned in Australia is modelled on Art. III s. 2(1) of the American Constitution. It states that the exclusive jurisdiction to entertain such disputes vests in the High Court of Australia (equivalent to Federal Supreme Court in America).[165] The High Court has held *"the Constitution treats the Commonwealth and the States as organisations possessing distinct identities having mutual legal relations and therefore, amenable to the jurisdiction of courts upon which the responsibility of enforcing the Constitution rests."*[166] Therefore, any such dispute is adjudicated by the High Court of Australia whose decisions are binding on all parties concerned.

In conclusion, the eight aforementioned features of federalism are present in the Australian federation, quite similar to the American position. The author concludes that the Australian Constitution does not permit unilateral amendment of the Constitution without the assent of the States and requires a referendum of the electors of the States as well. Secondly, the federation has a duty to protect the States from extinction, either internal or external, and it does not provide for the right to secede from the federation. Third, the federation has exclusive authority to enter into agreements

---

163 Section 51 (vi) r/w Section 51 (xxxix), Constitution of Australia.

164 S. Australia vs. Commonwealth (1942) 65 CLR 373

165 Cf. Commonwealth vs. N.S.W. (1923) 32 CLR 200; Cf. Australia vs. Victoria (1911) 12 CLR 667.

166 Bank of N.S.W. vs. Commonwealth (1948) 76 CLR 1 (363); Australia vs. Victoria (1962) 108 CLR 130.

or treaties with foreign countries. Fourth, the federal supremacy gains immense importance in Australia due to a very wide concurrent sphere, as a necessary corollary of which, the Constitution provides federal supremacy over State laws. Fifth, the States are permitted to enact their own respective Constitutions provided they adhere to the constitutional limitations imposed on such State Constitutions. Further, the federal government can neither exercise direct control over State legislations nor can it exercise control over State administration. However, as discussed in the preceding paragraphs, the federal government indirectly exercises control over State administration and legislation through conditional grants. Lastly, the Australian Constitution provides for establishment of the High Court of Australia to adjudicate upon disputes arising between the Union and the States or between the States inter se.

Canada

First, the Canadian Constitution requires assent of States for amendment of only those provisions of the Constitution which directly or indirectly affect the States. For all other provisions, the federal legislature can unilaterally amend the Constitution. This power to amend the Constitution was granted to the Canadian legislatures in 1949, prior to which, the Constitution could be amended only by the British Parliament.[167]

Through the Canada Act, 1982, the powers of the Canadian Parliament were further expanded as the British government abjured all its authority over Canada. Presently, the general procedure for amendment of the Constitution provides that the proclamation to amend shall be made by the Governor General after authorisation through resolutions of both Houses of the Federal Parliament accompanied with resolutions of State Legislatures of atleast 2/3rd of the provinces, having atleast 50% population of all provinces.[168] This procedure is however subject to the following:

1. The Federal Parliament has exclusive competence to amend the constitutional provisions relating to executive government or the Houses of Federal Parliament.[169]

---

167 British North American (No. 2) Act, 1949
168 S. 38, Constitution of Canada
169 S. 44, Constitution of Canada

2. The legislatures of the States are competent to amend their respective Constitutions.[170]

3. The amendment of provisions concerning both, the federation and the provinces, such as office of Governor General, Provincial Governors, Supreme Court etc. shall require unanimous consent of federal government and State governments i.e. all the provincial legislatures along with both Houses of Federal Parliament shall ratify such an amendment.[171]

4. The amendment of provisions which only affect a certain number of States, such as alteration of boundaries, require assent of both Houses of the Federal Parliament along with ratification by the legislature of the affected State.[172]

Therefore, the Constitution of Canada provides a slightly different provision from that of America and Australia. It requires the assent of the States in only those amendments which seek to affect the rights of the States. If the federation seeks to amend the provisions affecting only the federal government, it does not require the assent of the States. This procedure provides flexibility and efficiency to the federation by allowing expeditious amendments as and when required.

Second, the federation has a duty to protect the States from extinction. As discussed earlier, this has dual aspects – first, right to secede or withdraw from the Union and second, protection against external or internal violence or aggression. The British North America Act, 1867 does not provide for secession, therefore, the Constitution shall have to be amended if any State intends to secede. If secession had been permitted, the French speaking regions would have seceded from the federation, writes *Sawer*.[173] However, the Canadian Supreme Court has held that a province may be permitted to secede with support of an independence referendum however, the court did not comment on how such a secession shall be effected.[174] The court held that the unilateral secession was neither allowed nor denied by the Constitution. Second, the federation has an implicit duty to defend the

---

170 S. 45, Constitution of Canada
171 S. 41, Constitution of Canada
172 S. 43, Constitution of Canada
173 Sawer, Modern Federalism (1969) p. 97.
174 Reference Re Secession of Quebec, [1998] 2 SCR 217 at para 150

States considering that the States renounce their powers of defence in favour of the federation by virtue of the federal principle. However, unlike Australia and America, Canada does not provide for such a duty explicitly.

Third, Canada has a unique policy relating to foreign affairs, quite contrary to the federal systems in America and Australia. It is an established principle that powers pertaining to foreign affairs in a federation vest exclusively in the federal government however, in Canada the provinces are permitted to operate internationally, appoint agent generals to other nations and participate in foreign relations.[175] However, the provinces cannot legislate treaties. Therefore, Canadian provinces can participate in foreign affairs despite the renunciation of powers of foreign affairs in favour of the federation. This is in stark contrast to the federal principle in general wherein the federation exclusively controls the foreign affairs.

Fourth, the Canadian Constitution does not provide for a general federal supremacy clause, unlike the Australian and American Constitutions. There are some specific provisions which provide for federal supremacy in expressly laid down legislative fields. For example, Art. 95 of the British North America Act, 1867 provides for federal supremacy in legislations pertaining to agriculture and immigration. Similarly, Art. 94 & 94A provide for federal supremacy in laws relating to property and civil rights in Ontario, Nova Scotia and New Brunswick and laws relating to old age pensions, disability benefits, supplementary benefits etc. However, the judiciary has upheld the supremacy of the federal laws in Canada.[176] In *G.T.R. vs. A.G. Canada*[177], the court explicitly confirmed the federal supremacy by holding *"there can be a domain in which Provincial and Dominion legislation may overlap, in which case, neither legislation will be ultra vires, if the field is clear; but if the field is not clear, and in such a domain the two legislations meet, then the Dominion legislation must prevail."*

---

175 Elliot J. Feldman and Lily Gardner Feldman. "The Impact of Federalism on the Organization of Canadian Foreign Policy". Publius (Vol. 14, No. 4, Federated States and International Relations (Autumn, 1984)): 33–59.

176 A.G. Ontario vs. A. G. Canada (1894) AC 189 (200); Tennant vs. Union Bank (1894) AC 31 (45).

177 G.T.R. vs. A.G. Canada (1907) AC 65

Fifth, Canada does not permit the States to have their own Constitutions[178], unlike Australia and America. The provisions which one would usually find in a provincial Constitution in traditional federations are instead drafted into the Constitution of Canada itself and in specific statutes enacted by the States. For example, Part V of the Constitution Act, 1867 provides for the governmental structures for provinces. Similarly, some provinces were created through statutes themselves which contain the governing provisions of the province therein.[179] All provinces have enacted their own statutes which provide for their rules of governance including elections, executive functioning etc. which are deemed to be their respective Constitutions. It is pertinent to mention that such legislations do not supersede other provincial legislations i.e. they are at par with other legislations unlike a Constitution which is considered to be the supreme law of the land.

Sixth, unlike the American and Australian federations, the Canadian Constitution allows federal control over State legislations, quite contrary to the federal principal. Such control by the federal government is exercised in two ways – disallowance of provincial legislation or reservation of provincial legislation. First, the Federal Parliament has the power to disallow a provincial legislation.[180] This power, albeit sparingly used, is still available to the Parliament.[181] The Governor General is empowered to exercise such a power on the advice of Federal Parliament. There is no restriction on the grounds upon which a provincial legislation may be disallowed[182], thereby giving an arbitrary edge to the federal government. Such a prerogative vested in the Federal Parliament attenuates the federal principle. However, as we have seen in the preceding paragraphs, such control is exercised by the federal governments in traditional federations as well albeit indirectly.

Seventh, unlike American and Australia, the federal government in Canada exercises control over the State administration. The Governor of a province in Canada is appointed and removed by the Governor General,

---

178 Morton, F.L. Provincial Constitutions in Canada, Conference on "Federalism and Sub-national Constitutions: Design and Reform", Centre for the Study of State Constitutions, Rockefeller Center, Bellagio, Italy, March 2004.
179 Manitoba Act, 1870, SC 1870, c 3; Alberta Act, SC 1905, c 3; and Saskatchewan Act, SC 1905, c 42.
180 S. 56 and S. 60, British North America Act, 1867
181 This power was last used in 1943; Halsbury, 4th Edn. Vol. 6, para 931
182 Re. Disallowance and Reservation Powers (1938) SCR 71 (Can)

acting on advise of the federal government.[183] As a result, the Governor of a province is an agent of the federal government, often employed to exercise federal control over the provinces including reservation of a Bill for Governor-General's assent.[184] The federal government can exercise its federal powers in a State through its own employees.[185] However, an exception has been carved out in the recent years by the courts in Canada in pursuance of the doctrine of 'cooperative federalism', thereby allowing federal legislature to delegate or authorize the delegation of administrative functions to a provincial agency or authority even though the subject matter may not be within the States' legislative or administrative competence, upholding that the federation may require the cooperation of the States' agencies.[186] Through this mechanism, the federation exercises control over the State administration. As a result, similar to America and Australia, the federal government in Canada exercises control over the State administration indirectly, despite not being permitted to do so directly by the Constitution.

Lastly, as regards the dispute resolution mechanism for disputes between the federation and the States or between States *inter se*, the Constitution Act of Canada, 1867 is silent about the Federal Supreme Court however, it gives the discretion to the Federal Parliament to create a 'general court of appeal for Canada'. In pursuance of the same, the Federal Parliament set up the Supreme Court[187] and as a necessary corollary, the jurisdiction of the Supreme Court flows from the legislation which created it.[188] Peculiarly, the Supreme Court of Canada does not exercise original jurisdiction. The disputes between aforementioned parties are heard by the State courts[189] or the Federal Exchequer Court[190] in the first instance, and then heard by the Supreme Court by way of appeal.[191] Considering that the federal government has been constitutionally empowered to veto provincial legislations on any

---

183 Halsbury, 4th Edn. Vol. 6, para 822, 931

184 Dawson, Government of Canada, (1970) pg. 28.

185 Proprietary Articles Association vs. A. G. Canada (1931) AC 310 (327) (PC)

186 P.E.I. Potato Marketing Rd. vs. Willis (1952) 2 SCR 392 (Can.)

187 The Supreme Court Act, 1875

188 Crown Grain Co. vs. Day (1908) SC 504

189 Grant vs. St. Lawrence Authority (1960) 23 DLR (2d); Cf. Elect. Development Co. vs. A.G. Ontario (1919) AC 687

190 Cf. A.G. B.C. vs. A.G. Canada (1924) AC 222

191 Laskin, Bora, Laskin's Canadian Constitutional Law: Cases, Text and Notes on Distribution of Legislative Power, Carswell Co., 4th Edn., January 1, 1975.

ground whatsoever, the scope of disputes remains severely limited. As a result, disputes are rarely heard by the Supreme Court.

Therefore, the dispute resolution system in Canada is dissimilar to the ones in traditional federations. In the latter, there exists a Federal Supreme Court which adjudicates the disputes between the States *inter se* or between the Union and the States. In Canada, the disputes are heard by the State courts originally and can only be heard by the Supreme Court through an appeal. Therefore, the Canadian Supreme Court does not exercise original jurisdiction over such disputes, unlike America and Australia.

Withal, the aforementioned features are dealt with in Canada in a manner somewhat dissimilar to traditional federations. First, the author concluded that unilateral amendments are permitted in Canada without the consent of the States but only for provisions not affecting the States. For provisions which affect the States, the consent of the States is mandatory. Secondly, the federation has a duty to protect the States from extinction, either internal or external, and it does not provide for the right to secede from the federation. Third, unlike the American or Australian federation, States in Canada possess limited powers to deal with foreign affairs but cannot legislate treaties. Fourth, the federal supremacy has been granted to the federal government by virtue of judicial pronouncements, however, the Constitution remains silent on federal supremacy. Fifth, the States are not permitted to enact their own respective Constitutions provided however, the provisions governing States are present in the Constitution of Canada itself, thereby dispensing with the need for State Constitutions. Further, the federal government can exercise control over State legislation and over State administration. As discussed in the preceding paragraphs, the position in Canada is not different from that in America and Australia considering that these federations also exercise such control over States albeit indirectly. Lastly, Canada provides for a dispute resolution mechanism however, it is quite different from that of traditional federations. In Canada, the disputes are heard by the State courts, with an appeal lying to the Federal Supreme Court. The Supreme Court does not have original jurisdiction.

India

First, Article 368 of the Constitution of India specifically provides for addition, variation or repeal of any of the provisions[192] of the Constitution. Such an amendment can be initiated in either House of Parliament, passed by a majority of that House and two-third majority of the other House. As the reader may notice, an amendment to the Constitution of India, unlike the American or Australian Constitution, does not require the assent of the States. However, any amendment which affects the States shall require the assent of atleast one-half of the States of India. These provisions affecting the States specifically form a part of Art. 368[193]:

> *"(a) Article 54, Article 55, Article 73, Article 162, Article 241 or Article 279A or*
>
> *(b) Chapter IV of Part V, Chapter V of Part VI, or Chapter I of Part XI, or*
>
> *(c) any of the Lists in the Seventh Schedule, or*
>
> *(d) the representation of States in Parliament, or*
>
> *(e) the provisions of this article,"*

These provisions mandate the Union to seek consent of the States prior to amending provisions which particularly affect the States such as the federal structure itself or subjects common to both the Union and the States. These include the election of the President[194]; the extent of the executive power of the Union and the States[195]; the High Courts for Union Territories[196]; the Union judiciary and the High Courts in the States[197]; the distribution of legislative powers between the Union and the States[198]; the representation of States in Parliament; and the provision for amendment of the Constitution laid down in Article 368.

The intention behind seeking the assent of States for constitutional amendments in America and Australia is to ensure that the interests of the

---

192 This is however subject to the basic structure doctrine (see Kesavananda Bharti vs. State of Kerala (1973) 4 SCC 225; AIR 1973 SC 1461)
193 Article 368 (2) Proviso, Constitution of India
194 Article 54, Article 55
195 Article 73, Article 162
196 Article 241
197 Chapter IV of Part V, Chapter V of Part VI
198 Chapter I of Part XI, Seventh Schedule

States are protected. To the similar effect, the Constitution of India ensures that any matter, the amendment of which shall affect the States must receive the assent of atleast one-half of the States. As a result, the interests of the States are secured and the federal government cannot amend the Constitution to the detriment of the States without their assent. Further, seeking the assent of States only for such provisions allows the legislators in India much freedom to effectively and efficaciously amend the Constitution to suit the needs or demands of the country, thereby affording great flexibility and efficiency to law-makers.

Second, the federation has a duty to protect the States from extinction. As discussed earlier, this has dual aspects – first, right to secede or withdraw from the Union and second, protection against external or internal violence or aggression. The Constitution of India is silent on the right of a State to secede from the Union. Some judges of the Hon'ble Supreme Court have opined that the denial of right to secede is a part of the basic structure of the Constitution i.e. a State cannot secede even with a constitutional amendment.[199] However, in author's opinion, considering that the Constitution is completely silent on this aspect, a constitutional amendment may allow a State to secede theoretically. However, in practice, such a secession is nearly impossible unless by means of a revolution. The second aspect concerning the protection of States is addressed through Article 355 of the Constitution which provides:

"It shall be the duty of the Union to protect every State against external aggression and internal disturbance and to ensure that the government of every State is carried on in accordance with the provisions of this Constitution."

The Constitution of India therefore expressly provides that the Union has a duty to protect the States from both, the external aggression and from internal disturbances. This is similar to the traditional federations, each providing for a duty to protect the States.

Third, since the States renounce their powers pertaining to 'external affairs' in favour of the Union, the States cannot enter into any treaty or agreement with foreign States. This position is similar to the traditional federations. Any matter pertaining to foreign affairs or all matters which bring the Union into relation with any foreign country vest exclusively in

---

199 Golak Nath vs. State of Punjab (1967) 2 SCR 762 (834); Kesavanand Bharti vs. State of Kerala AIR 1973 SC 1461.

the legislative domain of the Parliament, to the complete exclusion of the States.[200]

Fourth, the Constitution of India prescribes for a 'federal supremacy' clause, similar to our traditional federations. This clause is often dubbed as the 'doctrine of repugnancy'. Article 254 of the Constitution of India provides:

"254. Inconsistency between laws made by Parliament and laws made by the Legislatures of States:

(1) If any provision of a law made by the Legislature of a State is repugnant to any provision of a law made by Parliament which Parliament is competent to enact, or to any provision of an existing law with respect to one of the matters enumerated in the Concurrent List, then, subject to the provisions of clause (2), the law made by Parliament, whether passed before or after the law made by the Legislature of such State, or, as the case may be, the existing law, shall prevail and the law made by the Legislature of the State shall, to the extent of the repugnancy, be void."

As the reader may see, this is not a 'general' federal supremacy clause. It provides for federal supremacy only for legislations which the Parliament is competent to enact or subjects mentioned in the Concurrent List. In order to further reduce the scope for disputes, the hon'ble Supreme Court of India has provided that an effort shall be made to reconcile the two laws in cases of inconsistency and only if they are completely irreconcilable should the doctrine of repugnancy be employed.[201] As the reader may observe, several provisions of the Constitution specifically provide federal supremacy to central legislations. For instance, provisions pertaining to emergency powers, alteration of State territories and compulsory acquisition of properties expressly provide for federal supremacy if a conflict persists with State laws. As a result, the Union cannot claim a general supremacy over the States in the absence of a specific provision which bequeaths it with such supremacy.[202] Therefore, compared to American and Australian provisions which provide for a blanket supremacy, the Indian Constitution limits

---

200 Entry 10, List I – Union List, Seventh Schedule, Constitution of India

201 Bharat Hydro Power Corpn. Ltd. vs. State of Assam (2004) 2 SCC 553; Central Bank of India vs. State of Kerala (2009) 4 SCC 94

202 D. D. Basu, Comparative Federalism, 2nd Edn. (2007), p. 80

federal supremacy to protect the interests of the States which is essential for federalism.

Surprisingly, a reader may notice that the Indian version of supremacy is more federal than that of America and Australia. In a traditional federation, it must be ensured that the federal and State governments are equal and one government is not superior to the other. However, in America and Australia, the Constitutions themselves provide for general blanket supremacy in favour of the federal government as opposed to India, which does not permit such supremacy unless expressly provided for.

Fifth, similar to Canada, the Constitution of India does not permit States to have their own Constitutions. However, peculiarly enough, the Constitutions of the States are present within the Constitution of India itself. If the reader may see, Part VI of the Constitution of India provides for complete provisions governing the internal functioning of a State, similar to the provisions which a State Constitution may have provided itself. It explicitly lays down the provisions for governance of the States in exactly the same way as it does for the Union. It provides for State legislatures, council of ministers of State, Advocate General, Governor, conduct of government business etc. It is pertinent to mention that any amendment to Part VI cannot be brought without consent of atleast one-half of the States. Further, the States have enacted their own legislations for legislating on areas not covered in the Constitution itself, for instance, the State government bodies such as State medical councils, education, police etc. Therefore, instead of giving the right to enact a Constitution to the States, the constituent assembly provided for a State Constitution within the Constitution of India itself and permitted the States to legislate upon other matters governing their internal functioning.

Sixth, the federal government in India exercises direct control over the State legislations, similar to the Canadian position. First, the Governor of a State being an appointee of the President of India, may reserve any Bill for the assent of the President, who enjoys absolute veto over such Bills.[203] Since the President acts on aid and advise of the council of ministers, the said Bill cannot be assented to by the President without the approval of Parliament. Further, some Bills may only be introduced in State legislatures

---

203 Article 201, Constitution of India

after prior consent of the Governor.[204] Second, each Bill passed in the State legislature requires the assent of the governor who may either withhold its assent or send the Bill back to legislature with changes.[205] Third, the Parliament may be permitted to legislate on any matter reserved for the States, mentioned in List II of Seventh Schedule of the Constitution. This can be effected either through a resolution by the State itself[206] or through a resolution by the Rajya Saba i.e. Upper House of the Parliament.[207] Fourth, the Parliament may make laws on subjects reserved for State legislature if these shall be implemented in pursuance of international agreements.[208] In addition to these, the Parliament is empowered to legislate on State subjects if an emergency under Art. 352, 256 or 360 is in operation in a State.[209] Through these means, the federal government exercises control over the State legislations. Such a system is similar to Canada but dissimilar to that of Australia and America, the latter not permitting such control. However, as seen in the preceding paragraphs, even these traditional federations exercise control over State legislations albeit indirectly.

Seventh, similar to Canada, the federal government exercises direct control over the State administration. The Governor of a State is appointed by the President of India on the advice of the Council of Ministers i.e. the Union government. As discussed in the preceding paragraphs, the Governor is empowered to withhold assent, recommend amendments or reserve Bill for the President, thereby exercising some control over State legislature. Governor of a State is considered to be the eyes and ears of the President and can recommend dismissal of a State government to the President. Further, the Union government has the power to ensure compliance of laws made by the Parliament and it may give directions to the States necessary for this purpose.[210] If such directions are not followed by the States, the State government can be dismissed by the President, on the recommendation of the Governor.[211] In addition to these, the Union government exercises control through the All India Civil Services such as

204 Article 207, Constitution of India
205 Article 200, Constitution of India
206 Article 252, Constitution of India
207 Article 249, Constitution of India
208 Article 253, Constitution of India
209 See Article 356, Constitution of India
210 Article 256, Constitution of India
211 Article 356, Constitution of India

IAS, IPS, IRS etc. The personnel in these services occupy the posts at the highest echelons of the government. Since these are employed and deployed by the Union government, the latter exercises substantial control over the State affairs through these personnel.[212] Technically, this position is in stark contrast to the ones in traditional federations however, as we have seen in the preceding paragraphs, in practice, the traditional federations also exercise such control indirectly over the State administrations.

Lastly, as regards the dispute resolution mechanism for disputes between the federation and the States or between States *inter se*, the Constitution of India specifically provides for dispute settlement mechanism. The dispute settlement mechanism is similar to the one in America and Australia i.e. a Supreme (or Federal) Court vested with original jurisdiction to adjudicate upon disputes between the Union and States or between two or more States *inter se*. Such jurisdiction has been vested in the Hon'ble Supreme Court by virtue of Art. 131, which states:

"131. Original jurisdiction of the Supreme Court Subject to the provisions of this Constitution, the Supreme Court shall, to the exclusion of any other court, have original jurisdiction in any dispute

(a) between the Government of India and one or more States; or

(b) between the Government of India and any State or States on one side and one or more other States on the other; or

(c) between two or more States, if and in so far as the dispute involves any question (whether of law or fact) on which the existence or extent of a legal right depends"

Therefore, the Supreme Court can hear disputes between the Union and States and between two or more States. No other court in the country can adjudicate upon such disputes. The Supreme Court of India is similar to the Federal Court in America and the High Court of Australia.

In conclusion, the preceding paragraphs analyse the eight features of federalism with regards to the rights of the States. First, for amendment of provisions which affect the rights or powers of a State, their consent is mandatory for such amendment. Second, the States in India do not have a right to secede from the federation, however, a constitutional amendment

---

212 Article 312, Constitution of India

may be employed to effect such a secession. Further, the Union has a constitutional obligation to protect the States from external or internal aggression. Third, foreign affairs are the exclusive domain of the federation to the complete exclusion of the States. Fourth, the federation does not enjoy a general supremacy over the State laws, unless expressly provided for by the Constitution. Fifth, the Constitution of India does not permit the States to enact their own Constitutions. The provisions which may have appeared in the Constitution of the States are instead present in the Constitution of India itself. Sixth, the federal government exercises direct control over the State government legislations. Seventh, the federal government exercises direct administrative control over the States as well. Lastly, any disputes between the Union and the States, or between two or more States is adjudicated upon by the Supreme Court of India, having exclusive jurisdiction to entertain such disputes.

Conclusion

In the preceding paragraphs, the author attempted to discuss the provisions pertaining to rights of the States in a federation and the protections afforded to these States by the Constitution. Considering that States renounce some of their powers while entering a federation, the Constitution of each federation ensures that some rights and protections are granted to these States essential for them to retain partial autonomy, so that they are not reduced to mere administrative units. In light of these, the following paragraphs will compare the Indian federal system with our target federations to conclude that the system in India is similar to these federations in substance, however, the form may vary in some instances.

First, we discussed the power of the federal government to unilaterally amend the Constitution to the detriment of the States. Such an amendment shall be ratified or approved by the States as well, considering that it is essential for a federation to ensure that States are not reduced to mere administrative units. Therefore, any amendment which is intended to vary or remove the powers or rights of States shall seek consent of majority of States for upholding the federal principle. The rationale underlying the aforementioned is protection of the rights of States. In America, constitutional amendments require 3/4th of the States to vote in favour of such amendments. Similarly, in Australia a more complex procedure is adopted to the effect that in addition to the approval of majority of State legislatures, the approval of majority of electors shall be obtained along with Parliamentary approval. Considering that the basic principle behind ratification of constitutional amendments by States is their protection, their consent shall be taken for such amendments. Canada adopts a different approach wherein the Constitution requires the assent of the States for amendment of only those provisions which affect the States. To the same effect, Indian Constitution provides that any amendment which affects the functioning or rights of the States such as election of the President, extent of the executive power of the Union and the States, judiciary, distribution of legislative powers between the Union and the States, representation of States in Parliament or the provision for amendment of the Constitution itself, shall require ratification by majority of the States in the country.

In the author's opinion, the position in India and Canada is the most efficient approach considering that if each amendment requires assent of States, it is extremely difficult to pass an amendment leading to extreme rigidity and policy paralysis. The Constitution is a living documents which shall change from time to time, considering the ever-changing circumstances in a nation. To cite an example, only eight (8) out of forty-four (44) amendments in Australia have been approved by all concerned parties. Such a position provides extreme rigidity and every amendment may involve expensive and time-consuming exercise of garnering support with States' legislators despite the fact that the amendment may not affect the interests of the States at all. The Indian and Canadian position on the other hand, provides great flexibility to the federal government while simultaneously ensuring that the interests of the States are protected. Therefore, similar to America and Australia, Indian Constitution provides for protection of States against unilateral amendments which affect the rights of the States. However, at the same time, the Indian Constitution allows the Parliament to unilaterally amend other parts of the Constitution not concerning States, thereby allowing substantial freedom and efficiency of administration to the Union government.

Second, it is implicit in the federal principle that the federal government has a duty to protect the States from extinction which includes protection from external or internal aggression and secession. The Constitutions of America, Australia and India expressly provide for the duty of the federal government to protect the States from such aggression. The Constitution of Canada, however, does not expressly provide for such a duty though the duty is implicit in the federal principle. With regards to secession, the American and Australian Constitutions are silent on the right to secede. It has been held by the courts that States cannot secede from the federation unless all the States of the federation consent to such secession or through a revolution. The Indian Constitution is similar to traditional federations so far as it is silent on secession. Theoretically, secession in India may be permitted if the Constitution is amended to that effect. However, in practice, secession is not permitted in India. The Canadian Constitution, in stark contrast to aforementioned federations, expressly permits secession. Any such secession would require assent of Federal Parliament along with ratification by 2/3rd of provinces and 50% of the population in all provinces. Though the secession is permitted, in practice it is nearly impossible considering the enormous assent required. Therefore, secession is not permitted in America, Australia and India though theoretically, it may be allowed through alternative means.

Third, one of the three main powers which the States renounce whilst entering the federation is dealing with foreign affairs. In other words, foreign affairs are exclusively dealt with by the federation. In furtherance of the same, America, Australia and India do not permit States to participate in foreign affairs of the Union. However, in Canada, the States are permitted to participate in foreign affairs and appoint agents to other nations though they cannot legislate treaties. Therefore, Canadian position is on one end of the spectrum with America, Australia and India occupying the other end.

Fourth, in case of conflict between federal and State laws, it is essential to have a supremacy clause to eliminate scope for disputes. As a result, the Constitutions of America and Australia expressly provide a general 'supremacy clause' stating that in case of an inconsistency between the federal and State laws, the former shall prevail. The position in Canada is similar to that of aforementioned federations however, the federal supremacy in Canada has been adopted by the judiciary and not by the Constitution itself. The position in India is similar to our target federations to the extent that Constitution of India provides for federal supremacy however, the supremacy is only limited to specific circumstances. In other words, it is not a blanket supremacy. The basic purpose behind 'supremacy clauses' is that they eliminate the scope for disputes in cases of inconsistency.

In furtherance of this purpose, the courts in India attempt to reconcile the laws in cases of repugnancy and only declare them to be irreconcilable if there is absolutely no scope to do so. Therefore, the Indian position is more aligned with the federal principle than that of aforementioned federations considering that the Indian provision prefers to secure the interests of the States to a vast extent, only providing for federal supremacy for specific purposes and wherein the laws cannot be reconciled.

Fifth, States in America and Australia are permitted to enact their own Constitutions, in addition to the federal Constitution. However, these Constitutions are subject to the federal Constitution i.e. in case of conflict, the latter shall prevail. On the other hand, Canada does not permit the States to enact their own Constitutions. Similarly, the Constitution of India does not permit enactment of Constitutions by the States either. However, peculiarly enough, the Constitutions of the States are present within the Constitution of India itself. If the reader may see, Part VI of the Constitution of India provides for complete provisions governing the internal functioning of a State, similar to the provisions a State Constitution may have provided itself. It explicitly lays down the provisions for governance of the States in exactly the same way as it does for the Union. It provides for State legislatures, council of ministers of State, Advocate General, Governor, conduct of government business etc. Further, the States have enacted their own legislations for legislating upon areas not covered in the Constitution itself, for instance, the State government bodies such as State medical councils, education, police etc. Therefore, instead of giving the right to enact a Constitution to the States, the constituent assembly provided for a State Constitution within the Constitution of India itself. As a result, similar to the federations of America and Australia, Indian Constitution also provides for State Constitutions albeit through different means. Therefore, the Indian position concerning State Constitutions is similar to America and Australia in substance, however the form is different.

Sixth, in America and Australia, the principle of dual government does not permit legislative interference of either government into the domain of the other. The federal government cannot interfere with legislative power of the State governments provided the State governments are empowered to legislate on such subjects. Further, the Governor of a State is empowered to veto a bill passed by State legislature akin to President's veto on a federal bill however, neither the Governor can veto a federal bill, nor can the President veto a State Bill. It is pertinent to mention that though these federations do not permit federal control over State legislations, the federal government still exercises considerable control over these legislations indirectly through conditional grants, infrastructure projects etc. In order to obtain such grants, States are directed to legislate upon a certain matter or amend their legislations.

On the other hand, the Canadian Constitution allows federal control over State legislations directly, quite contrary to the federal principal. Such control by the federal government is exercised through disallowance of provincial legislation by Federal Parliament or reservation of provincial legislation by the Governor. However, though such powers are available, these are sparingly used. As a result, Canada allows federal control over State legislations, thereby attenuating the federal principle. The Indian system is similar to Canada, allowing wide control to the federal government over State legislations. The rationale behind permitting the federation to exercise control over State legislations is to promote the collective integrity of the nation, national security and general welfare of the nation, which at times requires federal interference. Considering that nations like India are blessed with enormous religious, linguistic and cultural diversity, such powers must be provided to the federal government in interest of the collective integrity and growth of the nation. As a result, though Indian position is different from that of America and Australia in form, substantially even these federations permit federal control over State legislations albeit indirectly. Thus, all our target federations exercise control over State legislations either directly or indirectly.

Seventh, similar to federal control over State legislations, control over the State administration is an anti-thesis of the federal principle. As a necessary corollary, such control or interference shall not be permitted, being considered a derogation of the federal principle. However, in practice, all target federations exercise substantial control over State administration through direct or indirect means. On one end of the spectrum is America and Australia wherein the control over State administration is exercised through indirect means such as grants-in-aid, conditional grants etc. wherein the federal government may pass mandatory directions to the States, only upon the fulfilment of which the grants shall be made. On the other hand, Canada and India exercise administrative control over the States directly through the Governor (being an agent of federal government), internal emergency powers, central civil services, withholding assent for Bills etc. Through these means, the federal government tends to dictate the administrative setup of the States, however, such powers are not exercised frequently but rather sparingly, often for political reasons. The reader may notice here that all the target federations exercise administrative control over the States, either through direct or indirect means, exercising control nonetheless. The only difference is that of form, America and Australia exercise such control indirectly whereas Canada and India do so directly, the substance or purpose of this control being the same. Therefore, all federations tend to control State administration in substance albeit through different forms.

Eighth, on many an occasion, the three organs of a government – executive, legislature and judiciary may exceed their domain and enter that of the other organ. In such cases, it is essential for a special forum to adjudicate the disputes to avoid anarchy and complete chaos. The respective Constitutions of America, Australia and India specifically provide for a Federal Supreme Court, High Court and Supreme Court respectively, exclusively empowered to hear and adjudicate disputes between the Union and States or between States *inter se*. In Canada, the Supreme Court does not possess original jurisdiction, as a result of which, the disputes between the federation and States and States *inter se* are heard by State courts. The parties may appeal the decisions of these State courts before the Supreme Court. However, since the federal government is empowered to veto any State legislation on any ground whatsoever, the scope for disputes is extremely narrow. Therefore, the position of India is exactly similar to that of America and Australia.

Finally, as seen in the preceding paragraphs, the position of India with respect to the rights of States vis-à-vis the Union are similar to that of American and Australia, traditional federations of the modern world. The author discussed provisions against unilateral amendment of the Constitution, federal duty to protect the States from extinction, foreign affairs, federal supremacy, States' Constitutions, legislative control of federation over States, administrative control over States and dispute resolution mechanism. It was seen from the discussion that the provisions in India are similar to the aforementioned federations, serving the same purpose albeit through slightly different means. Hence, as regards the rights of States vis-à-vis the Union, India is on par with the American and Australian federations.

CHAPTER 7

Emergency Powers of the Union

One of the major objectives of a federal system of governance is to preserve the autonomy of the States while maintaining national unity and integrity. However, many a time, certain situations arise where national unity or security takes precedence over preservation of autonomy of States. Some leading examples of such situations may be external aggression, riots, war etc. wherein all the resources of the federation need to be directed towards countering these situations through diversion of funds, engaging State law enforcement personnel, suspension of civil rights etc. In such situations, the federal government assumes complete control over the nation including States. There is little doubt that in a war effort or defence, a unified, effective and prompt action is hindered if resources and decision-making authorities are divided into two separate and coordinate governments. In other words, during such emergencies, the Constitution turns unitary from federal. However, this situation is an anti-thesis to the federal principle, considering that preservation of autonomy of States is a key aspect of federalism.

When the American federation came into existence, such instances requiring transfer of power to the federation by the States for a specific period to counter an emergency did not exist. As a result, traditional federal Constitutions do not provide for emergency powers expressly through their respective Constitutions. During the two World Wars i.e. between the years 1916 and 1945, these federations realised that emergency powers are absolutely essential for war efforts, considering that the nation has to optimally utilize all resources at its disposal including finances and human capital. As a result, the judiciary had to create room for exercise of such powers, which had become the need of the hour in the 20th century. In the federal Constitutions which were enacted after the culminations of two World Wars, the emergency powers are expressly provided for therein.

However, such emergency powers are many a time abused by the union or federal governments. A classic example of such abuse is imposition of emergency in States where the ruling political party is different from that at the centre. In such cases, especially in India, the central government has declared emergency just to dismiss the ruling government in a State on multiple occasions. Considering the precedent this practice has set, it is essential that several safeguards should be present to deter the Union from utilizing emergency powers at its whims and fancies. Such declarations result in severe undermining of the federal principle.

This chapter discusses the existence of emergency powers of the federal governments in each of the target jurisdictions, analyses their impact on the federal principle and compares the ways in emergency powers are restricted or controlled. It discusses three types of emergencies declared by the federations – external, internal and financial. The first is declared in situations of war or defence, the second is declared during internal disturbances such as rebellions, riots etc. and the third is declared during severe financial crises. In the subsequent paragraphs, the author discusses provisions pertaining to each type of emergency in context of each of our target federations.

United States of America

First, the Constitution of America does not expressly provide for any provisions permitting the federal government to declare an external emergency. However, the judiciary has expanded the powers of federal government during situations of war through a liberal interpretation of federal war powers under the American Constitution.[213] Being a federation, the exclusive power of war or defence vests in the federal government considering that the President is the 'Commander-in-Chief' of the Army and Navy of the United States.[214] The Constitution of America specifically empowers the Congress to declare war through Art. I, s. 8 Cl. 11 to 14 which state:

"(11) To declare war, grants letters of marque and reprisal, and make rules concerning captures on land water.

(12) To raise and support armies, but no appropriations of money to that use shall be for a longer term than two years.

(13) To provide and maintain a navy.

---

213 Basu, D. D., Comparative Federalism, 2nd Edn. (2007), p. 276
214 Art. II, s. 2(1), Constitution of U.S.A.

(14) To make rules for the government and regulation of the land and naval forces."

These powers, with the support of judiciary, have been widely expanded by the federal government to invade the State sphere which is not permitted in normal circumstances. In *Hirabayashi v. U.S.*[215], the Federal Supreme Court held that the Constitution grants the exercise of war power and all powers necessary for war including "every matter and activity related to war as substantially to affect its conduct and progress" and "embraces every phase of the national defence". The war power of the Congress and the President is not subject to judicial review, as a result of which the judgement or decisions of the government taken under this power cannot be questioned in a court of law.[216] Although the Congress is not permitted to exercise emergency powers maliciously to legislate on matters it otherwise is not permitted to,[217] legislating on such matters under exercise of war powers or national defence is still permitted.[218] The powers reserved for the States under the 10th Amendment are suspended till the time such emergency powers are in force.[219]

The judiciary has extended the war power to include imposition of curfews and penalties[220], control of inter-state and intra-state rail roads[221], control of nationwide telephone lines[222], regulation of essential commodities[223], control over ships[224], output of factories[225] and conscription for military[226]. In addition to these, even after the termination of war or such emergency, the Congress is empowered to legislate or undertake measures under the

---

215 (1943) 320 US 81

216 Ludecke v. Watkins (1948) 335 US 160

217 McCullock v. Maryland (1819) 4 Wh 316; Linder v. U.S. (1926) 268 US 15

218 Ashwander v. T.V.A. (1936) 297 US 288

219 Cf. F.E.R.C. v. Mississippi (1982) 456 US 742; Oklahoma v. U.S. (1947) 330 US 127; Case v. Bowles (1946) 327 US 92; Ferinandez v. Weimer (1945) 326 US 340

220 Hirobayashi v. U.S. (1942) 320 U.S. 81

221 N. Pacific Ry. Co. v. North Dakota (1919) 250 U.S. 135

222 Dakota Central Tel. Co. v. South Dakota (1919) 250 U.S. 135

223 Yakus v. U.S. (1944) 321 US 414; Testa v. Katt (1947) 330 US 386; Bowles v. Willingham (1944) 321 US 503

224 The Lake Monroe, (1919) 250 US 240

225 Moore & Tierney v. Rexford Knitting Co. (1918) 250 Fed. 276

226 U.S.v. David (1968) 20 L Ed (2d) 672; Selective Draft Law Cases (1918) 245 US 366

garb of emergency powers to remedy the effects of war.[227] However, such measures are brought under closer scrutiny by the judiciary. [228]

As a result, the Federal government exercises substantial control over the State governments during an external emergency. Although such powers were not granted expressly by the Constitution itself, the judiciary has expanded the war powers to include things necessary for exercise of such powers, including interference with States' affairs.

Second, the Constitution of America does not expressly provide for declaration of an internal emergency either. However, Article IV, s. 4 provides that the federal government shall guarantee a republican form of government in States. If any State fails to form a republican form of government, the federal government shall be under an obligation to restore the republican form of government even by force, if required. For this purpose, the federal government acts on its own initiative.[229] Such a position exists in India as well wherein the federal government can suspend the State governments if the latter violates constitutional provisions or directions of the federal government. In light of this, noted constitutional scholar *Sh. H. M. Seervai* observed *"Article IV, s. 4 shows that it is not inconsistent with the federal principle that a State should be prevented from working its own Constitution contrary to the mandate of the U.S. Constitution."*[230] The powers granted to the federal government under Article IV, s. 4 are very wide. The Congress has the power to restore the republican form of government in States and the question as to whether the State government had ceased to be republican is not justiciable,[231] thereby leaving scope of utilising such powers maliciously or for furthering political agendas.

Further, it has often been pointed out that traditional federations do not permit federal interference in cases of internal emergencies, unlike India. Such a proposition is incorrect. Article IV, s. 4 provides that the federal government has a duty to protect the State from domestic violence. In case a situation arises wherein the State government is under internal violence including riots, rebellions etc., the federal government has been empowered

---

227 Hamilton v. Kentucky Districts (1919) 251 US 146

228 Woods v. Miller (1948) 333 US 138

229 Willis, Constitutional Law, p. 451

230 Seervai, H. M., Constitutional Law of India, 4th Edn., Universal Law Publishing, pp. 292

231 Luther v. Borden 7 How. 1

to intervene. In *Debs*[232], it was held that the United States had the power and the duty to use *"the entire strength of the nation…to enforce in any part of the land the full and free exercise of all national powers and the security of all rights entrusted by the Constitution to its care."*[233] This stance of the federal government is supported through two illustrations set out in Kelly and Harbinson's *'The American Constitution'.*[234]

The first instance occurred in 1957 in State of Arkansas. The Governor of Arkansas ordered the Arkansas National Guard to bar the black students from entering or enrolling in a white school in Little Rock, citing necessity of maintaining law and order. With this proclamation, the Governor disregarded several orders of the Federal Court permitting the entry of black students. As a result, President Eisenhower decided to intervene by sending several companies of the U.S. Army, effectively putting the city under martial law, thereby enforcing the entry and enrolment of black students. The second instance occurred in 1962 in the State of Mississippi. The Supreme Court had ordered one James Meredith, a black man to be admitted as a student in University of Mississippi against the wishes of the people. The Governor of Mississippi used the police and law enforcement to ensure that Meredith was not allowed to enter the University to register. In retaliation, the President issued a proclamation directing the State authorities to cease any interference with Meredith's admission and ordered the U.S. Marshals to escort Meredith into the building. Riots ensued in the State as a corollary of the President's proclamation. The President therefore ordered several thousands of troops to put down the resistance to federal law.

As the reader may see, these two instances show that the federal government interferes with the functioning of the State if the State is in violation of constitutional directions or federal laws. Even in a federal Constitution like that of America, the federal government has the power to ensure that the States function in accordance with the federal Constitution, failure of which entitles the federal government to rectification, even by force, so that the State government can function as it was intended to function. As *Sh. H. M. Seervai* observed, *"if such a power did not exist, the*

---

232 Debs, In Re 158 U.S. 564
233 Ibid p. 582; See also 'The Constitution of the United States of America, Revised and Annotated (1964) at p. 796
234 5th Edn., p. 864

Federal government would itself be at the mercy of one or more States. A power essential for the existence of the federal government cannot be said to impair the federal principle."[235] Withal, the American federation permits the federal government to proclaim an internal emergency even though it is not expressly permitted by the Constitution.

Third, the provisions for financial emergency in the Constitution of America are absent. However, the federal government has enacted the International Emergency Economic Powers Act (IEEPA), 1977[236] which authorizes the President to regulate a variety of economic transactions following a declaration of national emergency, in response to any outlandish or extraordinary financial threat to U.S.[237] This Act authorizes the President to counter any economic or financial situations which may affect the economic or financial health of the nation,[238] empowering the federal government to declare emergency, block transactions, confiscate property and freeze assets to counter any threats.[239] As of 1st July, 2020, the President has declared fifty nine (59) emergencies under this Act, thirty three (33) of which are still ongoing.[240]

As seen in the preceding paragraphs, though the Constitution of America does not expressly provide for declaration of these emergencies, the courts and the federal government have carved these emergency powers owing to their necessity. For the proper functioning of a federal government, these powers are absolutely essential, in the absence of which, the correct balance between the States and the federation would be disturbed. In other words, a power essential for the existence of federal government cannot be said to impair the federal principle. If such powers are absent, chaos would ensue in a federation which could only be quelled by emergency provisions. As a result, the emergency powers are exercised in the United States of America, despite being a traditional federation.

---

235 Seervai, H. M., Constitutional Law of India, 4th Edn., Universal Law Publishing, pp. 293
236 Title II of Pub.L. 95-223, 91 Stat. 1626
237 Casey, Christopher A.; et al. (March 20, 2019). *The International Emergency Economic Powers Act: Origins, Evolution, and Use.* Washington, DC: Congressional Research Service.
238 50 U.S.C. §1701(a)
239 See 50 U.S.C. §1702(a)(1)(B); 50 U.S.C. §1702(a)(1)(C)
240 U.S. Treasury, Office of Foreign Asset Control, Sanctions Programs and Country Information

First, there is no such provision in the Constitution of Australia permitting the imposition of an external emergency. It has instead been held that the federal nature of the Constitution is not lost during war.[241] Though the Constitution provides for the power of defence under s. 51(vi)[242], it is subject to the overriding limitation imposed in s. 51 stating that everything is 'subject to this Constitution'. As a result, the federal government cannot disrupt the federal structure by taking over functions of State governments.[243] However, the situation in practice is substantially different from the one enumerated above. The judicial interpretation of 'defence' under s. 51(vi) has substantially enlarged the powers of the Parliament enabling it to interfere with the jurisdiction of the States to the extent that the federal distribution of powers appears to be suspended during the times of war.[244] In other words, the imposition of external emergency is permitted though not specifically provided for in the Constitution. In light of this, the Royal Commission of 1929[245] observed during the First World War that the federation, for practical purposes, is a unified government in times of war. During the Second World War, the federal power of defence was further expanded by the judiciary for adoption of 'post war measures' provided that the said measures are 'with respect to defence'[246].

In case such measures are not concerned with 'defence' or are disguised under the garb of 'defence' i.e. there is an absence of causal connection between the measure and the needs of defence, the court is empowered to interfere and strike down such a federal measure, citing unconstitutional invasion into the sphere of the State.[247] In other words, a federal invasion is unjustified if the problem which the federal government seeks to deal

---

241 Australian Communist Party v. Commonwealth (1951) 83 CLR 1 (202)

242 Section 51 lays down the legislative powers of the Parliament

243 Nicholas, Australian Constitution, (1952), pp. 144; Gratwick v. Johnson (1945) 70 CLR 1; Andrews v. Howell (1941) 65 CLR 255

244 D. D. Basu, Comparative Federalism, 2nd Edn. (2007), p. 279.

245 Royal Commission on the Constitution of the Commonwealth (Australia). & Peden, John Beverley. & Australia. Inter-Imperial Relations Committee. 1929, *Report of the Royal Commission on the Constitution*

246 Nicholas, Australian Constitution, (1952), pp. 144; Gratwick v. Johnson (1945) 70 CLR 1; Andrews v. Howell (1941) 65 CLR 255

247 Cf. Victoria v. Commonwealth (1942) 66 CLR 488; R. v. University of Sydney (1943) 67 CLR 95

with is not required to be dealt with during the war and such a problem was present in normal times.[248] The power of judicial review is rarely exercised during a period of war[249] and significantly increases after the termination of war[250]. During time of peace, the judiciary does not tolerate any interference with activities which have no connection with the needs of defence[251] such as manufacturing of military uniforms[252].

The reader may note that this position is in contrast with the American position, in so far as the courts in Australia are empowered to investigate the measures taken during an emergency or rather, in the name of 'defence'. Though empowered, the courts do not generally review such decisions taken during war time. Therefore, the Australian courts provide limited judicial review of measures taken during an emergency unlike America, wherein such measures are beyond judicial review[253]. However, both these federations provide for external emergency powers, either through the Constitution itself or through the activism of judiciary.

Second, the Constitution of Australia does not expressly provide for declaration of an internal emergency either. An indirect power to declare such an emergency may be derived from s. 61 of the Constitution which empowers the Commonwealth to maintain the Constitution. This power is vested in the Governor-General who may utilise this power to protect the authority of the organs of the government.[254]

In addition to this, the judiciary has carved out an inherent power vested in the Federal Parliament to legislate for its own protection and of the Constitution against 'domestic attack'.[255] This power is derived from a conjoint reading of s. 51(xxxix) and s. 61 of the Constitution.[256] In *Burns v. Ransley*[257], the High Court broadened the scope of such power by including the power to suppress subversive activities and propaganda against the

---

248 Victorian Chamber v. Commonwealth (Industrial Lighting Regulations) (1943) 67 CLR 413

249 Stenhouse v. Coleman (1944) 69 CLR 457; Farey v. Burvett (1916) 21 CLR 433

250 R. v. Foster (1949) 79 CLR 43; Dawson v. Commonwealth (1946) 73 CLR 174

251 Commonwealth v. Australian Shipping Bd. (1926) 39 CLR 1

252 A.G. for Victoria v. Commonwealth (1935) 52 CLR 533

253 Ludecke v. Watkins (1948) 335 US 160

254 R. v. Sharkey (1949) 79 CLR 121

255 Australian Communist Party v. Commonwealth (1951) 83 CLR 1

256 ibid

257 Burns v. Ransley (1944) 79 CLR 101

federation, prevent and punish incitement against the government, revolutionary change in the form of government, punish any group or individual attempting to or encouraging the overthrow of government by force or violence. In fact, this power has been held to be as elastic as the 'defence power'[258] discussed earlier, thereby giving the federal government amply wide powers. However, it is strictly mandated that such internal emergency power shall not be used as a coercive measure against the State governments.[259]

Third, the Constitution of Australia does not provide for proclamation of financial emergency either. However, such an emergency has been contemplated under the incidental powers mentioned in s. 51 (xxxix) of the Constitution. For instance, following the global financial crisis of 2008, the issue of 'tax bonus' arose in *Pape v. Federal Commissioner of Taxation,* [260] wherein the majority of High Court observed "*the Executive Government is the arm of government capable of and empowered to respond to a crisis be it war, natural disaster or a financial crisis on the scale here.*" The court further added "*the executive power of the Commonwealth conferred by s. 61 of the Constitution extends to the power to expend public moneys for the purpose of avoiding or mitigating the large-scale adverse effects of the circumstances affecting the national economy*". As a result, the courts have stated that the federal government is empowered to expend or reallocate public money to face challenges occurring due to financial crises.

Further, the Federal Parliament has legislated towards declaration of a financial emergency, as and when required. For instance, the Financial Emergency Act of 1931[261] was enacted to declare a financial emergency. Its Preamble stated "*an Act to make necessary Provision for carrying out a Plan agreed on by the Commonwealth and the States for meeting the grave Financial Emergency existing in Australia, re-establishing Financial Stability, and restoring Industrial and General Prosperity.*" This legislation specifically laid down the regulation of public money with a view to avert the financial crisis.

---

258 Australian Communist Party v. Commonwealth (1951) 83 CLR 1
259 Commonwealth v. Colonial Combing Co. (1922) 31 CLR 421
260 (2009) 238 CLR 1
261 Act no. 10 of 1931

As the reader may notice, the federal governments has been empowered to declare a financial emergency, if required. The courts have expressly laid down that the government may adopt measures for financial control of public money during financial crises, in addition to the legislative power of the government to declare a financial emergency.

As seen in the preceding paragraphs, the Australian Constitution does not expressly provide for declaration of external emergency however, the courts have interpreted such a power into the legislative powers of the federal government. Similarly, despite the absence of any provision empowering the federal government to declare an internal emergency, the judiciary has expanded the scope of federal government's powers to include a declaration of such emergency. The financial emergency has been similarly read into the provisions of the Constitution by the judiciary. Therefore, despite the absence of specific provisions in the Constitution, the federal government is well empowered to declare all three kinds of emergencies.

Canada

Similar to the American and Australian Constitution, the Canadian Constitution does not expressly provide for declaration of an external emergency or the powers incidental thereto. Therefore, the Canadian government enacted the Emergencies Act, 1985[262] which authorises the Governor General of Canada to take special temporary measures to ensure safety and security during national emergencies.[263] It provides for review of an emergency by the Parliament, powers of revocation or continuation and the powers of the Federal Parliament during the invocation of such emergency. Further, it provides for judicial review of violations of civil rights in Canada during such emergencies. This Act lays down the detailed provisions pertaining to four types of emergencies in Canada – public welfare, public order, international and war emergency. It is pertinent to mention that the Emergencies Act has never been used till date.[264]

In addition to this, due to the absence of any constitutional provisions permitting proclamation of an external emergency, the courts expanded the

---

262 *Emergencies Act*, R.S.C. 1985, c. 22, as amended by S.C. 2001, c. 27

263 Forcese, Craig; West, Leah (2020-03-14). "Ch 8 -- Emergencies". *National Security Law 2d Ed*. Rochester, NY: Irwin Law

264 Bensadoun, Emerald (17 March 2020). "Coronavirus: How the Emergencies Act could help Canada's struggling economy". *Global News*.

federal powers of defence to give effect to such an emergency. S. 91(7) of the British North America Act, 1867 gives exclusive power to the Federal Parliament to legislate with respect to '*militia, military and naval service, and defence*'. To supplement this power, the courts have relied upon the general or residuary power extended to the Federal Parliament pertaining to '*peace, order and good government*',[265] to support the exercise of emergency powers.

In *Ref. re Wartime Leasehold Regulations*[266], the Privy Council held that during the war, the dominion could enact measures for economic and social control and regulation which in normal circumstances belonged to the jurisdiction of the provinces. The Privy Council employed the doctrine of aspect while justifying the extension of federal powers in the name of defence by holding that these subjects are not transferred to the federation from the provinces during the war but rather, these subjects assumed a national aspect during war times which can only be adequately dealt with by the federal government.[267] This view is supported by the observations of Lord Haldane in *Fort Frances*[268] wherein he stated "...*there may be cases arising out of some extraordinary peril to national life of Canada as a whole, such as the cases arising out of war, where legislation is required of an order that passes beyond the heads of exclusive provincial competency*". This power has been implied from the expression '*peace, order and good government*'.[269]

These powers acquired by the Federal Parliament during an emergency to deal with the national aspects of a certain subject do not affect the powers of the provinces to deal with other aspects of that subject in so far as it specially affects the concerned province only.[270] Further, the federal powers to interfere in State subjects do not necessarily cease on cessation of hostilities or end of war.[271] Such powers can continue in order to smoothly transit from war period to peace, for instance, the Canadian Supreme Court allowed war time regulation and control of rent[272] and chemicals four years

---

265 S. 91, British North America Act, 1867

266 (1950) SCR 124

267 Fort Frances Pulp Co. v. Manitoba Free Press (1923) SC 695; In re, Bd. of Commerce Act, 1919 (1922) 1 AC 191 (PC)

268 Fort Frances Pulp Co. v. Manitoba Free Press (1923) SC 695

269 S. 91, British North America Act, 1867

270 A.G. Ontario v. Canada Temperance Fed., (1946) AC 193

271 Fort Frances Pulp Co. v. Manitoba Free Press (1923) SC 695

272 Commonwealth v. Australian Shipping Edn., (1926) 39 CLR 1

after the cessation of hostilities[273]. Parliament is entitled to '*maintain such control as it finds necessary to ensure the orderly transition from war to peace*'.[274]

There are however certain restrictions on the acts done under emergency powers, laid down in *Board of Commerce*[275] case. First, the Federal Parliament cannot enact permanent laws relating to provincial subjects during such emergency. Second, such wartime restrictions continuing after cessation of hostilities cannot continue indefinitely. Third, it must be demonstrated that the circumstances are still abnormal thereby requiring interference with the provincial subjects.

The provisions for internal or financial emergency are not provided for in the Constitution either. However, s. 91(7) of the Constitution and Emergencies Act, 1985 envisage the declaration of these emergencies. For instance, the Emergencies Act, 1985 specifically provides for declaring an emergency for public order. No such emergency has ever been declared in Canada. Such a position is perfectly in line with the federal principle wherein the Constitution does not allow the federal government to supersede or suspend the provincial governments. The position is therefore similar to the one in America and Australia. These traditional federations provide for emergency powers through expansive reading of their constitutional provisions and specific legislations.

As seen in the preceding paragraphs, the Canadian Constitution does not expressly provide for declaration of external emergency however, the Federal Parliament has enacted the Emergencies Act 1985 which exhaustively deals with the declaration of emergencies. In addition to this, the courts have interpreted such a power of external emergency into the legislative powers of the federal government. However, the provisions for financial or internal emergency are completely absent from the Constitution, though the Emergencies Act, 1985 envisages the declaration of such emergencies. Such an instance of declaration of either an internal or financial emergency have never arisen in Canada. Therefore, the emergency provisions in the Canadian federation are in line with the acceptable emergency powers employed in traditional federations.

---

273 Ref. re Regulation of Chemicals (1943) SCR 1
274 Ref. re Wartime Leasehold Regulations (1950) SCR 124
275 In re Bd. of Commerce Act, 1919, (1922) 1 AC 191

India

Learning from the experiences of the traditional federations during the World Wars, the founding fathers of the Republic of India expressly laid down the provisions for declaration of an external emergency in India. As seen in the preceding paragraphs, the traditional federations did not have provisions for declaration of such emergencies in their respective Constitutions, as a result of which, the judiciary had to intervene and carve out such powers in the Constitution to enable the federal government to consolidate its efforts and resources during such emergencies. Therefore, it seemed appropriate to provide such provisions in the Constitution of India itself.

Article 352(1) of the Constitution of India expressly provides:

"(1) If the President is satisfied that a grave emergency exists whereby the security of India or of any part of the territory thereof is threatened, whether by war or external aggression or armed rebellion, he may, by Proclamation, make a declaration to that effect in respect of the whole of India or of such part of the territory thereof as may be specified in the Proclamation."

Therefore, Art. 352 empowers the President to declare an emergency if he is 'satisfied' that security of India or any part of India is threatened by war, external aggression or armed rebellion. These powers are to be exercised only in rare circumstances as it disturbs the normal fabric of the Constitution. Prior to 1978, the words 'internal disturbance' existed in place of 'armed rebellion'. However, due to its wide scope of interpretation and abuse[276], 'internal disturbance' was replaced by 'armed rebellion'.[277]

Not only does Article 352 provide for declaration of an emergency, it provides several safeguards against its abuse along with provisions for its approval by the Parliament, duration and its revocation. Learning from the experiences of the traditional federations, the Constituent Assembly ensured that the entire procedure devised by the judiciary in traditional federations is laid down in the Constitution itself to eliminate any scope for discrepancies, inconsistency or abuse of such powers.[278]

---

276 Naga People's Movement of Human Rights vs. Union of India AIR 1998 SC 431: (1998) 2 SCC 109
277 44th Constitutional Amendment, 1978.
278 See Chapter XIII, Constitution of India

The 44th Amendment brought with itself several safeguards against abuse of emergency powers. Article 352(3) was inserted which provides that a proclamation of emergency can be issued by the President only after a decision of Union Cabinet, including the Prime Minister, communicating the same to the President in writing. No unilateral proclamation of emergency can be issued by the President or the Prime Minister. This particular provision was inserted as an aftermath of the declaration of emergency in 1975, wherein the President of India had issued the proclamation on the advice of the Prime Minister only. Further, Art. 352(4) provides that any proclamation issued shall survive for a period of one month only (reduced from two months vide 44th Amendment), unless approved by both Houses of Parliament. As a result, if the proclamation is not approved by the Parliament within one month, the proclamation shall stand revoked. The Constitution imposes a high threshold for approval of such proclamations i.e. Art. 352(6) provides that the proclamation shall be approved by each House of Parliament by a majority of total membership of each House and not less than two-thirds of the majority of members present and voting. Prior to the 44th amendment, such a proclamation could be approved by a simple majority.

Upon its approval by the Parliament, the proclamation remains in force for a period of six months from the date of approval by the House voting on a later date, unless revoked.[279] If the emergency is required to be continued beyond a period of six months, such an approval of the Parliament shall be taken again. Another safeguard added through the 44th Amendment is that the proclamation can be revoked by the Parliament if the House of People (Lok Sabha) passes it with a simple majority.[280] Another major safeguard added by the 44th Amendment as Art. 352(8) provides that upon notice by 1/10th of total members of Lok Sabha, a special sitting of the House can be convened within fourteen days from receipt of such notice for the purpose of considering the proclamation of emergency or its extension or disapproving the same. As a result, the revocation is much easier than its proclamation, ensuring that the constitutional fabric is only disturbed in extraordinary circumstances.

---

279 Article 352(5), Constitution of India
280 Article 352(7), Constitution of India

Similar to America and Australia, the judicial review is permitted to a very limited extent with respect to emergency powers under Art. 352. In *Bhut Nath v. State of West Bengal[281]*, the Hon'ble Supreme Court stated that the proclamation under Art. 352 is "*a political, not justiciable issue and the appeal should be to the polls and not to the courts*", thereby barring judicial review. However, the recent view has supported judicial review of such proclamations. The 38th Amendment amended Art. 352 had inserting the words '*shall be final and conclusive*' and '*shall not be questioned in any court on any ground*' with respect to proclamation of an emergency, however, these words have been removed vide the 44th Amendment. This indicates that the general view has been to restore the judicial review of such powers. Since no emergency has been declared under Art. 352 after 1975, the Hon'ble Supreme Court has not had an occasion to decide whether such proclamations are amenable to judicial review or not. It is pertinent to mention that despite this, in *Minerva Mills[282]*, BHAGWATI, J. observed that whether the President in proclaiming the emergency under Art. 352 had applied his mind, or whether he had acted outside his powers, or acted malafide in proclaiming the emergency, the emergency could not be excluded from the scope of judicial review. Further, since the Hon'ble Supreme Court has held that a proclamation under Art. 356 is amenable to judicial review[283], it can be assumed that if a similar situation arises in context of Art 352, the court will hold the proclamation amenable to judicial review. Therefore, a proclamation under Art. 352 shall be amenable to judicial review albeit to a limited extent, similar to America and Australia.

Second, similar to the provisions for external emergency, the internal emergency powers have been expressly provided for in Art. 356 of Constitution of India. This provision remains one of the most controversial and litigated provisions of the Constitution. Art. 356 provides that the President, on receipt of a report from the Governor of a State or otherwise, if satisfied that a situation has arisen in which the government of a State cannot be carried on in accordance with the provisions of the Constitution, the President may by proclamation:

---

281 AIR1974 SC 806: (1974) 1 SCC 645
282 Minerva Mills v. Union of India AIR 1980 SC 1840
283 S. R. Bommai vs. Union of India 1994 AIR 1918, 1994 SCC (3)

1. Assume to himself all or any of the functions of the State government, or the powers of the governor, or any body or authority in the State other than the State legislature;

2. declare that the powers of the State legislature are to be exercised by the Parliament;

3. make such incidental provisions as may appear to him to be necessary or desirable for giving effect to the provisions of the proclamation; the President may even suspend in whole or in part the provisions of the Constitution relating to any body or authority in the State.

As a result, upon proclamation of an emergency under Art. 356, the powers and functions of the State government and State legislature are transferred to the President and Parliament respectively. The President however, shall act only on the advice of the Council of Ministers. Further, the President cannot assume the powers of the High Court of the concerned State.[284]

It is pertinent to mention that Art. 356 does not only provide for declaration of an internal emergency but also provides a detailed procedure for declaration, revocation, extension of emergency and powers of federal or State government including ancillary provisions thereto. Art. 356(1), as mentioned hereinabove, provides for the proclamation of internal emergency on grounds mentioned therein. Such a proclamation can be revoked or varied by a subsequent proclamation.[285] Every proclamation under Art. 356 ceases to operate at the expiration of two months unless prior to these two months, the proclamation has been approved by both Houses of Parliament.[286] A proclamation so approved shall, unless revoked, cease to operate on the expiration of a period of six months from the date of issue of such proclamation. Such a proclamation may be approved every six (6) months however, it shall not remain in force for more than three years.[287]

This provision was intended to be used only in rare circumstances as it strikes at the very foundation of a federal system. Dr. B. R. Ambedkar

---

284 Art. 356(1)(c), Constitution of India
285 Article 356(2), Constitution of India
286 Art. 356(3), Constitution of India
287 Art. 356(4), Constitution of India

described Art. 356 as a 'dead letter', meaning thereby that it is not intended to be used unless exceptional circumstances demand it.[288] Further, the *Sarkaria Commission* recommended that Art. 356 should be used "*very sparingly, in extreme cases, as a measure of last resort, when all the other alternatives fail to prevent or rectify a breakdown of constitutional machinery in the State.*"[289] However, in practice, Art. 356 is one of the most abused provisions of the Constitution. Many a time for political purposes, the central government dismissed the State governments wherein the latter were governed by an opposition political party. As a result, several litigations ensued in the Hon'ble Supreme Court of India pertaining to justiciability of such proclamations in cases where Art. 356 was employed with a malafide intention.

One of the early cases where the controversy regarding declaration of internal emergency under Art. 356 of the Constitution came to light was *State of Rajasthan vs. Union of India*[290]. In this case, the general elections for Lok Sabha were held in 1977 after the revocation of emergency of 1975 wherein the Congress Party was badly routed in several States by the Janata Party which won a large number of seats in Lok Sabha. As a result, the government at the centre decided to dismiss the State governments wherein the ruling party was Indian National Congress. The State of Rajasthan thus filed an original suit[291] in the Supreme Court against the Union of India praying for the court to declare this directive of the Home Minister unconstitutional and illegal. Peculiarly enough, the decision rendered by the Supreme Court was unanimous in dismissing the suit. The broad position adopted by the court was that it could not interfere with the centre's exercise of power under Art. 356 merely on the ground that it embraced 'political and executive policy and expediency unless some constitutional provision was being infringed.' It is pertinent to mention that this ruling came prior to the 44th Amendment which removed the words 'final and conclusive' from President's satisfaction.

In *State of Rajasthan vs. Union of India*, BHAGWATI, J. emphasised that the satisfaction of the President under Art. 356 is a subjective one and cannot be tested by reference to any objective tests or by judicially discoverable and

288 Dr. B. R. Ambedkar, Constitutional Assembly Debates
289 Chapter VI – Emergency Provisions, Sarkaria Commission Report, 1988
290 AIR 1977 SC 1361: (1977) 2 SCC 592
291 Under Art. 13, Constitution of India

manageable standards. The court cannot go into the question of correctness or adequacy of the facts and circumstances on which the satisfaction of the central government is based. However, he observed *"but one thing is certain that if the satisfaction is malafide or is based on wholly extraneous and irrelevant grounds, the court would have jurisdiction to examine it, because in that case there would be no satisfaction of the President in regard to the matter in which he is required to be satisfied."* As a result, despite the existence of Art. 356(5), the court allowed some scope of judicial review into a proclamation under Art. 356 of the Constitution.

The Hon'ble Supreme Court had the final word on judicial review of proclamations under Art. 356 in the landmark case of *S. R. Bommai vs. Union of India*[292]. The court held that the validity of proclamation under Art. 356(1) is justiciable on such grounds as - whether it was issued on the basis of any material at all, or whether the material was relevant, or whether the proclamation was issued in the malafide exercise of the power, or was based wholly on extraneous and/or irrelevant grounds. Therefore, there must be material before the President indicating that the concerned State government cannot be carried on in accordance with the Constitution. As JEEVAN REDDY, J. observed, *"It is not an absolute power. The existence of material which may comprise of or include the report of the Governor is a precondition. The President's satisfaction must be formed on relevant material."* In case such material does not exist the proclamation made by the president is open to challenge. Further, the Apex Court held that though the power under Art. 356 is formally exercised by the President, the power really belongs to the Council of Ministers. Further, the dissolution of the State assembly or dismissal of the government is not an automatic consequence of the proclamation, rather, the government merely remains suspended unless expressly dismissed by the proclamation. Once the proclamation runs its course, the State government may begin functioning again.

As a result, Art. 356 and subsequent judgements of the Supreme Court have substantially curbed the use of Art. 356, ensuring that the federal principle is not violated unless absolutely essential. *Sh. M.P. Jain* rightly analyses the impact of Art. 356 on federalism as *"since federalism has been designated as a basic value in the Indian Constitution, dismissal of duly*

---

292 AIR 1994 SC 1918: (1994) 3 SCC 1

elected State assembly by the central government is really a negation of the federal concept. The power under Art. 356 has thus to be exercised sparingly, scrupulously and with circumspection. Abuse or misuse of this power will damage the federal fabric and disturb the federal balance."[293]

As the reader may observe, the federal government has been empowered to declare internal emergency in a State however, such a power is not absolute. Art. 356 itself provides for several safeguards against the abuse of this power. In addition to these, the courts have held that a proclamation under Art. 356 is justiciable on grounds mentioned in the preceding paragraphs. Such a power can only be exercised sparingly and any abuse may render it amenable to judicial review. Therefore, considering that the power violates the federal principle, it is rarely exercised and only in circumstances which absolutely require its declaration. This power is similar to the ones provided in America and Australia, the only difference being that the Constitution of India expressly provides for such a power.

Third, the provisions for financial emergencies are expressly provided for in the Constitution itself. We have already seen that America and Australia provide for such emergencies, albeit through different means. This provision was adopted by the Constituent Assembly in light of the problems faced by other federations, particularly America, during the depression in 1930's which very much left the Congress or the federal government handicapped in taking economic measures.[294] Article 360 of the Constitution provides:

"360. Provisions as to financial emergency

(1) If the President is satisfied that a situation has arisen whereby the financial stability or credit of India or of any part of the territory thereof is threatened, he may by a Proclamation make a declaration to that effect."

When such a proclamation is made, the central government is empowered to give directions to any State to observe '*such canons of financial propriety*'[295], as the central government may specify. The central government may also pass directions which the President may deem necessary and adequate for the purpose.[296] Further, any direction may be passed requiring the reduction of salaries and allowances of all or any class

---

293 Jain, M.P., Indian Constitutional Law, 7th Edn. Lexis Nexis 2016 pp. 727
294 See XCAD, 361-72; Schechter Poultry Corp. v. United States 295 US 495
295 Jain, M.P., Indian Constitutional Law, 7th Edn. Lexis Nexis 2016 pp. 730
296 Art. 360(3), Constitution of India

of persons serving in connection with the affairs of a State; or requiring all Money Bills or other Bills to be reserved for the consideration of the President after they are passed by the Legislature of the State.[297] These provisions were inserted to keep a check on States' finances and ensure that the States cannot pass Money Bills, which are used for withdrawing money from the nation's finances without President's assent. It is pertinent to mention that this emergency has ever been declared since the Constitution of India came into force.

As seen in the preceding paragraphs, the Indian Constitution expressly provides for all three kinds of emergencies – external, internal and financial. Not only does it provide for declaration of such emergencies, it also provides several safeguards against its abuse, procedure of its approval, grounds for declaration and judicial review. The courts have actively reviewed the emergencies under Art. 356, being the most abused provision among the three. Through several constitutional amendments and judicial pronouncements, it has been ensured that the provisions for emergencies are not abused, considering that emergency provisions render States subordinate to the centre thereby acting as an anti-thesis of the federal principle. Thus, the position in India is similar to the traditional federations considering that the latter provide for emergency powers indirectly whereas the Indian Constitution provides such powers itself. Therefore, the form is different although the substance is the same.

In light of the preceding paragraphs, the proposition stating emergency powers are antithetical to federal principle and therefore, relegating India to the position of a quasi-federal nation due to the presence of emergency powers in the Constitution itself is completely incorrect. All our target federations provide for emergency provisions for declaration of all three emergencies albeit through different means. Therefore, the Indian position is on par with that of traditional federations.

Conclusion

The author attempted to analyse the provisions pertaining to emergency powers of the federal government in each of our target jurisdictions. Considering that the emergency powers are an anti-thesis of the federal principle which relegate the States to the status of subordinate units, their

---

297 Article 360(4), Constitution of India

existence in a federal government is highly questionable. However, seeing the peculiar conditions nations often find themselves in either due to war, internal riots, economic depression or armed rebellions, the federal governments require such powers to consolidate their efforts to counter such threats. As a necessary corollary, the federations require emergency powers for their own protection. The traditional federations do not provide for emergency provisions in their respective Constitutions however, the courts have carved out these emergency powers from the provisions of their Constitutions acknowledging their absolute essentiality. In light of these, the following paragraphs will compare the Indian federal system with that of other target federations to conclude that the system in India is substantially similar to the other federations, only the form may vary in some instances.

First, the American Constitution does not expressly provide for declaration of external emergencies. However, the courts have substantially expanded the 'federal war powers' to include declaration of external emergencies. These powers include every matter and activity related to war and other ancillary activities. Further, this power is not subject to judicial review and suspends the powers of the States till such emergency powers are in force. In some cases, the Congress is even allowed to legislate under emergency powers after the culmination of the emergency if such powers are exercised to remedy the effects of war.

Similarly, the Australian Constitution does not expressly provide for such emergency powers either. Therefore, the courts in Australia have expanded the powers in the Constitution to make scope for emergency powers by substantiating the scope of defence powers under s. 51(vi) of the Constitution. During the existence of external emergency, the federal distribution of powers remains suspended, giving the perception of a unified government similar to America. Further, it includes exercise of emergency powers even after its culmination for post-war measures. The Australian courts refrain from exercising judicial review of such powers however, in cases of blatant abuse of such powers, the courts do interfere. After the war ends, the courts actively review the actions of federal government taken under the garb of emergency powers.

Akin to America and Australia, the Canadian Constitution does not expressly provide for declaration of external emergency or the powers incidental thereto. The Canadian government therefore enacted the

Emergencies Act, 1985 which authorises the Governor General of Canada to take special temporary measures to ensure safety and security during national emergencies. In addition to these, the courts have also expanded the federal war power to include measures necessary for such efforts. These powers do not cease on conclusion of a war but continue for as long as necessary, subject to judicial review.

In India, the founding fathers of the nation experienced the developments of the aforementioned Constitutions and the problems faced by their subjects. Learning from these experiences, the Constituent Assembly specifically provided for external emergency powers in the Constitution along with its procedure, form of declaration, ratification, safeguards and provisions for its revocation. In fact, subsequent to the enactment of the Constitution of India, several amendments have been introduced to ensure that the emergency powers are not abused. These provisions provide the same kind of powers which are available in America and Australia. Further, the judicial review is also permitted to a limited extent, as is in traditional federations.

As the reader may notice, the provisions permitting external emergency in traditional federations of America and Australia provide for exactly the same kind of powers expressly provided for in the Constitution of India. It has been often argued that the emergency powers provided in the Constitution of India are an anti-thesis of federalism. However, as seen in the preceding paragraphs, the traditional federations also provide for similar powers albeit through different means. It is submitted that these 'different means' exist due to the fact that these Constitutions were created prior to the World Wars or global financial crises which demanded provisions for proclamation of emergencies. Therefore, in substance, the provisions for unifying and strengthening the nation in times of emergency exist in all the federations however, their form is different. Indian provisions pertaining to emergency powers are thus, on par with those of American and Australia.

Second, similar to external emergencies, the traditional Constitutions did not initially provide for internal emergencies however, such powers were carved out from the provisions of their respective Constitutions. In America, Art. IV, s. 4 which provides that the federal government shall guarantee a republican form of government in the States, provides ample scope to the federal government to remand the States considering that many a violation can be declared as not conforming to the republican principle, in absence of any specific definition. As a result, the federal government has very wide jurisdiction to impose conditions under the garb of Art. IV, s. 4. To further add to the detriment of the States, the decision whether the State government has ceased to be non-republican is not justiciable, as a necessary corollary of which, the scope for a malicious declaration of emergency measures increases. The author cited a few instances in the preceding paragraphs wherein the federal government was even allowed to resort to force to bring any adverse situation in a State under control. Similarly, the Australian Constitution is silent on the aspect of internal emergency. This emergency power however, has been derived from s. 61 of the Constitution which empowers the federal government to maintain the provisions of the Constitution. This power has been held to include the power to suppress subversive activities and propaganda against the federation, prevent and punish incitement against the government, revolutionary change in the form of government, punish any group or individual attempting to or encouraging the overthrow of government by force or violence. However, as opposed to the position in America, these powers are justiciable in Australia. Similarly, Canada provides for declaration of internal emergencies through Emergencies Act, 1985 which permits such a declaration for public welfare or security.

Coming to the Indian position, the Constitution of India expressly provides for declaration of an internal emergency. Learning from the experiences of the traditional federations, the provision for declaration of such an emergency provides for its declaration, revocation, extension, safeguards and the respective powers of federal and State governments during the subsistence of an emergency. As a result, instead of leaving it to the judiciary to adjust the provision according to the exigencies of time, the founding fathers of the Constitution decided to expressly provide for such details within the provision itself. Further, the proclamation of such an emergency is justiciable, albeit to a limited extent.

Therefore, the position in India is quite similar to the one in America and Australia. Both these traditional federations provide for the declaration of internal emergency however, such provisions are not expressly present in the Constitution itself. Over the period of two centuries, these federations realised the dire need for such powers to protect the States from internal actors essential for preserving unity of the federation. As a result, these provisions have been carved out of the existing provisions of the Constitution through an expansive interpretation by the judiciary. Nonetheless, all four federations - America, Australia, Canada and India provide for declaration of internal emergencies, albeit through different means despite the fact that such a declaration goes against the federal principle.

Third, akin to the external and internal emergencies, the provisions pertaining to declaration of financial emergencies are also absent from the American Constitution. As a result, the federal government enacted the International Emergency Economic Powers Act (IEEPA), 1977 which permits the President to regulate economic transactions in response to any financial threat to the country which may affect its economic or financial health. This mechanism adopted by the government permits it to impose measures which are similar to a financial emergency. Similarly, in Australia, an expansive reading of s. 51 (xxxix) has permitted imposition of financial measures in the absence of any express constitutional provision to that effect. In fact, the Australian High Court has held that the executive government is capable and empowered to respond to a financial crisis, including the power to *"expend public moneys for the purpose of avoiding or mitigating the large-scale adverse effects of the circumstances affecting the national economy"*. In addition to this, the Australian federation has also resorted to enacting specific legislations to counter a financial emergency, similar to the American position. As opposed to these, Canada does not provide for a financial emergency. However, Canadian government is empowered to enact a legislation similar to Emergencies Act, 1985 for such declarations.

The Constitution of India expressly provides for the declaration of a financial emergency. It empowers the federal government to direct the States to observe such conditions pertaining to finances as the former may impose. As a result, the federal government ensures that the States' finances are kept in check and money is not withdrawn from the nation's funds without the President's express approval. However, this emergency has never been declared in India.

As the preceding paragraphs demonstrate, the provision for declaration of financial emergency is present in America and Australia, as is in India. Despite the contention that a financial emergency may be against the federal principle, the traditional federations still provide for such powers at the behest of the federal government. Without the presence of such powers, it would be extremely onerous to counter any financial threat to the stability of a nation which may eventually result in disintegration of the federation. The great depression of the 1920's in America is the leading example of such measures, wherein several economic regulations and measures were adopted to ensure that the economy does not collapse *in toto*. These powers are absolutely essential, as a result of which, most federations provide for a declaration of financial emergency albeit through different means.

The reader may note that the traditional federations i.e. America and Australia provide for declaration of all three types of emergencies. Over a period of two centuries, many a situation arose wherein circumstances demanded a strong federal government to concentrate the resources and efforts for countering the threats, whether external, internal or financial. Since the respective Constitutions of these federations did not expressly provide for declaration of such emergencies, the judiciary read the emergency powers into the constitutional provisions through an expansive reading of the provisions thereby permitting unfettered powers to the federal government. Learning from these experiences, the Constitution of India, having had the advantage of coming into force after 150 years from the enactment of the American and Australian Constitutions, specifically provided for the emergency powers in the Constitution itself, instead of leaving it to judicial pronouncements which often result in lack of uniformity and brings uncertainty. As a result, the Indian Constitution provides for all kinds of emergency measures similar to the traditional federations though the means of adopting such measures are different. Thus, it is incorrect to state that India is less federal or quasi-federal due to the fact that the Constitution provides for emergency powers thereby putting the federal government on a pedestal higher than the States, as similar powers are present in traditional federations which laid down the contours of federal principle.

CHAPTER 8

Legislative Lists and Distribution of Powers

A federation is a union of several States desiring union but not unity.[298] Building upon this proposition of *Dicey*, it is accurate to conclude that the powers of these States have to be demarcated as the States are clearly distinct entities from the federal government. As a necessary corollary, the Constitution of each of these federations specifically provides a List of powers which shall be exercised exclusively by the federation or by the States, as the case may be. In the absence of such enumeration of powers, there is a very wide scope of disputes between the States and the federation as either may legislate upon any matter, many a time resulting in concurrent legislations leading to utter chaos. Therefore, such an enumeration of powers is an essential feature of federalism. Every federation in the world provides for such an enumeration of powers.

The distribution of powers is enumerated in each Constitution in two respects – the distribution between the legislature, executive and judiciary; and between the States and the federal government. For the purpose of this chapter, we shall confine our discussion to the effect on the federal principle. Therefore, the discussion shall be limited to the latter part i.e. distribution of legislative powers between the federal government and the State governments.

It is pertinent to mention that the pattern of distribution of powers in our target federations is distinct vis-à-vis one another however, there is a similarity to the extent that each of these federations provide a list of enumerated powers of the federation and the States. As a general rule, the legislative powers concerning matters of national importance are vested in the federal government whereas, the States have jurisdiction over the matters of regional concern.

---

298 Dicey, 10th Edn., pp. 141-43

In the following discussion, the author shall discuss the position in each federation with respect to the Legislative Lists and distribution of powers through four limbs – the structure and types of Lists provided in the Constitution, concurrent sphere, vesting of residuary powers i.e. powers not enumerated in any List and lastly, the extent of interference with the powers enumerated in another List.

United States of America

In America, the Constitution simply enumerates the powers assigned to the Federal Parliament only i.e. there is a single enumeration of powers.[299] As a result, the scheme of the American Constitution provides that the powers of the federal legislature have been enumerated specifically and the rest of the powers are left to the States. However, the scheme is more complicated than it seems.

The powers enumerated for the exercise by the federal legislature are provided for in Art. I, s 8. Art. I, s. 9 prohibits the federal government from doing certain acts whereas Art. I, s. 10 prohibits the States from exercising certain powers. In addition to this, the 10th Amendment provides that the powers not delegated to the federal government and not prohibited under Art. I belong to the States. These four provisions, Art. I, s. 8, 9 and 10 along with the 10th amendment will be discussed in the following paragraph, to ascertain the scheme of distribution of powers in U.S.A.

The federal government has no general powers to enact laws for the people. It can only legislate on the matters enumerated in Art. I. s. 8. As Woodrow Wilson stated, *"the State governments are the ordinary governments of the country, the federal government is its instrument only for practical purposes."*[300] Though the author disagrees with this quote, keeping in mind the preceding chapters showcasing the federal government's control over the States, the quote nonetheless displays the scheme of distribution of powers in the American Constitution. These enumerated powers include foreign affairs, treaties, declaration of war, coinage etc. Although the rest of the powers not enumerated in Art. I, s. 8 were available to the States, Art. I, s. 10 prohibited the States from exercising some of these powers.

---

299 Jennings, Characteristics of the Indian Constitution (1953); Schulz, Essentials of Government (1958)

300 Woodrow Wilson, Constitutional Government; New York vs. United States (1946) 326 US 572

These powers were essential for exercise by the federal government, keeping the national interests in mind. These include taxation, foreign or interstate agreements, monetary system etc. Apart from these, the rest of the powers, either express or implied, can be exercised by the States within their respective territorial limits.[301] As opposed to this, Art. I, s. 9 enumerates the powers prohibited to the federal government including power to grant nobility, taxing imports, giving preference to a particular State(s) over others and suspension of habeas corpus writ.

The residuary powers vest in the States by virtue of the 10th amendment. It is pertinent to mention that residuary powers are the powers not enumerated in the Constitution. The powers neither delegated to the federal government by the Constitution nor prohibited by it to the States are reserved for the States.[302] In the words of Marshall, C.J., "*the genius and character of the whole government seems to be, that its action is to be applied to all the external concerns of the nations, and to those internal concerns, which affect the States generally, but not to those which are completely within a particular State, which do not affect other States and with which it is not necessary to interfere for the purpose of executing some of the general powers of the national government.*"[303] Therefore, the residuary powers vest in the States.

It is pertinent to mention that the Constitution of America does not provide for a concurrent sphere i.e. the legislative matters which can be legislated upon by both – the federal government and the State government. However, the judiciary has created this sphere by holding that as long as the federal government does not legislate on a certain matter, the State government may legislate[304], subject to the doctrine of repugnancy. This concurrent sphere has resulted from the application of the doctrine of implied powers, founded upon the 'necessary and proper' clause in Art. I, s. 8(18) which permits the federal government to legislate upon matters outside its legislative competence, which are necessary and proper for execution of powers enumerated in Art. I, s. 8.[305] It must however be mentioned that any

---

301 Carter v. Cater Coal Co. (1936) 298 US 238; Colorado Symes (1932) 286 US 510
302 10th Amendment, Constitution of America
303 Gibbons v. Ogden (1824) 9 Wh (195)
304 *Ibid*
305 Heart of Atlanta v. U.S. (1964) 379 US 241; McCulloch v. Maryland (1819) 4 Who 316; U.S. v. Curtiss-Wright Corp (1936) 299 US 304

power which is not granted to the federal government, either expressly or by necessary implication, cannot be exercised by it.[306] In other words, the powers not granted to the federal government are prohibited to it.[307] It has been held that the 10th Amendment will invalidate the federal law if it seeks to regulate the States as States.[308]

The governments often attempt to interfere with the sphere of legislative powers of the other government. As a necessary corollary, Constitutions provide for tools and devices to be employed in order to resolve such conflicts. In addition to this, the judiciary has devised several mechanisms to eliminate the scope of conflicts. First and foremost is the 'federal supremacy clause' which ensures that any law validly enacted by the federal legislature shall prevail over the State law.[309] It follows from this provision that the Congress must have competence to legislate upon the matter to claim supremacy under this provision. Second, the 'doctrine of implied powers' which provides that the federal government not only has the powers expressly provided to it but also the powers necessary to carrying out or implementing the express powers.[310] Therefore, the federal government may indirectly invade the State's legislative sphere through the 'necessary powers'.[311] Third, the 'doctrine of occupied field' provides that the States are enabled to legislate in this sphere by reason of the fact that the federal government does not exercise its enumerated power fully or over the entire field of the subject matter under its jurisdiction.[312] To the extent of federal inaction, the State may exercise the power reserved for the federal government.[313] These devices and tools provide leeway to both the

---

306 Ashton v. Cameron County (1936) 298 US 513; U.S. v. Butler (1936) 297 US 1

307 Virginia v. Tennessee (1893) 148 US 503

308 National League of Cities v. Usery (1976) 426 US 833

309 Art. VI, s. 2, Constitution of America

310 First Fed. Savings Assocn. V. Loomis (1939) 305 US 666; U.S. vs. S.E. Underwriters' Assocn. (1944) 322 US 533; City of Cleveland v. U.S., (1944) 323 US 329; City of Burbank v. Lockheed (1973) 411 US 624; Bailey v. Drexel Furniture Co., (1922) 249 US 20; Steward Machine Co. v. Davis (1936) 301 US 548; Helvering v. Davis (1936) 301 US 619.

311 See Hodel v. Virginia Assocn. (1981) 452 US 264; E.E.O.C. v. Wyoming (1983) 460 US 226

312 Sagar, Arun. "Federal Supremacy and the Occupied Field: A Comparative Critique." *Publius*, vol. 43, no. 2, 2013, pp. 251–274.

313 Parker v. Brown (1943) 317 US 341; S. Carolina Highway Dept. v. Barnwell (1938) 303 US 177

governments in their legislative endeavors and ensures that the conflicts are minimized by permitting interference under limited circumstances.

Withal, the United States of America provides for only one List i.e. under Art. I, s. 8 which expressly lays down the legislative powers of the federal government. The 10th Amendment provides that all the residuary powers or powers not enumerated in the Constitution vest in the States. However, any power incidental or necessary for the exercise of powers under Art. I, s. 8 can also be exercised by the federal government even if it is reserved for the States. As a result, several powers can be exercised by both, the federal government and the State governments. Any conflict which may arise from such exercise of powers is resolved by the judiciary which has, in addition to the constitutional devices, devised mechanisms to permit interference under limited circumstances.

Australia

Similar to the American position, the Constitution of Australia provides for a single enumeration of powers i.e. the legislative powers of the federal government are enumerated in the Constitution itself.[314] S. 51 of the Australian Constitution enumerates the powers of the federal government, however, these powers are not exclusive.[315] Ss. 52, 90, 111, 114 and 115 provide for powers 'exclusively' vested in the federal government. These include the powers pertaining to customs, excise, bounties, naval and military defence and armed forces, coinage, seat of the federal government, federal public service and surrendered territory.

It is pertinent to mention that there exists a concurrent sphere in the Australian federation as well, however, there is no Concurrent List as such. Surprisingly, the concurrent sphere in the Australian federation is much wider than the one in America, such that the powers of the States extend even to the matters enumerated in s. 51, to the extent that the federal government has not enacted any legislation in exercise of that power.[316] S. 51 of the Constitution does not mention that the powers of the federal government enumerated therein are exclusive, unlike s. 52 which provides for the 'exclusive' powers of the federal government. As a result, the powers

---

314 S. Australia v. The Commonwealth (1942) 65 CLR 373; James v. Commonwealth (1936) AC 578
315 Melbourne Corporation v. Commonwealth (1974) 74 CLR 31
316 D. D. Basu, Comparative Federalism, 2nd Edn. (2007), p. 210

under s. 51 are considered to be concurrent. S. 107 of the Constitution thus provides:

"Every power of the Parliament of a Colony which has become or becomes a State, shall, unless it is by this Constitution exclusively vested in the Parliament of the Commonwealth or withdrawn from the Parliament of the State, continue as at the establishment of the Commonwealth, or as at the admission or establishment of the State, as the case may be."

In simpler words, s. 107 provides that the State government can legislate on the entire legislative sphere provided in s. 51. If the federal government has enacted a law under s. 51, the State government cannot enact a law under that power and the latter will lose its jurisdiction. If the State law was enacted prior to the federal law, the doctrine of repugnancy shall apply. The doctrine of repugnancy with respect to the Constitution has been provided for in s. 109 of the Constitution. However, if the federal government has not enacted any legislation on that enumerated matter, the State law will hold good.[317] The concurrent powers however do not apply to matters exclusively vested in the federal government including ss. 52, 90, 111, 114 and 115. As a result, the concurrent sphere in Australia is much wider than in America.

The residuary power in the Australian federation vests in the States, similar to the American federation.[318] The States can exercise all the powers not vested exclusively in the federal government, subject to s. 109 of the Constitution and doctrine of repugnancy. On a bare reading of s. 107, the reader may see that it expressly provides for vesting of residuary powers in the States, unless exclusively vested in the federal government. These residuary powers include local government, irrigation, education, price control etc.[319]

Coming to the interference by the federal and State governments into one another's respective legislative spheres, the doctrine of implied powers, occupied field and federal supremacy ensure that the interference by either sphere is governed by these doctrines, enforced by the High Court of Australia. These doctrines are expressly mentioned in the Australian Constitution itself. To this effect, as discussed in the preceding chapter, s. 107 and s. 109 provide for doctrine of implied powers, federal supremacy

---

317 O'Sullivan v. Noarlunga Meat Ltd. (1956) 3 All ER 177 (183) PC
318 Peterswald v. Bartley (1904) 1 CLR 497
319 See A.G. Colonial Refining Co. (1913) 17 CLR 644; R v. Foster (1949) 79 CLR 43

and occupied field. In other words, the legislative powers of the federation and the States with respect to matters mentioned in s. 51 are concurrent, subject to the supremacy of the prevalent federal legislation in the field if State legislation is inconsistent thereto.[320] Therefore, the federal law shall prevail over the State law in the concurrent field. It must however be mentioned that the Federal Parliament cannot expressly repeal a State law itself.[321] Subsequently, if the federal law is repealed in the future, the inconsistent State law shall become operative again. These ensure that either government does not interfere with the domain of the other, and if it does, the courts are empowered to strike down the legislation in contravention of the constitutional mandate.

As the reader may see, the position in Australia is quite similar to that in America, considering the fact that the former borrows heavily from the latter.

Canada

Deviating from the prevalent practice in the traditional federations i.e. America and Australia, the Canadian federation provides for two Lists, each providing the legislative powers of the federal legislature and of provincial legislatures. The Canadian federation attempted to exhaust the field of legislation to minimise the scope for disputes between the governments. S. 91 of the Constitution provides for the list of subjects which can be legislated upon by the federal legislature exclusively. This List contains matters which are of national importance[322] including currency, banking, shipping, criminal legislations, family matters and defence. On the other hand, s. 92 provides for the legislative powers of the provincial governments including prisons, hospitals, public land, property and civil rights and incorporation and governance of companies. This List basically enumerates matters which are of local concern.

It is pertinent to mention the absence of any Concurrent List in the Canadian Constitution. S. 91 provides that in case of any overlapping

320 Commonwealth v. Bogle (1953) 89 CLR 229; Federated Saw Mill v. James (1909) 8 CLR 465; Lamshed v. Lake (1957) 99 CLR 132; Spratt v. Hermes (1965) 114 CLR 226
321 R. v. Credit Tribunal (1977) 137 CLR 545; Carter v. Egg Marketing Board (1942) 66 CLR 557
322 A.G. for Ontario vs. A.G. for Canada (1896) AC 248; In re Aeronautics (1932) AC 54 (70)

between s. 91 and s. 92, the interpretation shall be held in favour of the federal legislature i.e. in case both the governments are empowered to legislate on the same subject, the federal legislation shall prevail. This position is strengthened by the perorating words of s. 91 which state "*any Matter coming within any of the Classes of Subjects enumerated in this Section shall not be deemed to come within the Class of Matters of a local or private Nature comprised in the Enumeration of the Classes of Subjects by this Act assigned exclusively to the Legislatures of the Provinces*". It must be mentioned that unlike the position in Australia wherein the provincial legislation under s. 51 is permitted if there exists no such federal legislation on the subject, the Canadian position is different to the extent that even if the federal government has not legislated upon the matters in s. 91, the provincial government still cannot legislate upon those subjects.[323] Further, in case there is any overlapping between the subjects mentioned in s. 91 and s. 92, the latter shall yield to the former i.e. the federal government shall have jurisdiction over those subjects.[324]

Further, the legislations under s. 91 are permitted to interfere or trench upon the matters enumerated under s. 92.[325] There is however a caveat here. The legislation, if trenching upon the matters in s. 92, shall only be to the extent necessary for furthering the object of legislations enacted under s. 91 or for national importance or during emergency,[326] but cannot legislate directly on the matters enumerated in s. 92.

In stark contrast to the American and Australian position, the residuary powers in Canada vest in the federal government and not the provinces. S. 91 expressly provides that the federal legislature can legislate for the '*peace, order and good government of Canada*' on all matters which do not come under the purview of s. 92. Further, if any subject is not mentioned either in

---

323 Union Colliery v. Bryden (1899) AC 580; A.G. for Alberta v. A.G. for Canada AIR 1943 PC 76

324 G.W. Saddlery Co. v. The King (1921) AC 91 (116)

325 A. G. of Canada v. A. G. of British Columbia (1930) AC 111; In re Aeronautics (1932) AC 54 (70)

326 A. G. for Ontario v. Canada Temperance Federation (1946) AC 193; A. G. for Canada v. A. G. for Ontario AIR 1937 PC 89; Johannesson vs. West St. Paul (1952) 1 SCR 292; Co-operative Committee on Japanese Canadians vs. A. G. for Canada (1947) AC 87

s. 91 or s. 92, the Federal Parliament shall have the jurisdiction to legislate upon that subject.[327]

The doctrine of aspect legislation, federal supremacy and ultra vires ensure that the scope of disputes between the federation and the States is minimal. As seen in the preceding paragraphs, the federal government has superiority over the provincial governments in general. Therefore, the courts tend to give primacy to the federal government in cases of conflict with the provincial government.

The Canadian federation, therefore, provides two Lists, as opposed to the American and Australian position. These Lists lay down the legislative powers of the federal government and the provincial governments. The concurrent sphere in Canada does not exist as the federal government has been given primacy over the provincial governments, thereby ensuring that the federal legislation prevails. Further, the residuary powers of the federation shall vest in the federal government, as opposed to the American and Australian position. Lastly, the courts employ the doctrine of aspect legislation, federal supremacy and ultra vires to minimise the scope of disputes between the concerned parties.

India

Owing to the extensive study of existing federal Constitutions throughout the world by the constituent assembly, the members of the assembly introduced a third List in the Constitution considering that the aforementioned federations underwent enormous volumes of litigation for interpretation of legislative powers of the government and the peculiarities pertaining to exercise of such powers including concurrent sphere, overlapping of legislations, supremacy, repugnancy and limiting the scope of residuary powers, among others. As *Sh. D. D. Basu* notes *"while other federal Constitutions, like the American, the Australian and the Canadian, specify only broad heads of legislation, leaving it to judicial interpretation to make deductions applicable to particular exigencies as they arise, the framers of our*

---

327 A.G. for Ontario vs. A.G. for Canada (1894) AC 189; Russel v. Queen (1882) 7 AC 829; Toronto Electric Commr. V. Snider (1925) AC 87; Co-operative Committee of Japanese Canadians vs. A.G. for Canada ((1947) AC 87; Johannesson vs. West St. Paul (1952) 1 SCR 292; A.G. for Ontario vs. Canada Temperance Federation (1946) AC 193; A.G. of Canada v. A.G. of British Columbia (1930) AC 111; In re Aeronautics (1932) AC 54

Constitution attempted to exhaust the whole field of legislation as they could comprehend, into numerous items, thus narrowing down the scope for filling up the details by the judicial process of amplifying the given item".[328]

As a result, the third List i.e. the 'Concurrent List' was added to the existing Schedule, in addition to the Central List and State List.[329] The Central List lays down 97 subjects including foreign affairs, defence, banking, currency etc., upon which the central government exclusively exercises its legislative powers. Similarly, the State governments can legislate upon 66 items listed under the State List such as public order and police, State taxes, sanitation, education etc. The Concurrent List on the other hand, lays down 44 legislative subjects upon which both the central and the State government can legislate. These subjects include economic and social planning, marriage, criminal law and procedure, labour etc. This system of having three Legislative Lists is unique to the Indian Constitution. To add to the pride of our constituent assembly members, the Constitution of Malaysia 1957 followed the Indian position and introduced three Lists in their Constitution as well.[330]

It is pertinent to mention that the introduction of the Concurrent List has with itself created scope for several conflicts between the central government and the States. For instance, if both the governments legislate upon the same subject, which legislation shall prevail? If one legislation prevails over the other, the other legislation is void *in toto* or can some part of it be saved? Article 254 of the Constitution of India titled 'inconsistency between laws made by Parliament and laws made by Legislatures of States' answers these questions. The said Article is reproduced hereinafter:

"254. Inconsistency between laws made by Parliament and laws made by the Legislatures of States

(1) If any provision of a law made by the Legislature of a State is repugnant to any provision of a law made by Parliament which Parliament is competent to enact, or to any provision of an existing law with respect to one of the matters enumerated in the Concurrent List, then, subject to the provisions of clause (2), the law made by Parliament, whether passed before or after the law made by the Legislature of such State, or, as the case may be, the existing

---

328 D. D. Basu, Comparative Federalism, 2nd Edn. (2007), p. 217
329 Schedule VII of Constitution of India, 1950
330 Schedule IX, Constitution of Malaysia, 1957

law, shall prevail and the law made by the Legislature of the State shall, to the extent of the repugnancy, be void;

(2) Where a law made by the Legislature of a State with respect to one of the matters enumerated in the concurrent List contains any provision repugnant to the provisions of an earlier law made by Parliament or an existing law with respect to that matter, then, the law so made by the Legislature of such State shall, if it has been reserved for the consideration of the President and has received his assent, prevail in that State: Provided that nothing in this clause shall prevent Parliament from enacting at any time any law with respect to the same matter including a law adding to, amending, varying or repealing the law so made by the Legislature of the State."

As per this provision, if there exists an inconsistency between the central and State laws, the State law shall be void to the extent of repugnancy i.e. to the extent it is contradictory to the central law. In other words, the powers of the States in the concurrent sphere are subject to powers of the Union Parliament.[331] However, there is one overriding condition here. If the law passed by the State is passed after the central law came into force, the State law may prevail if the President expressly gives his assent to the State law. If the Parliament thereafter enacts a central law again, the State law shall be void to the extent of repugnancy.[332] Therefore, the doctrine of repugnancy operates to quell any conflict between the governments, clearly portraying that the central law shall prevail over the State law.

Quite contrary to the prevalent positions in the traditional federations, the federal government in India is empowered to override the legislative powers of the State mentioned in State List under some circumstances. First, the Parliament can legislate upon a matter enumerated in State List in national interest. To this effect, the Council of States or Rajya Sabha has to pass a resolution with approval of 2/3rd of its members present and voting, thereby declaring that a Parliamentary legislation on the concerned subject is required in national interest.[333] This declaration is however, only valid for

---

331 See K.S.E. Bd. V. Indian Aluminum AIR 1976 SC 1031; Sudhir v. W.T.O. AIR 1969 SC 59; I.T.C. v. State of Karnataka (1985) Supp SCC 476; Subramaniyam v. Muthuswami AIR 1941 FC 47

332 See Zaverbhai v. State of Bombay AIR 1954 SC 752; U.P.E.S. AIR 1970 SC 237; Western Coalfields v. S.A.D.A. AIR 1982 SC 697

333 Article 249, Constitution of India; See Mittal v. Union of India AIR 1983 SC 1; State of Karnataka v. Union of India AIR 1978 SC 68

one year.[334] Second, the Parliament can legislate upon State subjects during the proclamation of emergency by the President.[335] The emergency may either be a national emergency under Art. 352 or an internal emergency under Art. 356. Such legislations promulgated under emergency powers are only in effect till the subsistence of the emergency.[336] Third, if two or more States expressly resolve that the power to make laws on a certain subject shall be vested in the Parliament, it shall be lawful for the Parliament to legislate upon those subjects, but only in those States which have consented.[337] Fourth, the Parliament may legislate upon the State subjects for implementing treaties or international agreements entered into by India.[338] In other words, the Legislative Lists shall not impede the powers of the Parliament to enforce a treaty or international agreements.[339]

Withal, it must be mentioned here that despite the precedence given to the Union legislations over the State legislations, the courts are empowered to ensure that the Parliament does not legislate upon subjects mentioned in the State List, unless the Parliament is expressly empowered to do so under the provisions mentioned in the preceding paragraphs. If the Parliament exceeds its jurisdiction, the courts will strike down the Union legislation being *ultra vires*.[340]

Further, the courts have devised principles and tools, in addition to doctrine of ultra vires, to ensure that the legislative powers of the governments do not overlap or enter each other's domains, unless permitted by the Constitution of India. Since the object of this research is not a constitutional law discourse, the author shall only discuss selective doctrines in brief. The most common of these doctrines is the doctrine of repugnancy, as had been discussed in the preceding paragraphs with regard to concurrent sphere.[341] The doctrine of repugnancy states that the State law repugnant or inconsistent with the central law shall be void to the

---

334 Article 249(2), Constitution of India
335 Article 250, Constitution of India
336 Article 250(2), Constitution of India
337 Article 252, Constitution of India; Union of India v. Basavaiah AIR 1972 SC 1415; R.M.D.C. vs. State of Mysore AIR 1962 SC 594
338 Article 253, Constitution of India
339 Maganbhai v. Union of India AIR 1969 SC 785
340 Ref. under Art. 143, AIR 1965 SC 745
341 Premnath vs. State of J&K AIR 1959 SC 749; Bar Council vs. State of U.P. AIR 1973 SC 231; Barai vs. Henry AIR 1983 SC 150; Deep Chand vs. State of U.P. AIR

extent of such inconsistency.[342] Second, the doctrine of pith and substance permits transgression on the legislative powers of the other governments if such transgression is incidental to the exercise of their legitimate legislative powers.[343] Third, similar to the doctrine of pith and substance, the doctrine of ancillary powers permits the legislature to go beyond its legislative powers to legislate upon matters which are necessary for proper and effective exercise of legislative powers of the government.[344] Fourth, the doctrine of ultra vires is supported by the doctrine of colourable legislation which strikes down the legislations which are beyond the legislative competence of a government. Often, the governments attempt to indirectly legislate upon the matters which are beyond their competence by inserting provisions in their legislations which affect the matters assigned to legislative domain of another government.[345] In other words, while purporting to legislate in exercise of a power assigned to it, the legislature transgresses those powers and encroached upon the jurisdiction of another legislature, thus subverting the federal system and constitutional mandate. Such legislations are struck down by the courts under the doctrine of colourable legislation. Lastly, the doctrine of reading down ensures that if a legislature has used wide or vague words which allow it to transgress the legislative domain of another legislature, instead of declaring the legislation *ultra vires*, the courts read down or narrow the scope of such provisions of the legislation.[346] As a result, the legislation is saved from being struck down. Cumulatively, these doctrines, among others, ensure that the scope of disputes is minimal between the legislatures and neither legislature transgresses the domain of the other.

1959 SC 648; Ukha vs. State of Maharashtra AIR 1963 SC 1531; L.T.C. vs. State of Karnataka (1985) Supp SCC 476; Hoechst vs. State of Bihar AIR 1983 SC 1020.

342 Article 254, Constitution of India

343 D.C.G.M. vs. Union of India AIR 1983 SC 937; Ganga Corp. vs. State of A.P. (1980) 1 SCC 223; Prem vs. Chhabra (1984) 2 SCC 302; K.S.E. vs. Indian Aluminium Co. AIR 1976 SC 1031; Khaitan Sugar Mills vs. State of U.P. AIR 1980 SC 1955; Southern Pharmaceuticals vs. State of Kerala AIR 1981 SC 1865

344 Joshi vs. Ajit Mills AIR 1974 SC 2278; Sodhi Transport vs. State of U.P. AIR 1986 SC 1099; C.P.O. vs. Abdulla AIR 1971 SC 792; Abdul vs. S.T.O. AIR 1964 SC 922

345 State of Bihar vs. Kameshwar AIR 1952 SC 252; Sonapur Tea co. v. Dy. Commr. AIR 1962 SC 137; Tara Prasad vs. Union of India AIR 1980 SC 1682; Gajapati vs. State of Orissa AIR 1953 SC 375

346 Union of India vs. Atic Industries AIR 1954 SC 1495; Monogram Mills vs. State of Gujarat AIR 1976 SC 2177

Unlike the American and Australian position, the Constitution of India provides for vesting of residuary powers in the federal government. This is similar to the position in Canada. Article 248 read with Entry 97 of List I of Seventh Schedule provides for the residuary powers. These provisions have been reproduced below:

"248. Residuary powers of legislation

(1) Parliament has exclusive power to make any law with respect to any matter not enumerated in the Concurrent List or State List"

List 1 of 7ᵗʰ Schedule

"97. Any other matter not enumerated in List II or List III including any tax not mentioned in either of those Lists."

These provisions establish that the legislative powers over any provision not mentioned in either the State List or the Concurrent List belong to the central government.[347] Thus, the residuary powers vest in the federal government and not the States.

Summarising the Indian position, the Constitution of India provides for three Lists, one each laying down the legislative powers of central and State government while the third List lays down subjects on which both the governments can legislate. However, if the central government legislates upon a subject in Concurrent List, the State governments cannot do so. This provision is similar to that of Canada. The residuary powers vest in the central government and not the States. In India, a Concurrent List specifically provides for matters upon which both governments can legislate. Since India follows a multi-party electoral system, on several occasions the State or the central government attempts to transgress the legislative domain of the other. Any conflict which may arise from such exercise of powers is resolved by the judiciary which has, in addition to the constitutional devices, devised mechanisms to permit interference under limited circumstances.

---

347 See State of Karnataka vs. Union of India AIR 1978 SC 68; J. R. G. Association vs. Union of India AIR 1970 SC 1589; Hari vs. Union of India AIR 1966 SC 619; Jalan Trading Co. vs. Mill Mazdoor Sabha AIR 1967 SC 691.

Conclusion

In this chapter, the author discussed the Legislative Lists and the distribution of powers in our target federations. In a federation, it is extremely important that the legislative powers of each government are separately demarcated to avoid any disputes or interference with each other's legislative domains. Each of our target federations provide enumeration of legislative powers of the governments, albeit not exhaustively. The general rule is that the matters necessary for the functioning of the nation are vested in the federal government while matters of regional importance are left to the States.

The preceding paragraphs discussed the Legislative Lists provided by each Constitution. It was observed that each Constitution provides a concurrent sphere wherein the legislative powers can be exercised by both the federal and the State governments. However, this sphere is not clearly defined which results in disputes and transgression of each other's legislative domains. As a necessary corollary, the Constitutions and the courts devised principles and doctrines to avoid conflicts and limit the scope for disputes. In addition to these, the author discussed the residuary legislative powers of the country. The following paragraphs shall discuss the Indian position in light of the provisions in our target federations to establish that the Indian position is similar to the traditional federations.

First, we observed that the American and the Australian federations only provide one List i.e. the legislative powers enumerated for the federal government. The American Constitution provides a single enumeration of powers, the rest of which are left to the legislative domain of the States. In addition to this, the Constitution prohibits the federal government and the State governments from exercising some powers specifically enumerated in Art. I, s. 9 and 10. Similarly, the Australian federation follows the American example by enumerating the powers of the federal government only. In addition to this enumeration, the Constitution provides certain powers which are exclusively vested in the Federal Parliament, similar to the American structure.

In contrast to the American and Australian positions, Canada provides for two Lists i.e. one enumerating the legislative powers of the federation and other enumerating legislative powers of the States. The rationale behind this is that the Canadian federation came into existence after the American and Australian federations, thereby learning from the experiences of these federations wherein the courts had to time and again adjudicate disputes pertaining to transgression of legislative powers or deciding which power vested in whom. As a result, the drafters of the Canadian Constitution attempted to exhaust the field of legislative powers.

India moved a step ahead of the Canadian federation, learning from the experiences of the aforementioned federations. As the reader may be well aware of the amount of research which formed the bedrock of the constituent assembly debates, it gave space to voluminous ideas and experiences of other federations. As a result, in an attempt to further exhaust the field of legislative powers, India introduced another List, in addition to the two Lists provided by the Canadian federation i.e. the Concurrent List. The Concurrent List lays down the legislative fields wherein both the central as well as State government could legislate.

Therefore, the position in India is not different from that of the traditional federations i.e. America and Australia in the sense that each of these federations attempted to provide a list of legislative powers in the Constitution itself. Over the years, it was realised that one list laying down the powers of the federal government leaves a huge scope for disputes and completely ignores the fact that the legislative fields are not water-tight compartments but often overlap each other. As a result, the courts in these federations had to step in to resolve conflicts and devise principles for exercise of legislative powers. Learning from these experiences, India did the exact same thing however, it incorporated the deliberations of the courts in America and Australia in the Constitution itself to eliminate any scope for conflicts. Therefore, all these federations attempted to lay down the legislative powers of the governments in the Constitution itself, the only deviations occurring due to the fact that these Constitutions came into existence in separate periods of time. In fact, the author is of the opinion that had the American and Australian Constitutions come into existence several decades later, they would have had multiple lists as well.

Second, all our target federations provide for a concurrent sphere albeit through different means. The traditional federations which came earlier in time i.e. America and Australia do not expressly provide for a concurrent sphere however, due to the exigencies and necessities displaying a dire need for such a sphere, the judiciary stepped in to carve out a concurrent sphere. In America therefore, the judiciary held that the federal government can legislate upon certain matters not enumerated in the Federal List wherein the federal government shall have supremacy over the State government. Similarly, the Australian federation does not expressly provide for a concurrent sphere however, the judiciary has carved such a sphere by expansively interpreting s. 51 of the Constitution. As a result, the concurrent sphere is very wide in the Australian Constitution, such that even the powers enumerated for the federal government in s. 51 are made concurrent in entirety i.e. the States can legislate on the powers listed in the Federal List. However, if the federal government has legislated on any of these subjects, the State government cannot legislate upon the same. Some legislative powers of the federal government have been made exclusive.

The Indian federation follows the same position in the American and Australian federations through the means of expressly providing for a Concurrent List in the Constitution itself. The List enumerates the legislative subjects upon which both the federal and the State governments can legislate. However, if the federal government has legislated upon any of these subjects, the State legislation upon the same subject shall be void, quite similar to the Australian position. The only difference is that the constituent assembly in India decided to include the Concurrent List in the Constitution itself, not leaving it for the judiciary to ascertain the concurrent sphere. As a result, the scope of disputes pertaining to concurrent sphere stands vastly diminished and brought certainty to the legislatures. Therefore, the position in India is similar to America and Australia. Canada, however, does not provide for a concurrent sphere either through the Constitution or through judicial acts.

Third, in the traditional federations, the residuary powers vest in the States and not the federal government. In America, the 10th Amendment expressly vests the residuary powers in the States. Similarly, in Australia, the residuary powers vest in the States. However, the Canadian position is contrary to the one in America and Australia. In Canada, the residuary powers vest in the federal government and not the States. The primary rationale attributed to this change is the mode of formation of the Canadian federation wherein a unified country was divided into provinces to form a federal structure. In such a structure, the governments have centralising tendencies due to absence of friction from States as the States were not completely independent territories prior to the formation of the federation. The Indian federation follows the Canadian structure wherein the residuary powers lie with the federal government.

Lastly, owing to the tendencies of the governments to interfere with or transgress the legislative spheres of the other governments, the Constitutions of our target federations or their respective judiciaries devised several legal principles and devices to ascertain the legal validity of such transgressions. These principles or devices bring stability and legal certainty to any action of the government. Further, these principles strengthen the federal principle by ensuring that the federal government does not interfere or overpower the State governments unnecessarily. These principles include doctrine of implied powers, doctrine of colourable legislation, doctrine of occupied field, federal supremacy clauses etc. These ensure that the governments conform to the constitutional limitations imposed on their respective legislative powers.

Th reader may note that the Indian federation is very much similar to the traditional federations vis-à-vis the legislative powers of the federal and State governments. Similar to America and Australia, the Indian federation provides for Legislative Lists, a concurrent sphere and tools and devices to ensure that the governments remain within their legislative spheres and do not transgress into the legislative powers not allotted to it. The only difference is with regards to the residuary powers. The Indian Constitution vests the residuary powers in the federal government whereas the traditional federations vest such powers in the States. However, this is of little consequence considering that most of the prominent features of federalism with respect to legislative powers in India are similar to the traditional federations. The intent of the members of the constituent assembly was to build up on the same footing as that of America and Australia however, these were achieved through different means. The essence remains the same.

CHAPTER 9

Important of Matters Allocated to States and State Citizenship

In the present chapter, the author discusses two crucial issues which have a bearing on federalism – the importance of matters assigned to the States and State Citizenship. However, these issues are quite miniscule, as a result of which, the author shall discuss them briefly without a comparative context. The scheme of this chapter is different from the preceding chapters wherein we discussed the features in each federation separately, followed by a comparative analysis in the conclusion. In this chapter, we shall only discuss the Indian position to counter the arguments against the federal nature of India.

First, it has been often stated that the matters assigned to the States' Legislative List are of least importance in the federation, thereby concluding that the India is more unitary than federal. *Prof. Wheare* observed "*...the powers granted in the exclusive Union List and in the Concurrent List cover, as in Western Germany, almost all subjects of importance, and what is left to the exclusive authority of the States tends to be of subordinate concern*".[348] As we observed in the preceding paragraphs, the States in each of the federations are subordinate to the federal governments considering that the powers of the federal governments have been significantly enlarged in order to provide a stronger centre to deal with external threats and maintaining internal harmony. However, on a plain reading of his work, it is clear that *Prof. Wheare* uses the term 'subordinate' as a synonym to 'unimportant'. The author begs to differ on this proposition, hence the present chapter.

It is highly unreasonable to state that the powers assigned to the States in India are unimportant as compared to the powers assigned to States in other federations. It is submitted that indeed the most important matters are assigned to the federal governments i.e. foreign affairs, defence, currency, communications etc. however, the situation is the same in each of the federations, not just India. The States in India have been granted important

---

348 Wheare, Federal Government, p. 27

powers as well including local government, public order, police and public health. In fact, even in the traditional federations, such powers are allotted to the States. In addition to these, the States have been granted the powers to legislate upon agriculture, water, and fisheries as well. Considering that India is an agrarian economy with nearly 40% of its population engaged in agricultural activities, the States play a crucial role in the economic development through regulation of agriculture, water and fisheries. To this effect, *H.M. Seervai* observed, *"…But India is a Union of States, and the functions assigned to the States are of high importance though of a different kind"*.[349]

Further, the States have vast powers of taxation as well, in addition to the grants received from the central government. The powers of taxation of the States and the Union are mutually exclusive, as a result of which, States can tax its subjects independently. States generate revenue from several taxes such as agricultural tax, property tax, sales tax and motor vehicle tax, among others. On average, Indian States generate more than 50% of their revenue through their own taxes while the rest is transferred by the central government.[350] Further, even the States in America depend upon federal funding as barely any State is able to generate enough funds to meet its own financial commitments. In fact, there are several States which completely depend on federal funding, for instance New Mexico obtains close to 100% funding from federal government whereas Alaska, Mississippi and North Dakota require over 70% of their funding from the federal government.[351] Such a provision is not peculiar to India as even the States in America are highly dependent on federal funding. Therefore, the States have wide powers of taxation such that the taxes imposed by the States generate a majority of their revenue. Relying on federal funding for the rest is not against the federal principal.

Further, as we have seen in the Indian political landscape, the States are indeed quite powerful vis-à-vis the centre such that even a political party coming to power with an absolute majority at the centre may not be able to win State elections against the local political parties. One of the

---

349 Seervai, Constitutional Law of India, Volume 1, pg. 297
350 State of State Finances Report, January 2018, PRS India; "How Indian States are Nearly Broke", Live Mint, 23.06.2020
351 Deb Gordon, Return on Statehood: How much value every State gets from Federal Government, Money Geek, February 9, 2021.

reasons for this may be the power States enjoy over its subjects including law enforcement, public administration etc., permitting them to influence or gather support of the populace.

Therefore, in light of the preceding paragraphs, the author disagrees with the view taken by *Prof. Wheare* stating that the powers granted to the States are of subordinate concern. It is submitted that the powers allotted to the States are of high importance, in the absence of which, the States may even fail to exist. Further, the taxation powers allotted to the States generate majority of their revenues. Can it still be said that the legislative powers of the States are subordinate or unimportant? The author's answer would be negative.

Second, it has often been said that federalism requires that each State has a separate citizenry to ensure the autonomy of the States. Traditional federations such as America, Australia and even Switzerland provide for a dual citizenship i.e. one for the federation and one for the State. *Livingston* however, doubts that such a proposition is an essential component of federalism.[352] Federations such as India, Canada and Nigeria do not provide for a dual citizenship.

In America, s. 1(1) of the 14th Amendment permits the citizens to have a dual citizenship i.e. one for the nation and one for the State.[353] Similarly, Australian Constitution provides for citizenship of a State as well.[354] On the other hand, the Canadian Citizenship Act, 1946 does not permit State citizenship in addition to the citizenship of Canada. Similarly, the Indian Constitution does not permit dual citizenship. Thus, it may be said that the position in India with respect to State citizenship is different from that of traditional federations. However, the author disagrees with the proposition. Indian position is actually quite similar to that of America and Australia.

For this purpose, we need to understand the very rationale behind providing a State citizenship. Citizenship of a State/province ensures that the citizens of a State are provided certain privileges and immunities by that State for the general welfare of its people. These privileges include right to vote, employment opportunities, general welfare schemes, educational benefits, agricultural schemes etc. If the State's people prosper due to these

---

352 Livingston, Federalism and Constitutional Change (1956), p. 11

353 Corwin, Constitution: What it Means Today (1973), p. 208

354 W. Anstey Wynes, Legislative and Executive Powers in Australia (1970), p. 420

welfare schemes, the State prospers as a whole. Therefore, the States provide citizenship to ensure that its citizens prosper through its schemes and privileges.

With this in mind, we come to the situation in India. The States in India provide the exact same privileges to the people residing in their respective territories. If a person is resident of a certain State, he gets the right to vote in that particular State. Further, the person gets access to employment opportunities which are exclusively reserved for the residents of a State. For instance, the State of Haryana recently announced that 75% of the jobs in private sector in the State shall be reserved for residents of Haryana only.[355] Similarly, Andhra Pradesh reserved 75% jobs for locals of their State.[356] On the educational front, most States reserve the seats in its State funded educational institutions for its own residents. For instance, Tamil Nadu reserved 85% of the seats in its medical colleges for local students.[357] Similarly, in Karnataka, several universities reserved anywhere between 25-40% of its seats for its residents.[358]

Therefore, the reader may observe that the functions which a State citizenship fulfils in traditional federations, the States in India fulfill the same functions albeit through different means. Many a document could establish the domicile of a person in a State, in lieu of State citizenship, on the basis of which a person is eligible to obtain the benefits of residing in the State. As a result of this, the States provide several benefits to its own residents or 'citizens' to enhance their standard of living and general welfare of the State. Withal, though the Indian States do not provide citizenship, they alternatively provide domicile identities which enable its residents/citizens to obtain benefits exclusively allotted to people of the concerned States.

---

355 "Haryana governor approves bill to reserve 75% of private sector jobs for locals", The Times of India, 02.03.2021

356 "Andhra passes Bill giving 75% job reservation for locals", The Economic Times, 25.07.2019

357 "How fair is it for Delhi and Tamil Nadu to reserve 85% college seats for residents?", Scroll.in, 01.07.2017

358 "Building a case against domicile reservation in private unaided universities", The Bastion, 24.12.2020

CHAPTER 10

Conclusion

At the inception of this book, we discussed the idea behind federalism and the rationale for its adoption by several nations. In brief, a federation is a union of several States, whether independent or not, which come together to form a Union, mutually benefitting each State while allowing them to retain some autonomy and simultaneously offering them protection from external aggression, whether military or economic. There exist two types of governments in a federal structure, the central or federal government comprising of representatives from each State and a separate provincial government for each State. The power structure and the relations between these governments are generally provided in the Constitution itself, from which these governments derive their powers. The Constitution provides certain rights and protections to the States, thereby ensuring their autonomy and protecting them against any abuse by the federal government.

As any other structure, federalism suffers from fallacies and inadequacies. Since there is a division of powers between the States and the federal government, there is often a power struggle between the two. Each government frequently attempts to interfere with the power of the other for multiple reasons including political vendettas, welfare of State, protectionist tendencies of States towards its people and unitarian tendencies of federal government. On some occasions, such conflicts have even led to civil wars. For instance, America witnessed a full-blown civil war due to the differences between the southern States and the federal government in 1860s[359] or the dismissal of nine State governments by the Indira Gandhi led government in 1980[360]. For these purposes, the federal courts have been set up which act as the guardians of the Constitution and ensure that the governments

---

359 Hubbard, Charles (2000). The Burden of Confederate Diplomacy. Knoxville: University of Tennessee Press. p. 55. ISBN 1-57233-092-9; *Tikkanen, Amy (June 17, 2020). "American Civil War". Encyclopedia Britannica.*

360 Arul B. Louis, Prabhu Chawla, PM Indira Gandhi dismisses governments in nine States, looks to put Congress in power, India Today, 06.02.2014

stay within their respective spheres of governance, as stipulated by the Constitution.

As mentioned in the preceding paragraph, each federation faces a multitude of problems associated with a federal structure. To counter these problems, each federation provides for ways and means to ensure that the federal structure remains intact while simultaneously benefitting each State and the federal government as a whole. Since each federation came into existence under different circumstances and exigencies, the provisions in each of their Constitutions are technically different however, they are intended to achieve the same objective, as observed in the preceding chapters. In other words, there are several differences between the federal Constitutions of each of our target federations, however, on a textbook study of these differences, one may conclude that each of these federations are similar to each other, different only in form but not in substance. This difference in form over substance forms the basic premise of this study. It is true that each federation is different from the other, those which came into existence later even more different than the traditional ones. However, we observed that over the period of two centuries since these traditional federations came into existence, their Constitutions were suitably amended to create a stronger central government arising from the unifying needs due to global crises such as the Great Depression of 1930's, World Wars, Cold War etc., which required rigorous shift of powers from the States to the federal government for the survival of the nation. Therefore, the centralising elements present in the modern federations such as India and Canada are also present in America and Australia i.e. the traditional federations. The federations which came into existence at a later stage had the good fortune of learning from the experiences of earlier federations, as a result of which, these were able to include the centralising elements into their Constitutions itself.

As we observed, the purpose of this study is to ascertain whether India is federal, quasi-federal or unitary. The Hon'ble Supreme Court of India has characterised India as a quasi-federal nation. Similarly, several jurists have propounded that India is not federal and at best, it is quasi-federal. The author of course, disagreed with the stated proposition. Therefore, we attempted to undertake a study to conclude that India is indeed a federal nation by examining the features of federalism in traditional federations –

America and Australia and assessing India's conformity to these features. Upon analysing the features of federalism discerned by several academicians, lawyers and judicial members, we concluded that the most important features of federalism which shall be present in any federation can be broadly categorised as - federal sentiment; formation of federation and its territory; States' rights vis-à-vis the Union; emergency powers; Legislative Lists; and importance of matters allocated to States and State citizenship. Several other issues were studied under these broad heads. It was also observed that most of the authors form a consensus on the assertion that if most of the federal features are present in any nation, it can be declared as a federation. In other words, it is not mandatory that all the features of federalism 'must' be present in any federation. On this assumption, we discussed each of the aforementioned principles of federalism.

In each chapter, we discussed an aforementioned feature with respect to each of our target federations and adduced the mechanism through which such a feature operates in their respective Constitutions. Apropos this assessment, the author discussed the feature in context of the Indian Constitution, thereby concluding that the feature is present in India as well, albeit the form of its presence is different though it serves exactly the same purpose. Overlying these assessments, the author continues with the underlying theme that all federations have exactly the same features present in them, albeit in different forms. If all these essential features of federalism are present in the Indian federation is well, there is not an iota of doubt that India is indeed federal in nature and any authority characterizing it as quasi-federal or unitary shall be reconsidered.

The first feature we assessed was the presence of a federal sentiment among the founding fathers of each nation. In other words, we analysed the history of each Constitution to ascertain whether there existed an intention to form a federation among the founding fathers or constituent assembly members of each nation. At the outset, we discussed a rather curious observation as to why the early federations were all former British colonies. The rationale behind this is that the very idea of federalism sprouted from the political structure of the British Empire wherein the Crown headed the government through the British Parliament, in charge of military, foreign affairs and communications whereas the rest of the governance issues such as sanitation, public works, policing, education, health etc. were left to the governments of concerned colonies. Similarly, in a federal structure, the federal government is mainly in charge of military, foreign affairs and communications whereas the rest are left to the State governments. Since almost every colony had been acquainted with the federal structure for a period of over one hundred (100) years prior to their independence, federalism was thought to be the most appropriate structure.

Focusing our attention upon the federal sentiment, we observed that the federal sentiment was present in each of the federations, even prior to the formation of their respective constitutional assemblies. Upon independence, United States of America comprised of several independent States which came together to form a confederation wherein the States enjoyed great autonomy and were superior to the confederate government. Due to their cultural and traditional differences, the States failed to agree on a unitary government as they believed such a structure would not adequately protect their interests. Therefore, a confederate system was adopted in U.S.A. However, a confederate system was short-lived as a substantially weak government at the centre proved highly ineffective with very limited powers, eventually leading to conflicts among the States and severe economic crises. As a result, the founding fathers convened another Constitutional Convention in 1787 to analyse the short comings of the confederate system. The convention concluded that a federal system would be most appropriate for the country as it would maintain the perfect equilibrium between the States and the federal government. Thus, a federal sentiment had been present among the founding fathers of American Constitution ever since the idea of confederation was discarded. George Washington, the founding father of the United States of America, was a federalist himself.

Similarly, pre-independent Canada was highly diverse comprising of an English-speaking upper Canada and a French-speaking lower Canada with each having a separate Parliament and often finding themselves at loggerheads with one another. In addition to the linguistic diversity, the Canadian administration apprehended a full-scale war between Britain and the United States of America. Therefore, the founding fathers of Canada deemed it fit to come together and form a federation to collectively counter any external threat and simultaneously ensure that the interests of English and French speaking groups are protected by granting autonomy to the provinces. Thus, federation was thought to be the most appropriate structure.

In any case, if another structure were proposed to be adopted, it would have failed to reach consensus among the two regions. Thus, Canada was always intended to be either federal or confederal. Eventually, the decision to enact a federal Constitution was taken at the Quebec Conference of 1864.

On the other hand, the federation of Australia was formed by coming together of six States - former colonies of the British Empire, largely due to economic considerations. These autonomous colonies had their own laws, tariffs, railways, commercial regulations, trade barriers etc. which resulted in hindering the growth of the Australian sub-continent as a whole. As a result, the founding fathers mooted the idea of federalism as early as 1880, despite the Constitution having been enacted in 1900. A series of conventions conducted in 1890's finally led to the decision to form a federation in Australia. Thus, the federal sentiment had been present in the founding fathers since 1880 which led to the enactment of a federal Constitution.

Coming to the existence of a federal sentiment among the constituent assembly members of India, a federal structure was envisaged for India as early as 1918, with the advent of *Montague-Chelmsford Reforms*. Subsequently, the idea of a federal nation was again mooted in *Simon Commission's Report* in 1929. However, since complete independence was not on the cards, a federal India seemed a distant prospect. The very existence of the wide diversity of religions, traditions, cultures, languages and races in itself demanded a federal structure to protect their respective interests. In addition to this, India comprised of over 500 princely States, most of whom wanted a federal structure as it permitted them to enjoy autonomy in their respective States. Relying upon these considerations, the British government enacted the Government of India Act, 1935, which provided a federal structure for India. Our Constitution borrows heavily from this Act. India was thus, intended to be federal ever since the *Montague Chelmsford Reforms* in 1918, the question was only about a loose or tight federal structure. With the advent of massacres following the announcement of partition, it became clearer that a confederation or loose federation is not desirable as a strong centre is required to control the atrocities. Therefore, the constituent assembly members set out to form a federal structure. Most of the discussions in the constituent assembly circled around a compact or loose federation, and not whether India should be a unitary or federal State.

Thus, a federal sentiment existed among the founding fathers of the India as well.

As we observed in the preceding paragraphs, in all our target jurisdictions i.e. America, Australia, Canada and India, there existed a federal sentiment among the founding fathers indicating that the Constitution was always intended to be federal.

This brings us to the second feature of federalism. Formation of the federation and the regulation of its territory form a crucial part of the federal principle. In this chapter, we discussed the modes of formation of a federation along with four ancillary issues which are crucial for upholding the federal principle – procedure for reorganisation of States, admission of new States, mode of acquisition of new territories and powers granted or restrictions imposed on newly admitted States.

We observed that there are two modes of formation of a federation, often referred to as centripetal and centrifugal modes. As seen in the preceding chapters, many scholars accept that there are indeed two modes of formation of a federation. The first mode involves several independent States coming together to form a Union through a voluntary agreement without giving up their independence or autonomy, for a common purpose which may either be defence against external powers, collective economic prowess or efficient administration. The prime examples of this mode of formation are United States of America and Australia. The second mode of formation involves transforming an existing Unitary State into a federation by dividing its territory into provinces and granting federal autonomy to these provinces. This mode was adopted by Canada which converted itself into a federation. India, however, is a mixture of both the modes of formation of a federation.

America was formed by a Union of thirteen States, later rising to fifty States. A wide variety of reasons effected the decision to form the Union including defence against external powers (primarily the British and the French), eliminating internal conflicts and economic interests. Similarly, Australia formed with a union of five States initially, with a sixth State joining thereafter. However, Australian States came together for economic and administrative reasons, instead of defence which formed the basic premise for entering into federation for American States. On the other hand, we observed that Canada was formed by breaking up the existing country into provinces, thereby converting it into a federation. Canada comprised of two highly divergent communities - the English speaking and French speaking Canadians. The very rationale behind this decision was that no other structure could suitably protect the interests of both communities while providing a unified government at the same time.

According to the author, India is a mixture of the two modes of formation of a federation. At the time of independence, India comprised of about 560 princely States enjoying enormous autonomy over their subjects, covering over 40% of the area and comprising of about 23% of the population in India. For economic and geographical reasons, it was essential to assimilate these States into the Union. Since these States had an option to join either India, Pakistan or Bangladesh (erstwhile East Pakistan), the Indian government sought agreements in the form of instruments of accession to assimilate these princely States in India. After extensive discussions with these States, they agreed to sign the instrument of accession. As a consideration for signing the agreement, these States were granted an annual compensation called privy purses. The other provinces became a part of India by default as they were already under the sovereignty of the British India. These provinces were granted federal autonomy while creation of States in India. Therefore, India comprises of States which joined through an agreement along with States which were divided or created to form a federation by granting them autonomy, as prescribed by the Constitution.

Since it is widely accepted that there are two modes of formation of a federation – through agreement between independent States or through converting a Unitary State into a federation, India definitely satisfies this feature of federalism. India is a mixture of both the modes of formation, therefore confirming the presence of this feature.

This brings us to the first of four ancillary issues under this head – procedure for reorganisation of States. This includes the constitutional limitations or lack thereof upon the federal government to destroy a State or unilaterally diminish the boundary of a State. Federalism demands that the States' boundaries cannot be unilaterally altered to their disadvantage without their express permission. Thus, the federal Constitutions provide adequate safeguards against any unilateral reorganisation.

In U.S.A., the States are considered to be indestructible i.e. the boundaries of the States cannot be altered without the express consent of the concerned States. The Constitution itself provides that the concerned States' express approval is mandatory for any reorganisation of their boundaries. Similarly, the Australian Constitution does not permit unilateral reorganisation of States, thereby mandating the express approval of the concerned States. However, in addition to this, the Australian federation adds another condition i.e. a majority of eligible voters of the concerned States shall vote in favour of the reorganisation. Therefore, the Australian federation goes a step ahead towards protection of the States by adding another condition to the approval of States. Correspondingly, Canadian Constitution provides that any such reorganisation shall be approved by both Houses of the Federal Parliament, accompanied by an approval by the legislatures of the concerned States.

In India, the situation is peculiarly different from that of the aforementioned federations. The Union Parliament in India has the absolute power to reorganise or alter the boundaries of any State or even eliminate a State altogether without the consent of the concerned State. However, the author strongly argued that even though the Parliament has the aforementioned powers, these have never been exercised unilaterally by the Parliament. Instead, it has always been the States and their residents which have forced the Union government's hands into creating a new State or reorganising the boundaries of the States. The author laid down several instances wherein wide-scale mass agitations and riots took place in States by residents demanding such alterations or creation of new States. Further, since the Union government itself comprises of representatives from each State in the Parliament, it is highly unlikely that the government will take such unilateral decisions without any opposition from the representatives of the States. The governments prefer not to take such decisions unilaterally due to political reasons as well, considering that the political party at the centre will lose the support of an entire State if it makes decisions detrimental to their interests. For these reasons, there has never been an instance wherein the States have been reorganised against the concerned State's own wishes.

As a result, India albeit different in form, complies with the requirement that the States' boundaries cannot be altered unilaterally without the concerned States' approval. In every case prior to 2019, all the reorganisations have been requested by the States themselves or a group of residents have forced the government's hand into reorganisation. Therefore, in substance, the position in India is exactly similar to our target federations. However, the form is quite different.

The second ancillary issue we discussed concerned the admission of new States. The Constitution of U.S.A. specifically allows admission of new States into the federation. The Congress may impose conditions for admission on the States however, after admission, each State is equal and no limitation can be imposed on any State. In stark contrast to the American position, the Constitution of Australia permits the Parliament to admit new States however, the Parliament can impose conditions or limitations on the newly admitted States even after their admission, to the extent that even their representation in the Parliament could be curtailed. Therefore, newly admitted States do not stand on par with original States by default, upon their admission. The Canadian position is somewhat different from the aforementioned federations. Though the Canadian Constitution permits admission of new States, it shall require a constitutional amendment to admit a new State, as the present provision does not envisage admitting new States.

The Indian position is similar to the one in Australia. Although the Indian Constitution provides for admission of new States, the Union Parliament has been empowered to impose such terms and conditions upon it as it may deem fit. Therefore, with respect to the admission of new States, Indian position is similar to Australia, which is considered to be a traditional federation. Withal, this feature is also present in the Indian federation.

Third, the American Constitution is silent on the modes of acquisition of new territories by the nation. As a result, the territories can be acquired as per the established rules of international law including purchase, cession, war, treaty, annexation etc. However, the Australian Constitution specifically provides for three modes of acquisition of new territories. First involves 'territories surrendered by any State and accepted by Commonwealth', second involves 'territories placed under the ambit of the Commonwealth by the Queen' and finally, 'territories otherwise acquired by the Commonwealth'. The third mode involves acquisition under the rules of international law such as war, treaty, annexation etc. The Canadian position is exactly similar to that of America, with acquisition only permitted through rules of international law.

Similar to the American and Canadian federations, the Indian Constitution is silent on acquisition of new States. New territories are acquired as per the rules of international law i.e. cessation, purchase, treaty, war etc. Therefore, the Indian position is exactly similar to America and Canada.

The fourth issue brings us to the very crucial question – whether the newly admitted States are on par or equal to the existing States? In America, even though the Congress is empowered to impose conditions prior to admission of new States, upon their admission, every State in the federation stands on an equal footing. In contrast to this, the Australian Constitution provides that the Federal Parliament can make laws for the governance of the acquired territories, without any constitutional limitations. Until such a territory is admitted as a 'State', it is merely a dependency upon which the Federal Parliament exercises full autonomy. It is pertinent to mention that even for full-fledged States, the Federal Parliament is empowered to impose conditions which may not put newly admitted States on equal footing with other States. Similar to the Australian position, the newly admitted States in Canada may not be granted full legislative powers assigned to the original States. Therefore, the Canadian federation does not guarantee equality to all States after their admission.

The Indian position is partly similar to the Australian position and partly to the American position. Once a territory is acquired, it may not be granted the status of a full-fledged State. Upon admission, it is governed by the Union government under the Foreign Jurisdiction Act, 1947 till such time it is granted the status of a State of the federation. Once the territory has been admitted to the federation, it is equal to the other States of the federation, similar to the American position.

As seen in the preceding paragraphs, the mode of formation of India is perfectly in consonance with the widely accepted modes of formation of a federation. Further, each of the ancillary issue is dealt with in India in a mode similar to our target federations, with minor differences. The form of dealing with these issues may be different in each federation however, as observed, the provisions dealing with these issues in each Constitution are substantially the same i.e. their objective is similar.

In the subsequent chapter, we discussed the rights of the States vis-à-vis the Union i.e. the rights granted to the States by the Constitutions against any interference by the union or federal government. These rights are absolutely essential for the upkeep of the federal principle and ensuring that the interests of the States are protected. As *Dicey* observed, a federation attempts to reconcile national unity along with preservation of States' rights. In the absence of these rights, the States are at the mercy of the federal government which may reduce the States to mere administrative units. Therefore, this chapter discussed eight features essential for upholding the federal principle, present in the traditional federations. These are protection against unilateral amendment of Constitution, protection against extinction, federal control over foreign affairs, federal supremacy in conflicting legislations, State Constitutions, federal control over State legislations, federal control over State administration and providing judiciary for settlement of disputes between federal and State governments or State governments *inter se*.

Coming to the first feature under this chapter, we observed that the federal government shall not be permitted to unilaterally amend the Constitution, as such a power may reduce States to mere administrative units rendering them severely vulnerable to any exploitation by the federal government. Both the traditional federations i.e. America and Australia provide that the Constitution cannot be unilaterally amended by the federal government without the express consent of the States. We further observed that the amendment of the Australian Constitution is even more onerous owing to the fact that any amendment also requires approval of majority of electors in a State, not just the State legislature. The Canadian position is different to the extent that it only requires assent of the States only when amending provisions which affect the States. The Indian position is similar to the Canadian position. In the author's opinion, the position is India and Canada is the most efficient approach considering that if each amendment requires assent of the States, it is extremely difficult to pass such an amendment. To cite an example, only eight out of forty-four amendments in Australia have been passed in its constitutional history. Such a position provides extreme rigidity and every amendment may involve expensive and time-consuming exercise of garnering support with State legislators despite the fact that the amendment may not affect the interests of the State at all. The Indian and Canadian position on the other hand, provides great flexibility to the federal government while simultaneously ensuring that the interests of the States are protected. Since the very objective of avoiding unilateral amendments is protection of interest of States, the objective is fulfilled by the Indian position as well, while providing greater flexibility and efficiency.

Second, we observed that the federation has a duty to protect the States from extinction i.e. the federal government shall protect the States from aggression, internal or external and a State cannot be eliminated through secession. The Constitutions of America, Australia and India expressly provide for a duty to protect the States from internal or external aggression. Canada does not provide for such a duty however, considering that one of the basic characteristics of federalism is protection of States by the federal government, the duty is implicit in a federal structure. With regards to secession, the American and Australian Constitutions are silent on the right to secede however, the courts in both these jurisdictions have held that the States cannot secede from the federation. On the other hand, Canada provides for secession however, it is practically impossible to effect it considering that it requires assent of Federal Parliament along with ratification of 2/3rd of States with approval of 50% of the population in provinces. The Indian position is similar to the American and Australian positions wherein the States are not permitted to secede. Theoretically, such a secession in India may be permitted if the Constitution is amended to that effect.

Third, since the powers to deal with foreign affairs are renounced by the States in favour of the federal government, federations across the world exclusively permit the federal governments to deal with foreign affairs. America, Australia and India follow this position wherein the States are not permitted to deal with foreign nations. On the other hand, Canada permits the States to participate in foreign affairs by appointing agents to other nations however, the States cannot legislate treaties. This position is the anti-thesis of the federal principle considering that federations do not allow States to participate in foreign affairs.

Fourth, the traditional federations provide for supremacy of federal law over State laws in case of conflict between the two. Both America and Australia provide for a general 'supremacy clause' stating that in case of an inconsistency between the federal and State laws, the former shall prevail. In Canada, the Constitution does not provide for federal supremacy however, the courts have declared that in case of such a conflict, the federal law shall prevail. The position in India is similar to that of above-mentioned federations to the extent that Constitution of India provides for federal supremacy however, the supremacy is only limited to specific circumstances. In other words, it is not a blanket supremacy. The basic purpose behind 'supremacy clauses' is that they eliminate the scope for disputes in cases of inconsistency. The courts first attempt to reconcile the two laws and only declare them to be irreconcilable if there is absolutely no scope to do so. As mentioned earlier, the Indian position is more federal than that of our target federations considering that the Indian provision prefers to secure the interests of the State to a vast extent, only providing for federal supremacy if no other alternative is possible.

Fifth, the traditional federations i.e. America and Australia permit States to have their own respective Constitutions, subject to the provisions of the federal Constitution. In Canada and in India, the States are not permitted to enact their own Constitutions. It was observed that the Constitutions of the States in these jurisdictions are present in the Constitution of the nation itself. If the reader may see, Part VI of the Indian Constitution lays down all the provisions pertaining to the affairs of the States which would have been a part of a State Constitution, had its enactment been permitted. It provides for regulation of State legislatures, council of ministers of State, Advocate General, Governor, conduct of government business etc. In addition to this, the States themselves enact their own legislations which regulate the affairs of all authorities under the domain of the State government, without any hindrance from the federal government. Even though the enactment of State Constitutions is not permitted in India, the provisions which would have found themselves in State Constitutions are present in the Constitution of India itself. The ancillary affairs are regulated by the States through its own legislations or delegated legislations. Withal, similar to the federations of America and Australia, Indian Constitution also provides for the State Constitutions albeit through different means. Therefore, in substance,

Indian position regarding State Constitutions is similar to America and Australia however, the form is different.

Sixth, it was observed that the federal principle does not technically permit interference of federal or State governments with the legislative domains of one another. The position in America and Australia is that the federal governments cannot interfere with the legislative powers of the States. However, it was observed that the federal governments do exercise indirect authority over the State legislations by providing conditional grants, which at times require States to enact particular legislations or amend legislations in order to receive grants. Further, in Australia, the federal governments have larger powers to invest in the State's economy for development, as a result of which, the federal government has leverage over the States thereby increasing its influence over the latter. Canada and India on the other hand, allow federal interference with the State legislations. It was observed that though the Indian Parliament does not enjoy direct control over State legislations, it can veto a legislation through the President of India, the consent of whom is necessary for any legislation to come into force. The rationale behind permitting the federation to exercise control over State legislations is to promote the collective integrity of the nation, national security and general welfare of the nation, which at times requires federal interference. Considering nations like India with enormous religious, linguistic and cultural diversity, such measures must be provided in interest of the collective integrity and growth of the nation. As a result, though Indian position is different from that of American and Australia in form, in substance it is similar to the aforementioned federations as even these indirectly exercise control over State legislations.

Seventh, it was observed that though the federal government is not permitted to exercise control over State administration, in practice, the traditional federations do exercise such control indirectly. America and Australia exercise such control through conditional grants, grants-in-aid, infrastructural investments in the State etc. Canada and India however, directly exercise such control over the administration of the States through the Governor, who is an agent of the federal government. Further, in India, the employees of the federal government are posted at senior-most administrative positions in States through the India Civil Services, which permits federal government to exercise control over State administration.

The reader may notice here that all the target federations exercise administrative control over the States, either through direct or indirect means, exercising control nonetheless. The only difference is that of form, America and Australia exercise such control indirectly whereas Canada and India do so directly, the substance or purpose of this control being the same. Therefore, in substance, all federations tend to control State administration but through different forms.

Eighth, it is necessary to have a dispute settlement mechanism for adjudicating disputes between the federal government and the States or between two or more States *inter se*. Since the governments often attempt to interfere with each other's domains, it is necessary to have a dispute settlement system to avoid anarchy or chaos. The respective Constitutions of America, Australia and India specifically provide for a Federal Supreme Court, High Court and Supreme Court respectively, exclusively empowered to hear and adjudicate such disputes. Canada, however, does not provide for original jurisdiction of its Supreme Court. The disputes between the federation and States and States *inter se* are heard by State courts with an appeal lying to the Supreme Court. However, since the federal government is empowered to veto State legislations on any ground whatsoever, the scope for disputes is extremely narrow. Therefore, the position of India is exactly similar to that of America and Australia.

As the reader may see, the Indian position is similar to the ones in traditional federations i.e. America and Australia. Though the form in which these features are addressed may be different, in substance, the object behind these features is still fulfilled, albeit through alternative means. For instance, India and Canada directly permit federal interference with State administration however, the federal governments in America and Australia interfere indirectly, interfering nonetheless. Therefore, Indian position is similar to the traditional federations with minor deviations in form.

Next, we discussed the provisions pertaining to emergency powers in each of our target federations. We observed that though the federal system is intended to preserve autonomy of the States while maintaining national unity and integrity, there exist circumstances which threaten the national security or integrity. In order to deal with these circumstances, emergency powers exist in these federations to channel the federation's resources into a unified effort towards eliminating threats. In this chapter, we discussed three emergency powers – external, internal and financial with respect to each of our target federations.

First, with regards to external emergencies, we observed that American and Australian Constitutions do not expressly provide for declaration of external emergencies. However, the courts in these countries have substantially expanded the ambit of constitutional provisions to create room for declaration of an emergency to counter any external threats. The courts have very limited powers of judicial review upon the declaration of such emergencies. Similarly, the Canadian Constitution does not provide for declaration of external emergency either, however, the federal government enacted the Emergencies Act, 1985 which empowers the federal government to declare emergencies for safety and security of the federation. In India, the constituent assembly members extensively studied the developments of the aforementioned Constitutions and the problems faced by their subjects. Learning from these experiences, the constituent assembly specifically provided for external emergency powers in the Constitution instead of leaving it to the judiciary, along with its procedure, form of declaration, ratification, safeguards and provisions for its revocation, to ensure that the emergency powers are not abused. These provisions provide the same kind of powers which are available in America and Australia.

Second, both the traditional federations i.e. America and Australia do not provide for internal emergencies either. However, the internal emergency powers were carved from the existing constitutional provisions by the courts and federal government, considering the circumstances over the years. In America and Australia, the powers under Art. IV, s. 4 and s. 61 of their respective Constitutions were expanded to permit an internal emergency and exercise control over the States if the situation so demands. Peculiarly, the proclamation of an internal emergency in America is not justiciable as opposed to Australia wherein it is justiciable. Similarly, Canada does not provide for constitutional provisions pertaining to internal emergencies however, the Emergencies Act, 1985 provides for declaring emergencies for public welfare and public order. Coming to the Indian position, the Constitution of India expressly provides for declaration of an internal emergency. Learning from the experiences of the traditional federations, the provision for declaration of such an emergency provides for its declaration, revocation, extension, safeguards and the respective powers of federal and

State governments during the subsistence of an emergency. As a result, instead of leaving it to the judiciary to adjust the provision according to the exigencies of time, the constituent assembly decided to expressly provide for such details within the provision itself. Therefore, the position in India is quite similar to the one in America, Australia and Canada. All these federations provide for declaration of internal emergencies, albeit through different means, despite the fact that such a declaration goes against the federal principle.

Third, neither of the traditional federations provide constitutional provisions related to financial emergencies. However, the federal government in America enacted the International Emergency Economic Powers Act (IEEPA), 1977 which permits the President to regulate economic transactions in response to any threat to the country which may affect its economic or financial health. Similarly, in Australia, an expansive reading of s. 51 (xxxix) has permitted imposition of financial measures in the absence of any express constitutional provision to that effect. Astonishingly however, Canada does not have any provision pertaining to declaration of financial emergencies. It must however be mentioned that the federal government is well empowered to enact legislations to regulate the economy against any external threats, similar to the American position. On the other hand, the Constitution of India expressly provides for the declaration of a financial emergency. It empowers the federal government to direct the States to observe such conditions pertaining to finances as the former may impose. As a result, the federal government ensures that the States' finances are kept in check and money is not withdrawn from the nation's funds without the President's express approval. However, this emergency has never been declared in India. Therefore, the declaration of financial emergencies is permitted in all our target federations, albeit through different means. Despite the contention that a financial emergency may be against the federal principle, the traditional federations still provide for such powers at the behest of the federal government. Without the presence of such powers, it would be extremely onerous to counter any financial threat to the stability of a nation, which may eventually result in disintegration of the federation.

At the conclusion of this chapter, we observed that the proposition stating emergency powers are antithetical to federal principle and therefore, relegating India to the position of a quasi-federal nation due to the presence of emergency powers in the Constitution itself is completely incorrect. All our target federations provide for emergency provisions for declaration of all three emergencies albeit through different means. Though such provisions are not mentioned in the Constitutions of traditional federations themselves, the emergencies are nonetheless declared through alternative means. Therefore, the Indian position is on par with that of traditional federations.

In the succeeding chapter, we discussed the Legislative Lists and the distribution of powers between the federation and their respective States. A federation requires a separation of legislative powers in order to avoid any dispute or interference with each other's domains. Therefore, each federation provides a list of legislative powers in the Constitution itself. We discussed four aspects in this chapter – Legislative Lists in each Constitution; concurrent sphere; vesting of residuary powers; and mechanism for resolving disputes involving interference upon another's legislative domain.

First, we observed that all our target federal Constitutions provide for Legislative Lists in one form or the other. The traditional federations, America and Australia, each provide for one List only i.e. the legislative powers of the federal government. In addition to this, each of these Constitutions expressly exclude exercise of certain powers by the States, thereby vesting them in the federal government 'exclusively'. On the other hand, Canada provides for two Lists i.e. one enumerating the legislative powers of the federation and other enumerating legislative powers of the States. The rationale behind this is that the Canadian federation came into existence after the American and Australian federations, thereby learning from the experiences of these federations wherein the courts had to time and again adjudicate disputes pertaining to transgression of legislative powers or deciding which power vested in whom. As a result, the drafters of the Canadian Constitution attempted to exhaust the field of legislative powers. Since the Indian Constitution came into existence after each of the aforementioned Constitutions, the constituent assembly attempted to further exhaust the legislative field by providing three Lists – Central List, State List and Concurrent List, the latter being legislative powers upon which either of the governments could legislate. Therefore, the position in India is exactly similar to the target federations. In author's opinion, had the American and Australian Constitutions come into force much later, they would have contained three Lists as well, seeing the efficacy of the arrangement.

Second, we observed that each of our target federations provide, either directly or indirectly, for a concurrent sphere i.e. legislative powers upon which both the federal and State governments can legislate. The American Constitution does not expressly provide for a concurrent sphere. However, owing to the exigencies and necessities demanding a concurrent sphere, the courts carved out the sphere from the existing provisions. Therefore, we observed that the federal government can legislate upon certain matters not enumerated in the Constitutional List wherein the federal government shall have supremacy over the State government. The Australian Constitution, however, has a very wide concurrent sphere such that even the powers enumerated for the federal government under s. 51 are made concurrent in entirety i.e. the States can legislate on the powers listed in the Federal List. However, if the federal government has legislated on any of these subjects, the State government cannot legislate upon the same.

The Indian federation follows the same position as in the American and Australian federations, albeit by expressly providing for a Concurrent List in the Constitution itself. The List enumerates the legislative subjects upon which both the federal and the State governments can legislate. However, if the federal government has legislated upon any of these subjects, the State legislation upon the same subject shall be void. Therefore, the author concluded that the position in India with respect to the concurrent sphere is similar to the traditional federations i.e., America and Australia. The only difference is that the constituent assembly in India decided to include the Concurrent List in the Constitution itself, thereby not leaving it for the judiciary to ascertain the concurrent sphere. As a result, the scope of disputes pertaining to concurrent sphere stands vastly diminished and brought certainty to the legislatures. Therefore, the position in India is similar to America and Australia. Canada, on the other hand, does not provide for a concurrent sphere, either through the Constitution or through judicial acts.

Third, we observed that the traditional federations vest the residuary powers in the States whereas India and Canada vest these powers in the federal government. In America and Australia, the residuary powers are expressly vested in the States by the Constitution itself. On the other hand, in Canada and India, the residuary powers are vested in the federal governments considering that the situation under which these federations came into existence demanded a stronger central government. In author's opinion, the situation in America and Australia with respect to residuary powers would have been the same as the Indian position if the former had come into existence in mid 20th century, in light of the fact that federations during this period, after the culmination of two World Wars followed by the Cold War required a stronger central government. This strong centre was provided to the federal governments in America and Australia through interpretation of the constitutional provisions expanding the powers of the federal governments, as seen in the preceding chapters wherein the author attempted to display that constitutional developments in traditional federations have favoured a stronger centre.

Fourth, we observed that since the governments have tendencies to transgress the legislative powers of the other governments, it is essential to have legal principles to ascertain the legal validity of any such transgression or interference with another's legislative powers. These principles or devices bring stability and legal certainty to any action of the government and strengthen the federal principle by ensuring that the federal government does not interfere or overpower the State governments. These principles include doctrine of implied powers, doctrine of colourable legislation, doctrine of occupied filed, federal supremacy clauses etc. These ensure that the governments conform to the constitutional limitations imposed on their respective legislative powers. We concluded that such principles are present in each of our target federations, including India.

At the culmination of the chapter, we concluded that the Indian federation is very much similar to the traditional federations vis-à-vis the legislative powers of the federal and State governments. Similar to America and Australia, the Indian federation provides for Legislative Lists, a concurrent sphere and tools and devices to ensure that the governments remain within their legislative spheres and do not transgress into the legislative powers not allotted to it. The only difference is with regards to the residuary powers. The Indian Constitution vests the residuary powers in the federal government whereas the traditional federations vest them in the States. However, this is of little consequence considering that most of the prominent features of federalism with respect to legislative powers in India are similar to the traditional federations. The intent of the members of the constituent assembly was to build up on the same footing as that of America and Australia however, these were achieved through different means. The essence remains the same.

Lastly, we discussed two features of federalism which may not be crucial however, still have a bearing on the federal aspect of a federation. First, we attempted to quell the observation that the matters assigned to the States in Legislative Lists are subordinate or unimportant, as a result of which, the Indian Constitution is more unitary since the federal government possesses powers to legislate upon crucial matters. We observed that crucial matters such as currency, foreign affairs, defence, communications etc. are assigned to the federal governments in traditional federations as well therefore, these are not peculiar to India. Further, the States in India have been granted important powers including local government, public order, police and public health, among others. In fact, even in the traditional federations, such powers are allotted to the States. In addition to these, the States have been granted the powers to legislate upon agriculture, water, and fisheries as well. Considering that India is an agrarian economy with nearly 40% of its population engaged in agricultural activities, the States play a crucial role in the economic development through regulation of agriculture, water and fisheries.

Further, the States in India have been granted wide powers of taxation as well, such that a majority of their revenue is generated through their own taxes. The States are empowered to impose taxes such as agricultural tax, property tax, sales tax and motor vehicle tax, among others. Similarly, in USA, most States rely on federal funding, some even completely reliant on funds from the federal government. Therefore, relying on federal funding is not peculiar to federalism. We further observed that in the Indian political landscape, the States are indeed quite powerful vis-à-vis the centre such that even a political party coming to power with an absolute majority at the centre may not win State elections against the local political parties. One of the reasons for this may be the power States enjoy over its subjects including law enforcement, public administration etc., permitting them to influence or gather support of the populace with relative ease. Therefore, it is incorrect to state that the States in India are granted subordinate or unimportant legislative powers, relegating them to an inferior position vis-à-vis the centre.

Second, we discussed the absence of State citizenship in India. The traditional federations provide that a person can have citizenship of a State of the federation in addition to the national citizenship. We observed that even though the Indian States are not permitted to grant citizenship, they still provide benefits to its residents in a manner similar to the traditional federations wherein the States provide similar benefits to its citizens. For instance, we observed that the Indian States provide employment quotas which ensure that a certain percentage of jobs in the State are reserved only for the residents/citizens of that State. Similarly, the States provide such reservations in State-funded educational institutions as well. The States provide identities such as Aadhar Card which may be used to establish domicile in a certain State, on the basis of which, the States provide such benefits to its residents/citizens. Therefore, the reader may observe that the functions which a State citizenship fulfills in traditional federations, the States in India fulfill the same functions albeit through different means. Though the Indian States do not provide citizenship, they alternatively provide domicile identities which enable its residents/citizens to obtain benefits exclusively allotted to people of the concerned States. The form of State citizenship is India is different to the one in traditional federations however, substantially their objective is the same.

At this juncture, the author would revert to the second chapter of this book. We observed that most scholars of federalism agree that a predominance of federal features is sufficient to characterise a nation as federal and any requirement of existence of 'all' the features is not necessary. The most prominent proponent of federalism, *Prof. Wheare* suggested that in order to classify a Constitution as federal, a predominance of federal principal and not religious adherence to it is required. Similarly, *Prof. Wagner* stated that whether a State is federal or unitary is one of degree and the answer will depend on how many federal features it possesses. *Livingston* wrote that any theory which asserts that there are certain inflexible characteristics without which a political system cannot be federal ignores the fact that institutions are not the same things in different social and cultural environments, thereby concluding that federalism is different in each nation. Similarly, *Freidrich, Davis* and *Austin* agreed that federalism is a dynamic concept and cannot be circumscribed to say that such and such features shall be present to declare a Constitution as federal. It is essential to ascertain whether the federal principles are predominant.

Building on the premise mentioned in the preceding paragraph, we ascertained the features of federalism which are present in the traditional federations. With these features, we analysed the respective positions of our target federations i.e. U.S.A., Australia, Canada and India. At the end of each chapter, we concluded that India possesses almost all of the features of federalism which are present in the traditional federations, albeit in a different form however, substantially these features are the same. Hence, in each chapter, we studied each federal feature and its presence in each of our federations.

First, we studied the presence of a federal sentiment and concluded that the federal sentiment was present among the founding fathers of each of our federations, as a necessary corollary of which, these nations became federations. Second, we studied the formation of a federation and regulation of its territorial integrity. In this chapter, we discussed five features i.e. mode of formation; admission of new States; reorganisation of territories of States; mode of acquisition of new territories; and powers of newly admitted States. We observed that India possesses all of these federal features either directly or indirectly, but these are nonetheless present in the Constitution. Third, we discussed the rights of the States vis-à-vis the Union. We studied eight aspects under this feature – participation of States in constitutional amendment process; protection of States; foreign affairs; federal supremacy; State Constitutions; federal control over State legislations; federal control over State administration; and dispute settlement mechanism. In this chapter as well, we observed that the position in India is similar to the ones in traditional federations i.e. America and Australia. There exist minor differences in the way these federations deal with these issues but substantially, they are similar.

Fourth, we studied the emergency powers of the federations. We observed that though the emergency powers are not expressly granted in the traditional federations, the provisions permitting their proclamation have been made by the governments and judiciary subsequently. The only difference herein lies in the fact that the Indian Constitution expressly provides for emergency powers however, in traditional federations, the courts and governments carved out such powers from the constitutional provisions. The position is therefore the same, albeit the form is different. Fifth, we studied the Legislative Lists in our target federations. We discussed four aspects of this feature – the structure and types of Legislative Lists; concurrent sphere; residuary powers; and extent of interference with legislative powers. We concluded that the Indian position is similar to the ones in traditional federations but for one feature i.e. residuary powers. The residuary powers in India vest in the central government whereas in traditional federations, these vest in the States. Therefore, to the exception of one feature, the rest of the features are similar to the traditional federations. Lastly, we discussed two minor issues pertaining to the importance of legislative powers granted to the States and the State citizenship. We concluded that the legislative powers allotted to the States are very important and that the State citizenship does exist in India, albeit in a different form.

Therefore, we concluded that all the features of federalism studied in the present work are present in India. Though the form in which such features are provided may differ, substantially the Indian federation provides for each of these features in a manner similar to the traditional federations i.e. America and Australia. Referring to the second chapter, we observed that most authorities on federalism accept that no two federations are alike. Therefore, the predominance of the federal principle is to be ascertained, not water-tight adherence to the federal principle as it existed in America over two centuries ago. Keeping this in mind, Indian federation possesses all of these federal features with slightly different form but substantially fulfilling the same objective. Can the Indian federation then be characterised as quasi-federal or unitary? Relying on the conclusion in the preceding paragraphs, the author's answer would be negative.

CHAPTER 11

Critique of the Indian Position

In chapter 4, we discussed the position of federalism in India in brief. This chapter examines the observations of the Indian courts which have time and again characterised the Constitution as unitary or quasi-federal. The author discusses each observation of the justices of the apex court in each of the following judgements. In light of the discussion in the preceding chapters, the author undertakes this critique to establish the inaccuracy of these observations and that India is indeed a federal nation, not unitary or quasi-federal. It is pertinent to mention that the author disagrees with the present position as it is contrary to the modern-day concept of federalism.

The following paragraphs discuss the relevant parts of the aforementioned judgements which comment on federalism.

i. State of West Bengal vs. Union of India

The *West Bengal* case affirmed the view that the Indian Constitution is indeed federal in nature. The Apex Court identified six features of federalism present in the American federation – i. several autonomous States; ii. division of legislative powers between federal and State governments; iii. direct operation (sovereignty) of each government in its own sphere; iv. provision of each center with complete apparatus of law enforcement; v. supremacy of national government within its assigned sphere; and vi. dual citizenship.

In light of these six features, the court observed *"The aforesaid elements are no doubt present in the American Constitution, but it is not possible to contend that unless all the said criteria exist a Constitution cannot be described as a federal one. Though on paper the American Constitution is a typical federation, in practice the Supreme Court of the United States of America by evolving and developing many legal doctrines and implied powers has invested the Federal Government with large powers to enable it to interfere indirectly in the States field. Even in regard to judicial power, though the American Supreme Court was originally conceived to be a Federal*

Court concerning itself with federal laws, in fact it authoritatively interprets the State laws when they come into conflict with federal laws. The point is that even in America there is no federation in the orthodox sense of the term. So too, the Constitution of Australia clearly demarcates the exclusive fields of the Commonwealth and the States and jealously guards the State rights, but in practice the States have been reduced to the position of agencies of the Commonwealth Government. This was brought about because of the financial grip the Centre has over the State."

The court continued with the analysis of the Canadian federation. It observed *"But in Canada the position is the reverse. Though the Centre and the Provinces have their distinctive Lists of powers, the Central Government has certain limited powers of control over the governments of the ten Provinces of Canada; the residuary powers are given to the Centre and not to the States. Though undoubtedly some elements of unitary form of government are present, the constitutional custom evolved practically a federal State and, as one author puts it, "no dominion government which attempts to stress the unitary elements in the Constitution at the expense of the federal elements would survive." It is, therefore, clear that in every federal Constitution there are either textually or customarily some unitary elements.* **The real test to ascertain whether a particular Constitution has accepted the federal principle or not is whether the said Constitution provides for the division of powers in such a way that the general and regional governments are each within its sphere substantially independent of the other.** *The reservation of the residue of power or the power to interfere with States' affairs in emergencies in the Union may affect the balance of power in a federation, but does not destroy its character. Some Constitutions show a marked bias towards the Federation and the others towards the States, but notwithstanding the varying emphasis they accept the federal principle as their basis."* (emphasis supplied)

Finally, the Apex court observed *"Though some authors, accepting the American Constitution as the yardstick for a federation, prefer to describe Constitutions with a bias towards Union as quasi-federations, I do not think it is inappropriate to describe all Constitutions which substantially accept the federal principle as Federations. Applying this test, I have no doubt that the Indian Constitution is a federation, as the units in normal times exercise exclusive sovereign powers within the fields allotted to them…The Indian Constitution accepts the federal concept and distributes the sovereign powers between the co- ordinate constitutional entitles, namely, the Union and the States. This concept implies that one cannot encroach upon the governmental functions or instrumentalities of the other, unless the Constitution expressly provides for such interference. The legislative fields allotted to the units cover subjects for legislation and they do not deal with the relationship between the two co-ordinate units functioning in their allotted fields: this is regulated by other provisions of the Constitution and there is no provision which enables one unit to take away the property of another except by agreement. The future stability of our vast country with its unity in diversity depends upon the strict adherence of the federal principle, which the fathers of our Constitution have so wisely and foresightedly incorporated therein. This Court has the Constitutional power and the correlative duty-a difficult and delicate one to prevent encroachment, either overtly or covertly, by the Union of State field or vice versa, and thus maintain the balance of federation.*

......The Indian Constitution accepts the federal concept and distributes the sovereign powers between the co- ordinate constitutional entitles, namely, the Union and the States. This concept implies that one cannot encroach upon the governmental functions or instrumentalities of the other, unless the Constitution expressly provides for such interference. The legislative fields allotted to the units cover subjects for legislation and they do not deal with the relationship between the two co-ordinate units functioning in their allotted fields: this is regulated by other provisions of the Constitution and there is no provision which enables one unit to take away the property of another except by agreement. The future stability of our vast country with its unity in diversity depends upon the strict adherence of the federal principle, which the fathers of our Constitution have so wisely and foresightedly incorporated therein. This Court has the constitutional power and the correlative duty-a difficult and delicate one to prevent encroachment, either overtly or covertly, by the Union of State field or vice versa, and thus maintain the balance of federation."

Lastly, the court discussed the integrated system of judiciary in India, as opposed to the dual judicial system in America wherein the State and federal courts are different. The court observed, *"Every State has its judiciary and the highest court in a State is the High Court of judicature. The expenditure of the State judiciary is charged on the consolidated fund of the State concerned but the judges of the High Court are appointed by the*

President; and appeals lie to the Supreme Court of India in certain matters and it has also extraordinary powers to entertain appeals in other matters or to issue writs to enforce fundamental rights. But both the High Courts and the Supreme Court interpret the State and the Union laws and resolve conflicts, if any. An integrated system of judiciary has been accepted by the Constitution and the judicial control operates both ways, though the final word is with the Supreme Court. That cannot by itself affect the federal principle, as even in Australia an appeal lies to the Privy Council, under certain circumstances, from the decisions of the High Court of the Common. wealth of Australia."

As the reader may see, the Supreme Court held that the Indian Constitution is indeed federal in nature. The discussions were quite elaborate in the judgement and are self-explanatory. The court expressed that it is not mandatory that all the federal features shall be present in a Constitution to characterise it as federal. Even the American Constitution and the courts therein have invested large powers in the federal government over the years, in light of the various situations, both external and internal, which require consolidation of powers in the federal government for the security and economic well-being of the nation. Therefore, even the American Constitution cannot be characterised as federal in its orthodox sense. Similarly, in Australia, the States have been reduced to mere agencies of the federal government over the years. In contrast to these, the court observed that though the Canadian federation has some elements of unitary form of government, it is largely federal in nature. **It must be understood that each federation has either textually or customarily some federal features**. The real test, according to the court, is whether the said Constitution provides for the division of powers in such a way that the general and regional governments are each within its sphere substantially independent of the other. The emphasis has been largely on the division of powers and the supremacy in their respective spheres. More importantly, the court observed that vesting of residuary powers in the federal government does not destroy its federal character. Therefore, relying on the same, the court eventually concluded that the Indian Constitution is federal in nature, despite some authors characterising it as quasi-federal.

ii. Kesavananda Bharti vs. State of Kerala (1973) 4 SCC 225

Kesavananda Bharti case is widely renowned as the single most important case in the constitutional history of India. In this case, the doctrine of basic structure was propounded wherein it was held that the amending power of the Parliament is not absolute and some basic features of the Constitution cannot be amended or done away with through a constitutional amendment. Through this decision, the Hon'ble Supreme Court put an end to the marauding attempts of the Indian government to act at its whims and fancies, violating multiple constitutional provisions and human rights without any interference or reprimand from any law enforcement authorities. A peculiar feature of this decisions was that it was heard by a bench of thirteen (13) judges, the largest ever in the history of Supreme Court of India and decided by a majority of 7:6 judges. Had one judge dissented from the seven who delivered the majority verdict, the course of this nation could have been much more different from now, of course to the detriment of all concerned, including the author.

The Supreme Court elaborately discussed federalism in the judgement, largely in context of the amending powers of the Parliament. The court examined whether a federal Constitution empowers the sovereign Parliament to amend the Constitution thereby depriving it of its basic features including federalism itself? This question was answered by the court in negative in its lengthiest ever judgement. More importantly, the Apex court held that federalism is a part of the basic structure of the Indian Constitution and therefore, cannot be done away with through an amendment. For the purposes of this Chapter, the author shall only discuss the portions which deliberated upon the federal or quasi-federal nature of the Constitution.

In the beginning of the discussion, the court agreed that the Indian Constitution is indeed federal in nature. It observed "…*this Part, according to B.N. Rao; is like an Instrument of Instructions from the ultimate sovereign, namely, the people of India (B.N. Rao, India's Constitution in the Making p. 393). **The Constitution has all the essential elements of a federal structure as was the case in the Government of India Act 1935, the essence of federalism being the distribution of powers between the federation or the Union and the States or, the provinces.** All the legislatures have plenary powers but these are controlled by the basic concepts of the Constitution itself and they function within the limits laid down in it Per Gajendragadkar C.J. in Special Reference No. 1 of 1964, [1965] 1 S.C.R. 413 at p. 445. All the functionaries, be they legislators, members of the executive or the judiciary take oath of allegiance* *to the Constitution and derive their authority and jurisdiction from its provisions. The Constitution has entrusted to the judicature in this country the task of construing the provisions of the Constitution and of safeguarding the fundamental rights Ibid p. 446. It is a written and controlled Constitution. It can be amended only to the extent of and in accordance with the provisions contained therein, the principal provision being Article 368.* **Although our Constitution is federal in its structure it provides a system modelled on the British Parliamentary system.**" In Para 568, the court continued by stating **"our Constitution is federal in character, and not unitary."** (Emphasis supplied)

At the outset, as the reader may note from the discussion in the preceding paragraphs, there is a lot more to federalism than merely having a distribution of powers between the federation or the Union and States. Several features shall be present in a discussion on federalism which play a deciding role in whether a State is federal or not. The court however, accepts that our Constitution is federal in nature albeit without elaborating the reasons. Further, the court held that federalism is a part of the basic structure of the Constitution and therefore, cannot be done away with through a constitutional amendment. It observed:

"620. The basic structure of the Constitution is not a vague concept and the apprehensions expressed on behalf of the respondents that neither the citizen nor the Parliament would be able to understand it are unfounded. If the historical background, the Preamble, the entire scheme of the Constitution, the relevant provisions thereof including Article 368 are kept in mind there can be no difficulty in discerning that the following can be regarded as the basic elements of the constitutional structure. (These cannot be catalogued but can only be illustrated).

1. *The supremacy of the Constitution.*

2. *Republican and Democratic form of Government and sovereignty of the country.*

3. *Secular and **federal character of the Constitution**.*

4. *Demarcation of power between the legislature, the executive and the judiciary.*

5.   *The dignity of the individual (secured by the various freedoms and basic rights in Part III and the mandate to build a welfare State contained in Part IV.*

6.   *The unity and the integrity of the nation."*

(Emphasis supplied)

Resultantly, the court further observed *"what follows from this conclusion is the next question to be considered. It is submitted that an amendment should not alter the basic structure of the Constitution or be repugnant to the objectives set out in the Preamble and cannot be exercised to make the Constitution unidentifiable by altering its basic concept governing the democratic way of life accepted by the people of this country. If the entire Constitution cannot be abrogated, can all the provisions of the Constitution leaving the Preamble, or one article, or a few articles of the original Constitution be repealed and in their place other provisions replaced, whereby the entire structure of the Constitution, the power relationship inter se three Departments, the federal character of the State and the rights of the citizens vis-a- vis the State, are abrogated and new institutions, power relationships and the fundamental features substituted therefor? In my view, such an attempt would equally amount to abrogation of the Constitution, because any such exercise of the power will merely leave the husk and will amount to the substitution of an entirely new Constitution, which it is not denied, cannot be done under Article 368."*

As a result, the court held that the federal character of India is a part of the basic structure of the Constitution and cannot be done away with. Any attempt to eliminate the federal principle from the Constitution shall amount to abrogation of the Constitution itself. In addition to the aforementioned, the court referred to the Indian Constitution as federal many a time throughout its observations. Since these observations are in consonance with the author's views, these shall not be much deliberated upon here. However, at one point, the court mentioned that the Indian Constitution is quasi-federal without any reasons whatsoever.

While deliberating upon the extent of research relied upon by the constituent assembly members, the Apex court observed *"they knew the Unitary and Federal types of Constitutions and the Parliamentary and Presidential systems of Government. They knew what Constitutions were* *regarded as "Flexible" Constitutions and what Constitutions were regarded as "rigid" Constitutions. They further knew that in all modern written Constitutions special provision is made for the amendment of the Constitution. Besides, after the Government of India Act, 1935 this country had become better acquainted at first hand, both with the Parliamentary system of Government and the frame of a Federal Constitution with distribution of powers between the centre and in the State. **All this knowledge and experience went into the making of our Constitution which is broadly speaking a quasi - Federal Constitution** which adopted the Parliamentary System of Government based on adult franchise both at the centre and in the States."* (Emphasis supplied)

Here, as one may notice, the court makes a unreasoned observation that the Indian Constitution is quasi-federal, without any justification whatsoever. In the preceding paragraphs, the court maintained that India is federal however, this paragraph suddenly characterises it as quasi-federal. For this very reason, the author mentioned in the preceding paragraphs that the discussion of *Kesavananda Bharti* is not very important considering that it barely talks about the federal character in general, but only in light of the amending power of the federal government.

iii. Shamsher vs. State of Punjab

Shamsher is another case wherein the Supreme Court labelled the Indian Constitution as quasi-federal in nature. This case arose from alleged wrongful termination of services of two members of Punjab Civil Services and involved the adjudication upon discretionary powers of the Governor of a State. In the course of the judgement, the Apex Court commented on the nature of the Constitution. However, similar to the observations in *Kesavananda Bharti*, the court merely branded the Constitution as quasi-federal without indulging in the discussion as to why the Indian Constitution is quasi-federal and not federal.

The court observed *"...what are the basic fabric, the animating spirit, and juridical ideas of our constitutional structure and dynamics? The law of our Constitution, any student of Indian political history and of comparative constitutional systems will agree, is partly eclectic but primarily **an Indo-Anglian version of the Westminster model with quasi-federal adaptations,** historical modifications, geopolitical mutations and home spun traditions-basically a blended brew of the British Parliamentary system, and the*

Government of India Act, 1935 and near-American, nomenclature-wise and in some other respects." The court continued *"..Nehru, Patel, Munshi, Sir B.N. Rao,. Sir Alladi Krishnaswamy Aiyar and, above all, Dr. Ambedkar, who was Chairman of the Drafting Committee, spoke in one voice, with marginal variations on points immaterial to our major purpose. What emerges from such a study is that, with minimal innovations,* **a Parliamentary-style quasi-federalism was accepted***, rejecting the substance of a Presidential- style executive."* (Emphasis supplied)

What is apparent from these observations is that apart from merely stating that the Constitution is quasi-federal in nature, the Hon'ble Apex Court failed to provide any reasons whatsoever as to why the Indian Constitution is quasi-federal. As seen in the preceding chapters, the characterisation of a Constitution is much more technical and involves an assessment of several features essential to federalism. Even among these features, each federation adapts them in a different manner, in their own modified way to tackle indigenous issues. Therefore, it is unreasonable to brand the Constitution as federal or quasi-federal without deliberating upon the features discussed in the preceding chapters.

iv. State of Rajasthan vs. Union of India

The case in *State of Rajasthan* was filed under Art. 131 of the Constitution of India which permits the States to approach the Supreme Court when a conflict arises between the State and the central government. The State of Rajasthan sought the quashing of a certain directive of the central government with which the State refused to conform to. In addition to this, the State sought injunction to restrain the central government from invoking emergency under Art. 356 for non-compliance of the direction. States of Madhya Pradesh, Himachal Pradesh, Punjab, Bihar and Orissa sought similar reliefs. As mentioned in the preceding paragraph, the discussion shall be limited only to the observations on federalism.

The Supreme Court observed *"we are reluctant to embark on a discussion of the abstract principles of federalism in the face of express provisions of our Constitution. Nevertheless, as the principles have been mentioned as aids to the construction of the Constitution whose basic structure may, no doubt, have to be explored even when interpreting the language of a particular provision of the document which governs the destiny of the nation, we cannot avoid saying something on this aspect too. A conspectus of the provisions of our Constitution will indicate that, whatever appearances of a federal structure our Constitution may have, its operations are certainly, judged both by the contents of power which a number of its provisions carry with them and the use that has been made of them, more unitary than federal."*

The court continued, *"…but, the extent of federalism in it is largely watered down by the needs of progress and development of a country which has to be nationally integrated, politically and economically coordinated, and socially, intellectually and spiritually up-lifted. In such a system, the States cannot stand in the way of legitimate and comprehensively planned development of the country in the manner directed by the Central Government. The question of legitimacy of particular actions of the Central Government taking us in particular directions can often be tested and determined only by the verdicts of the people at appropriate times rather than by decisions of Courts. For this reasons, they become, properly speaking, matters for political debates rather than for legal discussion. If the special needs of our country, to have political coherence, national integration, and planned economic development of all parts of the country, so as to build a welfare State where "justice, social, economic and political" are to prevail and rapid strides are to be taken towards fulfilling the of her noble aspirations, set out in the Preamble, strong central directions seems inevitable."*

It is pertinent to mention that the court did not study the features of federalism prior to commenting on whether it is unitary or federal. It is submitted that had a study been conducted into the other federations, it would be apparent that even the traditional federations are more unitary than federal. As we have seen in the preceding chapters, the traditional federations have all become more unitary over the course of time. For instance, the internal emergency can be imposed by in America and Australia despite the absence of a constitutional provision permitting the same. Further, the observation that *'if we are to build a welfare State where "justice, social, economic and political" are to prevail and rapid strides are to be taken towards fulfilling the of her noble aspirations, set out in the Preamble, strong central directions seems inevitable'* is flawed. It is submitted that all these objectives are present in any given federal Constitution. As a result, the federal governments in all our target federations legislate towards the fulfilment of these aspirations themselves, rather than leaving it to the States.

For instance, the statutes providing basic human rights are uniform all across the federations and do not vary from one State to another. Therefore, it cannot be said that since the involvement of the federal government is key for development, the Constitution is more unitary than federal. If this were the case, the traditional federations would also be quasi-federal.

The court further goes on to observe *"in our country national planning involves disbursements of vast amounts of money collected as taxes from citizens residing in all the States and placed at the disposal of the Central Government for the benefits of the States without even the "conditional grants" mentioned above. Hence, the manner in which State Governments function and deal with sums placed at their disposal by the Union Government or how they carry on the general administration may also be matters of considerable concern to the Union Government."*

As we have seen in the preceding chapters, States generate over 50% of their revenues through their own powers of taxation. Further, we observed that even in America and Australia, the federal governments exercise considerable powers over the States through these grants as even in these federations, States heavily rely on the federal governments for their revenues. In fact, some States in America obtain over 70% of their funds from the federal government. Therefore, this observation is flawed in the sense that it uses the federal government's control over States through financial disbursements as a criterion for federalism.

Lastly, the court observed, with respect to emergency powers, *"The constitutional implications of a declaration of emergency under Article 352, clause (1) are vast and they are provided in Articles 250, 353, 354, 358 and 359. The emergency being an exceptional situation, arising out of a, national crisis, certain wide and sweeping power-, have been conferred on the Central Government and Parliament with a view to combat the situation and restore normal conditions. One such power is that given by Article 250 which provides that while a Proclamation of Emergency is in operation, Parliament shall have the power to make laws for the whole or any part of the territory of India with respect to any of the matters enumerated in the State List. The effect of this provision is that the federal structure based on separation of powers is put out of action for the time being. Another power of a similar kind is that conferred by Article 353 which says that during the time that Proclamation of Emergency is in force. the executive power of the Union shall extend to the giving of direction to any State as to the manner in which the executive power thereof is to be exercised. This provision also derogates from the federal principle which forms the basis of the Constitution."*

The author highly disagrees with the observations in the preceding paragraph. It is submitted that the emergency powers which permit the federal government to gain enormous control over the affairs of the States, including the legislative powers, are present in the traditional federations as well. As we have seen in chapter 8, our target federations provide for emergency powers wherein the federal government can legislate upon the subjects under States' legislative powers. Therefore, it is incorrect to conclude that emergency powers contribute to the unitary nature of the federation. If that were the case, America and Australia are unitary as well.

As the reader may see, even *State of Rajasthan* does not correctly assess the federal features and conduct a study into their presence or absence from the Indian Constitutions vis-à-vis traditional federations. It is submitted that federalism is a dynamic concept, in light of which, it cannot be stated that if a certain feature is not present, the nation is not federal. A wholistic study of the concept and the traditional federations is required to assess the dominance of federalism in a certain nations. Such a study has been undertaken in the preceding chapters.

v. Pradeep Jain vs. Union of India 1984 AIR 1420

In *Pradeep Jain*, the Apex Court observed "*Moreover, it must be remembered that India is not a federal State in the traditional sense of that term. It is not a compact of sovereign States which have come together to form a federation by ceding a part of their sovereignty to the federal States. It has undoubtedly certain federal features but it is still not a federal State and it has only one citizenship, namely, the citizenship of India. It has also one single unified legal system which extends throughout the country. It is not possible to say that a distinct and separate system of law prevails in each State forming part of the Union of India. The legal system which prevails through-out the territory of India is one single indivisible system with a single unified justicing system having the Supreme Court of India at the apex of the hierarchy, which lays down the law for the entire country.*"

It is submitted that the observations of the court are incorrect. First, the territories did in fact cede sovereignty to India. If the reader may recall, the princely States were not ipso facto part of India and instruments of accession had to be signed with these States. Would this not be equivalent to ceding sovereignty to India? The answer would be affirmative. Second, in chapter 6, we observed that the States in India indeed provide for a State citizenship, however in a different form to that of States in traditional federations. As we observed in the preceding chapters, it is crucial to assess the objective which is accomplished by these features and not the form in which these are accomplished. The form shall vary from one federation to another but in substance, these are the same. Third, the legal system is the same in traditional federations as well. If the States are permitted to enact different laws as per their circumstances, it cannot be said that there exist several legal systems. The laws enacted by the federal government uniformly apply to each State. The State laws may differ from one another in traditional federations but even in India, the position is the same. For instance, Andhra Pradesh provides for special trials for cases involving rape and murder of women however, such a law is absent from other States. The unified justice system however, is not a prominent feature of federalism, as we saw in the preceding chapters wherein none of the jurists consider a unified judiciary crucial for federalism.

vi. S. R. Bommai vs. Union of India (1994) 3 SCC 1

The most important judgement in the federal history of India is *S.R. Bommai*. This case arose out of the incessant declaration of emergencies under Art. 356 of the Constitution, mostly due to political vendettas. The petitioner's government had been elected to power in State of Karnataka, however, due to some defections, the President dismissed the government. Therefore, the petitioner sought interference from the Apex Court to declare such unreasonable declarations of Art. 356 as void or unconstitutional. In this case, the hon'ble justices of the Supreme Court studied the federal structure in detail to eventually conclude that India is quasi-federal. However, some of the judges though in agreement with the verdict, preferred to give separate opinions. The author shall discuss the relevant parts of the judgement in the following paragraphs.

Let us first consider the observations of Hon'ble Mr. Justice A.H. Ahmadi. It was observed *"the essence of a federation is the existence of the Union and the States and the distribution of powers between them. Federalism, therefore, essentially implies demarcation of powers in a federal compact......the oldest federal model in the modern world can be said to be the Constitution of the United States of America. The American Federation can be described as the outcome of the process of evolution, in that, the separate States first formed into a Confederation (1781) and then into a Federation (1789). Although the States may have their own Constitutions, the Federal Constitution is the suprema lex and is made binding on the States. That is because under the American Constitution, amendments to the Constitution are required to be ratified by three-fourths of the States. Besides under that Constitution there is a single legislative List enumerating the powers of the Union and, therefore, automatically the other subjects are left to the States. This is evident from the Tenth Amendment. Of course, the responsibility to protect the States against invasion is of the Federal Government. The States are, therefore, prohibited from entering into any treaty, alliance, etc., with any foreign power. The principle of dual sovereignty is carried in the judicial set-up as well since disputes under federal laws are to be adjudicated by federal courts, while those under State laws are to be adjudicated by State courts, subject of course to an appeal to the Supreme Court of the United States. The interpretation of the Constitution is by the United States Supreme Court."*

In the preceding paragraph, Ahmadi, J. highlights the features of federalism present in the American Constitution. In the preceding chapters, we have observed that the constitutional amendments in India which affect the States require assent of atleast one-half of the States and therefore, it is not a feature absent from our Constitution. Second, the Indian Constitution also enumerates the legislative powers of the federal government, along with that of the States. Third, the Indian Constitution provides a duty to protect States against invasion. Fourth, the States are prohibited from engaging in foreign affairs. Fifth, as concerns the dual sovereignty being carried out in the judicial set up, it is submitted that the judiciary in India has a similar set up, albeit not the same. The respective High Courts of the concerned States are empowered to deal with the State laws only, of course to the exception of the Supreme Court. However, as our readers would know, the Supreme Court on most occasions refuses to hear matters which fall under the jurisdiction of the concerned High Court. The Apex Court has time and again held that it is the court of last resort after exhaustion of all remedies.[361] Even for the protection of fundamental rights, the court refuses

---

361 Dr. Rajeev Dhawan, Court of Last Resort, India Today, July 1, 2013; Upendra Baxi, Taking Suffering Seriously: Social Action Litigation in the Supreme Court of

to entertain jurisdiction under Art. 32 if the remedy under Art. 226 has not been exhausted. Therefore, if a certain legislation in State of Karnataka is to be challenged, only the High Court of Karnataka can hear the challenge, to the exception of all other High Courts. The position therefore, is similar to the United States.

He continued *"Parliament can, therefore, without the concurrence of the State or States concerned change the boundaries of the State or increase or diminish its area or change its name. These provisions show that in the matter of Constitution of States, Parliament is paramount. This scheme substantially differs from the federal set-up established in the United States of America. The American States were independent sovereign States and the territorial boundaries of those independent States cannot be touched by the Federal Government. It is these independent sovereign units which together decided to form into a federation unlike in India where the States were not independent sovereign units but they were formed by Article 1 of the Constitution and their areas and boundaries could, therefore, be altered, without their concurrence, by Parliament. With respect to residuary powers, he observed "the residuary power has been conferred on the Union. This arrangement substantially differs from the scheme of distribution of powers in the United States of America where the residual powers are with the States."*

It is submitted that though the Parliament has been empowered to unilaterally alter the boundaries of the States, we observed that it does not happen without the internal pressures from the concerned States itself. We observed that in each of such boundary adjustments, the demand came from the State itself owing to the cultural or linguistic differences. Several examples were cited including Andhra Pradesh, the first State to be formed on a linguistic basis after independence[362], State of Telangana carved out from the State of Andhra Pradesh in 2014,[363] State of Jharkhand[364], State

---

India, 4(1) Third World Legal Studies 107 (1985).

362 "SRC submits report". *The Hindu*. Chennai, India. 1 October 2005.

363 "Pro-Telangana AP govt employees threaten agitation". *The Economic Times*. 10 February 2012; Telangana Students Suicides Increase in Hyderabad http://www. politicsdaily.com/2010/02/25/telangana-protests-student-suicides-increase-in-hyderabad-durin/

364 History of Jharkhand, Jharkhand History". *traveljharkhand.com*; "Tributes pour in for Justice Shahdeo", The Pioneer, 10 January 2018.

of Uttarakhand[365], State of Chhattisgarh[366] and State of Nagaland[367]. We further observed that if such unilateral boundary adjustments are made without the consent of the State, the political parties in power at the centre will lose the support of an entire State. From a political standpoint, such a move may bring disrepute and disapproval which could result in adverse results for the ruling party from the people of the State. Similarly, the Parliament has representatives of all the States in each House who are elected to ensure that the interests of their respective States are accounted for in every decision that is taken. If any such decision is taken against their interests, such members ensure that the word of disapproval reaches the government. To cite an example, the Smt. Harsimrat Kaur Badal resigned as a Union Minister due to the centre's alleged violation of rights of the farmers in State of Punjab.[368] In fact, in practice, the opposition parties usually join the protests from such members against unilateral alterations to pressurise the Union government to not undertake such alterations. Withal, there are several practical limitations imposed on the Union government which discourages it from unilaterally altering or reorganizing the boundaries of the States. Hence, if the reader looks at the substance and not the form of alteration of boundaries, it is clear that the Union cannot unilaterally alter such boundaries, which is in line with the position in America. However, it must be conceded that the position pertaining to residuary powers is dissimilar to the American position.

Ahmadi, J. continued "...*noticed that the executive power of every State must be so exercised as not to impede or prejudice the exercise of the executive power by the Union. The executive power of the Union also extends to giving such directions to a State as may appear to the Government of India to be necessary for those purposes and as to the construction, maintenance of means of communication declared to be of national or military importance and for protection of railways. The States have to depend largely on financial assistance from the Union. Under the scheme of Articles 268 to 273, States are in Certain cases allowed to collect and retain duties imposed by the Union; in*

---

365 Kumar, P. (2000). The Uttarakhand Movement: Construction of a Regional Identity. New Delhi: Kanishka Publishers.

366 Prithak Chattisgarh, 4 July 2010

367 Inoue, Kyoko, Integration of the North East: The State Formation Process, IDE JETRO Publication.

368 Harsimrat Kaur Badal resigns as Union Minister protesting over farm bills, Live Mint, September 17, 2020

other cases taxes levied and collected by the Union are assigned to the States and in yet other cases taxes levied and collected by the Union are shared with States. Article 275 also provides for the giving of grants by the Union to certain States. There is, therefore, no doubt that States depend for financial assistance upon the Union since their power to raise resources is limited."

It is submitted that the observations in the preceding paragraph are devoid of the actual position in the United States of America. All States in America depend upon federal funding as barely any State is able to generate enough funds to meet its own financial commitments. In fact, there are several States which completely depend on federal funding i.e. New Mexico obtains close to 100% funding from federal government whereas Alaska, Mississippi and North Dakota require over 70% of their funding from the federal government.[369] Therefore, even the States in America are highly dependent on federal funding. We observed in the preceding paragraphs that barely any State in India is completely dependent on federal funding. In fact, prosperous States such as Maharashtra and Karnataka generate over 50% of their revenues themselves. Therefore, this position is similar to the one in India.

It was further observed *"as economic planning is a concurrent subject, every major project must receive the sanction of the Central Government for its financial assistance since discretionary power under Article 282 to make grants for public purposes is vested in the Union or a State, notwithstanding that the purpose is one in respect to which Parliament or State Legislature can make laws. It is only after a project is finally sanctioned by the Central Government that the State Government can execute the same which demonstrates the control that the Union can exercise even in regard to a matter on which the State can legislate. In addition to these controls Article 368 confers powers on Parliament to amend the Constitution, albeit by a specified majority. The power extends to amending matters pertaining to the executive as well as legislative powers of the States if the amendments are ratified by the legislatures of not less than one-half of the States. This provision empowers Parliament to so amend the Constitution as to curtail the powers of the States. A strong Central Government may not find it difficult to secure the requisite majority as well as ratification by one half of the legislatures if*

---

369 Deb Gordon, Return on Statehood: How much value every State gets from Federal Government, Money Geek, February 9, 2021.

It is submitted that even in the United States, the States rely on federal funding for infrastructure projects. We already observed that many States fulfil over 50% of their funding requirements through the federal governments grants. Not just this, in U.S.A., the federal government exercises control over the State legislations and the State administration indirectly, as we have seen in the preceding chapters. Therefore, it is incorrect to state that since central government can exercise control over States through funding, the position is different from that in America. The same position persists in America as well. Further, the author believes it to be incorrect to propound that a strong central government can easily obtain the consent of one-half of the States to be of detriment towards the federal character. It is submitted that even in U.S.A., there have been instances wherein the ruling political party has had majority in over three-fourth of the States. For instance, in 1988 elections, President George H. W. Bush won in over 40 States i.e. majority in 80% of the States. If Ahmadi, J.'s proposition were true, the years that followed under the Bush administration, America must have been quasi-federal. But I believe everyone concerned has been of the view that America has been federal forever.

Concluding his observations on federalism, Ahmadi, J. observed *"it would thus seem that the Indian Constitution has, in it, not only features of a pragmatic federalism which, while distributing legislative powers and indicating the spheres of governmental powers of State and Central Governments, is overlaid by strongly 'unitary' features, particularly exhibited by lodging in Parliament the residuary legislative powers, and in the Central Government the executive power of appointing certain constitutional functionaries including High Court and Supreme Court Judges and issuing appropriate directions to the State Governments and even displacing the State Legislatures and the Governments in emergency situations, vide Articles 352 to 360 of the Constitution.*

It must also be realised that unlike the Constitution of the United States of America which recognises dual citizenship [Section 1(1), 14th Amendment], the Constitution of India, Article 5, does not recognise the concept of dual citizenship... The concept of citizenship assumes some importance in a *federation because in a country which recognises dual citizenship, the individual would owe allegiance both to the Federal Government as well as the State Government but a country recognising a single citizenship does not face complications arising from dual citizenship and by necessary implication negatives the concept of State sovereignty."*

It is submitted that if we assume that Indian Constitution is overlaid with unitary principles, albeit not accepting the same, the position is more or less the same in America as well. In the preceding chapters, we observed that even the American and Australian federations provide emergency powers to the federal governments and exercise enormous control over State legislations and State administrations. Further, we observed that though dual citizenship is not permitted in India, the States in India alternatively provide for privileges that one may get under State citizenship in States in America. For instance, the State citizenship confers voting rights and privileges such as employment reservations, educational opportunities, welfare schemes etc. The States in India provide these privileges to people domiciled in the concerned State. Therefore, although the Indian Constitution does not permit such dual citizenship, substantially it permits States to provide privileges to its residents, thereby indirectly providing State citizenship.

In addition to the observations of Ahmadi, J., K. Ramaswami, J. highlighted another aspect of the federal principle which the author believes to be important, although the author does not agree with the observation. He observed *"In the context of the Indian Constitution, federalism is not based on any agreement between federating units but one of integrated whole, as pleaded with vision by Dr B.R. Ambedkar on the floor of the Constituent Assembly at the very inception of the deliberations and the Constituent Assembly unanimously approved the resolution of federal structure."* It is submitted that India was actually formed by agreement with the princely States and through assimilation of the already existing provinces of the Union. The princely States were given an option to either join India or not.[370] Considering that there were about 565 princely States in India (covering around 40% of the area; 23% of the population)[371], the agreement with

---

370 Ishtiaq Ahmed (1998). *State, Nation and Ethnicity in Contemporary South Asia.* London & New York. p. 99; Ravi Kumar Pillai Kandamath (2016) Yaqoob Khan Bangash. A Princely Affair: The Accession and Integration of the *Princely States of Pakistan, 1947-1955, Asian Affairs, 47:2, 316-319,*

371 *Datar, Arvind P. (18 November 2013). "Who betrayed Sardar Patel?". The Hindu.*

these States to retain their allegiance to India was necessary for national security, maintenance of internal peace and retaining a larger geographical area. Therefore, several instruments of accession were signed between the princely States and the Union, which act as an agreement between the two. In fact, even a consideration in the form of privy purses was given to these princely States for acceding to India. Therefore, the formation of India actually required agreements with princely States which occupied about 40% of the land.

In contrast to the aforementioned views, P.B. Sawant, J., writing for himself and for Kuldip Singh, J., seemed to disagree with the observations of Ahmadi, J. however at the conclusion, Sawant, J. refused to characterise the Constitution as either federal, quasi-federal or unitary stating that these are merely theoretical labels. He relied on the findings of *Seervai*[372] which the author believes to be highly important to ascertain federalism in India. These are:

(a) It is no objection to our Constitution being federal that the States were not independent States before they became parts of a Federation. A federal situation existed, first, when the British Parliament adopted a federal solution in the G.I. Act, 1935, and secondly, when the Constituent Assembly adopted a federal solution in our Constitution;

(b) Parliament's power to alter the boundaries of States without their consent is a breach of the federal principle, but in fact it is not Parliament which has, on its own, altered the boundaries of States, By extra-constitutional agitation, the States have forced Parliament to alter the boundaries of States. In practice, therefore, the federal principle has not been violated;

(c) The allocation of the residuary power of legislation to Parliament (i.e. the Federation) is irrelevant for determining the federal nature of a Constitution. The U.S. and the Australian Constitutions do not confer the residuary power on the Federation but on the States, yet those Constitutions are indisputably federal;

(d) External sovereignty is not relevant to the federal nature of a Constitution, for such sovereignty must belong to the country as

---

372 H.M. Seervai, Constitutional Law of India, 3rd Edn, p. 166

a whole. But the division of internal sovereignty by a distribution of legislative powers is an essential feature of federalism, and our Constitution possesses that feature. With limited exceptions, the Australian Constitution confers overlapping legislative powers on the States and the Commonwealth, whereas List 11, Schedule VII of our Constitution confers exclusive powers of legislation on the States, thus emphasising the federal nature of our Constitution;

(e) The enactment in Article 352 of the emergency power arising from war or external aggression which threatens the security of India merely recognises de jure what happens de facto in great federal countries like the U.S., Canada and Australia in times of war, or imminent threat of war, because in war, these federal countries act as though they were unitary. The presence in our Constitution of exclusive legislative powers conferred on the States makes it reasonable to provide that during the emergency created by war or external aggression, the Union should have power to legislate on topics exclusively assigned to the States and to take corresponding executive action. The Emergency Provisions, therefore, do not dilute the principle of Federalism, although the abuse of those provisions by continuing the emergency when the occasion which caused it had ceased to exist does detract from the principle of Federal Government. The amendments introduced in Article 352 by the 44th Amendment have, to a considerable extent, reduced the chances of such abuse. And by deleting the clauses which made the declaration and the continuance of emergency by the President conclusive, the 44th Amendment has provided opportunity for judicial review which, it is submitted, the courts should not lightly decline when as a matter of common knowledge, the emergency has ceased to exist. This deletion of the conclusive satisfaction of the President has been prompted not only by the abuse of the Proclamation of emergency arising out of war or external aggression, but, even more, by th e wholly unjustified Proclamation of emergency issued in 1975 to protect the personal position of the Prime Minister;

(f) The power to proclaim an emergency originally on the ground of internal disturbance, but now only on the ground of armed rebellion, does not detract from the principle of federalism because such a power, as we have seen exists in indisputably federal constitutions. *Deb Sadhan Roy v. State of W.B. (AIR 1972 SC 1924)* has established that internal violence would ordinarily interfere with the powers of the federal Government to enforce its own laws and to take necessary executive action. Consequently, such interference can be put down with the total force of the United States, and the same position obtains in Australia;

(g) The provisions of Article 355 imposing a duty on the Union to protect a State against external aggression and internal disorder are not inconsistent with the federal principle. The war power belongs to the Union in all Federal Governments, and therefore the defence of a State against external aggression is essential in any Federal Government. As to internal disturbance, the position reached in Deb case28 shows that the absence of an application by the State does not materially affect the federal principle. Such application has lost its importance in the United States and in Australia;

(h) Since it is of the essence of the federal principle that both federal and State laws operate on the same individual, it must follow that in case of conflict of a valid federal law and a valid State law, the federal law must prevail and our Constitution so provides in Article 254, with an exception noted earlier which does not affect the present discussion;

(i) It follows from what is stated in (g) above, that federal laws must be implemented in the States and that the federal executive must have power to take appropriate executive action under federal laws in the State, including the enforcement of those laws.

Whether this is done by setting up in each State a parallel federal machinery of law enforcement, or by using the existing State machinery, is a matter governed by practical expediency which does not affect the federal principle. In the United States, a defiance of Federal law can be, and, as we have seen, has been put down by the use of Armed Forces of the U.S. and the National Militia of the States. This is not inconsistent with the federal principle in the United States. Our Constitution has adopted the method of empowering the Union Government to give directions to the States to give effect to the Union law and to prevent obstruction in the working of the Union law. Such a power, though different in form, is in substance the same as the power of the Federal Government in the U.S. to enforce its laws, if necessary by force. Therefore, the power to give directions to the State Governments does not violate the federal principle;

(j) Article 356 (read with Article 355) which provides for the failure of constitutional machinery was based of Article 4, Section 4 of the U.S. Constitution and Article 356, like Article 4, Section 4, is not inconsistent with the federal principle. As stated earlier, these provisions were meant to be the last resort, but have been gravely abused and can therefore be 28 (1972) 1 SCC 308: 1972 SCC (Cri) 45: AIR 1972 SC 1924 said to affect the working of the Constitution as a Federal Government. But the recent amendment of Article 356 by the 44th Amendment, and the submission to be made hereafter that the doctrine of the political question does not apply in India, show that the courts can now take a more active part in preventing a mala fide or improper exercise of the power to impose a President's rule, unfettered by the American doctrine of the political question;

(k) The view that unimportant matters were assigned to the States cannot be sustained in face of the very important subjects assigned to the States in List 11, and the same applies to taxing powers of the States, which are made mutually exclusive of the taxing powers of the Union so that ordinarily the States have independent source of revenue of their own. The legislative entries relating to taxes in List 11 show that the sources of revenue available to the States are substantial and would increasingly become more substantial. In addition to the exclusive taxing powers of the States, the States become entitled either to appropriate taxes collected by the Union or to a share in the taxes collected by the Union."

Sawant, J. concluded "*The above discussion thus shows that the States have an independent constitutional existence and they have as important a role to play in the political, social, educational and cultural life of the people as the Union. They are neither satellites nor agents of the Centre. The fact that during emergency and in certain other eventualities their powers are overridden or invaded by the Centre is not destructive of the essential federal nature of our Constitution. The invasion of power in such circumstances is not a normal feature of the Constitution. They are exceptions and have to be resorted to only occasionally to meet the exigencies of the special situations. The exceptions are not a rule."* Therefore, Sawant, J. and Singh, J., both were of the view that India is indeed federal in nature.

Similarly, B.P. Jeevan Reddy, J. had view similar to that of Sawant, J. and Singh, J. He observed *"The fact that under the scheme of our Constitution, greater power is conferred upon the Centre vis-a-vis the States does not mean that States are mere appendages of the Centre. Within the sphere allotted to them, States are supreme. The Centre cannot tamper with their powers. More particularly, the courts should not adopt an approach, an interpretation, which has the effect of or tends to have the effect of whittling down the powers reserved to the States. It is a matter of common knowledge that over the last several decades, the trend the world over is towards strengthening of Central Governments be it the result of advances in technological/scientific fields or otherwise, and that even In USA the Centre has become far more powerful notwithstanding the obvious bias in that Constitution in favour of the States. All this must put the court on guard against any conscious whittling down of the powers of the States. Let it be said that the federalism in the Indian Constitution is not a matter of administrative convenience, but one of principle the outcome of our own historical process and a recognition of the ground realities."*

Therefore, the observations of Ahmadi, J. are prevalent while considering the federal character of the Indian Constitution. As a result, the Indian Constitution has been characterised as a quasi-federal Constitution.

vii. Ganga Ram Moolchandani vs. State of Rajasthan

In *Ganga Ram Moolchandani*, the Apex Court dealt with the challenge to the Rajasthan Higher Judicial Service Rules, 1963 which made only those advocates eligible for consideration to the post of Rajasthan Higher Judicial Service who are practising in the Rajasthan High Court and courts subordinate thereto, on grounds, inter alia, that the same were violative of fundamental rights guaranteed to a citizen of India enshrined under Articles 14 and 16 of the Constitution. In this case, the court observed *"Indian Constitution is basically federal in form and is marked by the traditional characteristics of a federal system, namely, supremacy of the*

Constitution, division of power between the Union and States and existence of an independent judiciary."

It is submitted that the observation of the Hon'ble Supreme Court is flawed as these features are present in each and every federation, including some Unitary States which provide for a division of powers but provides for an exceptionally dominant central government. Therefore, such an assessment is incorrect as the features mentioned herein are inadequate. As we have seen in the preceding chapters, there are numerous other features and aspects of federalism which shall be assessed to ascertain the federal character of a nation.

Through this chapter, the author attempted to discuss the various observations of the Hon'ble Supreme Court in its judgements since the Constitution came into force. The author humbly submits that the observations of the apex court are inconsiderate towards the ever-changing nature of the federal principle and the evolution of the federations in America and Australia which are more or less similar to India in the present day. Further, in many cases, the court did not discuss the features of federalism in detail but rather made unsubstantiated observations on federalism. Therefore, the author hopes the reader received a sound take away on the federal character of India. India is indeed a federation!

References

Books

1. A.V Dicey: General Characteristics of English Constitutionalism: Six Unpublished Lectures

2. A.V. Dicey, An Introduction to the Study of Law of the Constitution 141 (10th Edn. 1959)

3. A.V. Dicey, Law of the Constitution, 10th Edn. (1885)

4. Alan Gledhill, The Republic of India, London: Stevens and Sons, Ltd. (1951)

5. C.H. Alexandrowicz, Constitutional Developments in India, Bombay: Oxford University Press, 1957

6. Aparna Pande, Explaining Pakistan's Foreign Policy: Escaping India, Taylor & Francis (2011), ISBN 978-1-136-81893-6

7. Austin, Indian Constitution (1966)

8. Kuldip Singh Bajwa (2003), Jammu and Kashmir War, 1947–1948

9. D.D. Basu, Commentary on the Constitution of India, 9th Edn (2014)

10. D.D. Basu, Comparative Federalism, Lexis Nexis, India (2007)

11. Bouton, Terry (2012). "The Trials of the Confederation". In Gray, Edward G.; Kamensky, Jane (eds.). The Oxford Handbook of the American Revolution ISBN 9780199746705

12. Bruchesi, Jean, 'Canada', Ryerson Press, Toronto, Ontario (1956)

13. C.F. Strong, Modern Political Constitutions, 6th Edn., London (1963)

14. Carl J. Friedrich, Trends of Federalism in Theory and Practice (1968)

15. Carter & Herz, Major Foreign Powers, (1972)

16. Casey, Christopher A.; et al. (March 20, 2019). The International Emergency Economic Powers Act: Origins, Evolution, and Use. Washington, DC: Congressional Research Service

17. Warren Reed West, American Government (1946)

18. Ogg & Ray, Essentials of American Government, (1965)

19. Colquhoun, A. H. (1964). The Fathers of the Confederation. Toronto, Ontario, University of Toronto Press

20. Corwin, Constitution: What it Means Today (1973)

21. Creighton, Donald (2012). Canada's First Century, 1867-1967. Toronto: Oxford

22. Dawson, Government of Canada, (1970)

23. De Smith, Constitutional Law, (1973)

24. Deaking, Alfred, The Federal Council of Australasia, 1895, University of Sydney Library, 2000

25. Driedger, Elma A. (1976). The Consolidation of the North America Acts. Ottawa: Department of Justice

26. Hugh Evander Willis, Constitutional Law of the United States (1936)

27. Encyclopedia Britannica

28. Fajgenbaum & Hanks, Australian Constitutional Law, (1980)

29. Fincher, Government of the U.S. (1976)

30. Finlay, John L (1991). Pre Confederation Canada. Scarborough, Ontario: Prentice-Hall

31. Forcese, Craig; West, Leah (2020-03-14). "Ch 8 -- Emergencies". National Security Law 2d Ed. Rochester, NY: Irwin Law

32. Founding Fathers: The Essential Guide to the Men Who Made America. John Wiley & Sons. ISBN 978-0-470-11792-7

33. Francis, R.D. (2013). Origins. Toronto, Ontario: Nelson Education

34. Freeman, History of Federal Government

35. Friedmann, Constitutional Government (1950)

36. G. Austin, Working a Democratic Constitution, The Indian Experience (1999)

37. Garner, Political Science and Government (1951)

38. Geoffrey Sawer, Modern Federalism (Watts and Co. London 1969)

39. Gettel, Political Science (1967)

40. Granville Austin, The Indian Constitution: Cornerstone of a Nation (1966)

41. Griffith, Impasse of Democracy, (1939)

42. Gwyer and Appadorai, Speeches and Documents on the Indian Constitution, Vol. 1

43. Halsbury, 4th Edn. Vol. 6

44. Harvey Flaumenhaft, "Hamilton's Administrative Republic and the American Presidency," in The Presidency in the Constitutional Order, ed. Joseph M. Bessette and Jeffrey K. Tulis (Baton Rouge and London: Louisiana State University Press, 1981)

45. *Hubbard, Charles (2000). The Burden of Confederate Diplomacy. Knoxville: University of Tennessee Press. ISBN 1-57233-092-9*

46. Hugh T. Lefler and Albert R. Newsome, North Carolina: The History of a Southern State (3rd ed., 1973); William S. Powell, North Carolina through Four Centuries (1989); Scott, Joseph and Smith, Daniel. "A map of the Tennessee government, formerly part of North Carolina, taken chiefly from surveys by Gen. D. Smith & others." [Philadelphia]

47. Ishtiaq Ahmed (1998). State, Nation and Ethnicity in Contemporary South Asia. London & New York

48. Ivor Jennings, Some Characteristics of the Indian Constitution (1953)

49. J. A. La Nauze, The Making of the Australian Constitution (Carlton: Melbourne University Press, 1972)

50. *Jalal, Ayesha (2014), The Struggle for Pakistan: A Muslim Homeland and Global Politics, Harvard University Press,* ISBN 978-0-674-74499-8

51. *Jensen, Merrill (1940). The Articles of Confederation: An Interpretation of the Social-Constitutional History of the American Revolution, 1774–1781. ISBN 9780299002039*

52. *Jensen, Merrill (1950). The New Nation: A History of the United States During the Confederation, 1781–1789. ISBN 9780930350154*

53. Kennedy, The Constitution of Canada (1922)

54. Krikorian, Jacqueline (2017). Roads to Confederation. The Making of Canada, 1867. Toronto, Ontario: University of Toronto Press

55. Laforest, Guy (2015). The Constitution that Shaped Us. Montreal, Quebec: McGill-Queen's University Press

56. Laskin, Bora, Laskin's Canadian Constitutional Law: Cases, Text and Notes on Distribution of Legislative Power, Carswell Co., 4th Edn. (1975)

57. Lipson, Great Issues in Politics (1981)

58. Livingston, Federalism and Constitutional Change (1956)

59. M.P. Jain, Indian Constitutional Law, Vol. 1, 5th Edn., (2003)

60. Moore, Christopher (2015). Three Weeks in Quebec City. New York, New York: Allen Lane

61. Neumann, European and Comparative Government (1960)

62. Nicholas Aroney, The Constitution of a Federal Commonwealth: the making and meaning of the Australian Constitution (New York: Cambridge University Press, 2009)

63. Nicholas Henry, Governing at the Grassroots (1980)

64. Nicholas, Australian Constitution, (1952)

65. Oxford Dictionary of Law (7th edn, OUP 2013)

66. Political and Military Perspective, New Delhi: Hari-Anand Publications Limited, ISBN 9788124109236

67. Prof. W.T. Wagner, Federal States and their Judiciary, Mouton & Co. (1959)

68. Ravi Kumar Pillai Kandamath (2016) Yaqoob Khan Bangash. A Princely Affair: The Accession and Integration of the Princely States of Pakistan, 1947-1955, Asian Affairs

69. Reagan, The New Federalism (1972)

70. Rep. of the Royal Commission of Inquiry on Constitutional Problems (Quebec, 1956) Vol. II

71. Robert Schutze, Political Philosophy of Federalism, Max Planck Encyclopedia of Comparative Constitutional Law (2016)

72. S. R. Davis, The Federal Principle: A Journey through Time in Quest of a Meaning (1978)

73. Sawyer, Modern Federalism (1969)

74. Schulz, Essentials of Government (1958)

75. Seervai, H. M., Constitutional Law of India, 4th Ed. Volume 1, Universal Law Publishing

76. Stedman, State and Local Governments (1976)

77. The Constitution of the United States of America, Revised and Annotated (1964)

78. The Federalist: a Collection of Essays, Written in Favour of the New Constitution, as Agreed upon by the Federal Convention, September 17, 1787, in two volumes (1st ed.). New York: J. & A. McLean. 1788

79. The Oxford History of the British Empire: Historiography, edited by R. W. Winks. Oxford: Oxford University Press ISBN 978-0-19-820566-1

80. Trotter, Reginald George (1971). Canadian Federation. New York, New York: Russel & Russel

81. W. Anstey Wynes, Legislative and Executive Powers in Australia (1970)

82. W.G. McMinn, Nationalism and Federalism in Australia (Oxford: Oxford University Press, 1994)

83. Waite, P. B. (1972). Confederation, 1854-1867. Toronto, Ontario: Holt, Rinehart and Winston of Canada

84. Warner, Donald (1960). The Idea of the Continental Union. Lexington, Kentucky: University of Kentucky Press

85. K.C. Wheare, Federal Government, Oxford University Press, London (1964)

86. K.C. Wheare, Legislatures (1962)

87. K.C. Wheare, Modern Constitution (1966)

88. Woodrow Wilson, Constitutional Government, (1908)

89. Wynes Legislative and Executive Powers, (1956)

90. Wynes, Legislative, Executive and Judicial Powers (1970)

Articles

1. Deb Gordon, Return on Statehood: How much value every state gets from Federal Government, Money Geek, 09.02.2021

2. Pro-Telangana AP govt employees threaten agitation, The Economic Times, 10.02. 2012

3. Telangana Students Suicides Increase in Hyderabad

4. Proclamation 100 – Admitting West Virginia Into the Union, John T. Woolley and Gerhard Peters, The American Presidency Project "Archived copy". Santa Barbara, CA. 20.04.1863

5. Andhra passes Bill giving 75% job reservation for locals, The Economic Times, 25.07.2019

6. Building a case against domicile reservation in private unaided universities, The Bastion, 24.12.2020

7. Govt launches pilot project to increase forestcover in 5 states, Live Mint, 17 June 2019

8. Haryana governor approves bill to reserve 75% of private sector jobs for locals, The Times of India, 02.03.2021

9. How fair is it for Delhi and Tamil Nadu to reserve 85% college seats for residents?, Scroll.in, 01.07.2017

10. Arul B. Louis, Prabhu Chawla, PM Indira Gandhi dismisses governments in nine states, looks to put Congress in power, India Today, 06.02.2014

11. Blackton, Charles S., Australian Nationality and Nativism: The Australian Natives' Association, 1885-1901, The Journal of Modern History, Vol. 30, No. 1 (1958)

12. Boyd, Eugene, 'American Federalism, 1776 to 1997: Significant Events', 06.01.1997

13. Elliot J. Feldman and Lily Gardner Feldman. "The Impact of Federalism on the Organization of Canadian Foreign Policy". Publius (Vol. 14, No. 4, Federated States and International Relations (Autumn, 1984))

14. Furber, Holden *(1951), "The Unification of India, 1947–1951", Pacific Affairs, Pacific Affairs, University of British Columbia, 24 (4)*

15. Harsimrat Kaur Badal resigns as Union Minister protesting over farm bills, Live Mint, September 17, 2020

16. History of Federalism in United States, Brewminate – A History of Federalism in the United States

17. History of Jharkhand, Jharkhand History". traveljharkhand.com;

18. Tributes pour in for Justice Shahdeo, The Pioneer, 10.01.2018

19. Inoue, Kyoko, Integration of the North East: The State Formation Process, IDE JETRO Publication

20. Jain, M.P., Indian Federalism: A Background Paper, Constitutional Developments since Independence.

21. *Jensen, Merrill (1943). "The Idea of a National Government During the American Revolution". Political Science Quarterly. 58 (3)*

22. Kentucky: Secretary of State – Land Office – Kentucky County Formations

23. How Kentucky Became a State, Puerto Rico 51st. 08.08.2014

24. Kumar, P. (2000). The Uttarakhand Movement: Construction of a Regional Identity. New Delhi: Kanishka Publishers

25. Lijphart, Arend. "Non-Majoritarian Democracy: A Comparison of Federal and Consociational Theories." Publius, Vol. 15, No. 2, (1985)

26. J. Duane Squires, Lincoln and West Virginia Statehood, Volume 24, Number 4 (July 1963)

27. McLaughlin, Andrew C., 'The Background of American Federalism', The American Political Science Review, Vol. 12, No. 2 (May, 1918)

28. Middlebury, Vermont; 1823

29. Morton, F.L. Provincial Constitutions in Canada, Conference on "Federalism and Sub-national Constitutions: Design and Reform", Centre for the Study of State Constitutions, Rockefeller Center, Bellagio, Italy, March 2004

30. Sagar, Arun. "Federal Supremacy and the Occupied Field: A Comparative Critique." Publius, Vol. 43, No. 2 (2013)

31. Samad, Yunas *(2014)*. *"Understanding the insurgency in Balochistan"*. *Commonwealth & Comparative Politics*

32. See India's Nationally Determined Contributions (NDCs), submitted under the United Nations Framework Convention on Climate Change (UNFCCC)

33. Selective Draft Law Cases (1918) 245 US 366

34. Slade, William, Jr., Compiler. Vermont State Papers: Being a Collection of Records and Documents Connected with the Assumption and Establishment of Government by the People of Vermont, Together with the Journal of the Council of Safety, the First Constitution, the Early Journals of the General Assembly, and the Laws from the Year 1779 to 1786, Inclusive.;

35. Telangana bill passed in Lok Sabha; Congress, BJP come together in favour of new state". Hindustan Times.

36. Upendra Baxi, Taking Suffering Seriously: Social Action Litigation in the Supreme Court of India, 4(1) Third World Legal Studies 107 (1985)

37. Van Zandt, Franklin K.; Boundaries of the United States and the Several States; Geological Survey Professional Paper 909. Washington, D.C.; Government Printing Office; 1976

38. Dr. Rajeev Dhawan, Court of Last Resort, India Today, 01.07.2013

39. Sir Henry Parkes's Tenterfield Oration, 1889, ABC Online. 14.02.2007

40. SRC submits report, The Hindu. Chennai, India. 01.10.2005

41. Buckner, Phillip A, "Québec Conference". Historica Canada. (07.02.2006)

42. http://www.politicsdaily.com/2010/02/25/telangana-protests-student-suicides-increase-in-hyderabad-durin/

43. Prithak Chattisgarh, 04.07.2010

44. *Datar, Arvind P. (18 November 2013). "Who betrayed Sardar Patel?". The Hindu*

45. Maine's Path to Statehood, PR51st.com, 31.05.2017

46. State of State Finances Report, January 2018, PRS India; "How Indian States are Nearly Broke", Live Mint, 23.06.2020

47. Bensadoun, Emerald ("Coronavirus: How the Emergencies Act could help Canada's struggling economy", Global News, 17.03. 2020

48. Tikkanen, Amy, 'American Civil War', Encyclopedia Britannica

Case Laws

1. A.G. B.C. vs. A.G. Canada (1924) AC 222

2. A.G. Colonial Refining Co. (1913) 17 CLR 644

3. A.G. for Alberta v. A.G. for Canada AIR 1943 PC 76

4. A.G. for Australia vs. Colonial Sugar Refining Co. (1914) AC 237

5. A.G. for Commonwealth vs. Colonial Sugar Refining Co. (1914) AC 237 (252-54)

6. A.G. for Ontario vs. A.G. for Canada (1894) AC 189

7. A.G. for Ontario vs. A.G. for Canada (1896) AC 248

8. A.G. for Ontario vs. Canada Temperance Federation (1946) AC 193

9. A.G. for Saskatchewan vs. Canadian Pacific Ry., (1953) 2 All ER 970 (PC)

10. A.G. for Victoria v. Commonwealth (1935) 52 CLR 533

11. A.G. N.S. vs. A.G. Can. (1951) SCR 31 (Can.)

12. A.G. of Canada v. A.G. of British Columbia (1930) AC 111

13. A.G. Ontario v. Canada Temperance Fed., (1946) AC 193

14. A.G. Ontario vs. A. G. Canada (1894) AC 189 (200);

15. Abdul vs. S.T.O. AIR 1964 SC 922

16. AIR 1963 SC 1241

17. AIR 1977 SC 1361: (1977) 2 SCC 592

18. AIR 1994 SC 1918: (1994) 3 SCC 1

19. AIR1974 SC 806: (1974) 1 SCC 645

20. American Ins. Co. vs. Canter (1828) 1 Pet 528

21. Andrews v. Howell (1941) 65 CLR 255

22. Ashton v. Cameron County (1936) 298 US 513

23. Ashwander v. T.V.A. (1936) 297 US 288

24. Australia vs. Victoria (1911) 12 CLR 667

25. Australia vs. Victoria (1962) 108 CLR 130

26. Australian Communist Party v. Commonwealth (1951) 83 CLR 1

27. Australian National Airways vs. Commonwealth (1945) 71 CLR 29 (79)

28. Bailey v. Drexel Furniture Co., (1922) 249 US 20

29. Balzac vs. People of Porto Rico (1922) 258 US 298

30. Bank of N.S.W. vs. Commonwealth (1948) 76 CLR 1 (363)

31. Bar Council vs. State of U.P. AIR 1973 SC 231

32. Barai vs. Henry AIR 1983 SC 150

33. Bharat Hydro Power Corpn. Ltd. vs. State of Assam (2004) 2 SCC 553

34. Bonanza Creek Co. vs. The King (1916) 1 AC 566

35. Bowles v. Willingham (1944) 321 US 503

36. Buchanan vs. Commonwealth (1913) 16 CLR 315

37. Buckley v. Valeo (1976) 424 US 1 (90-91)

38. Burns v. Ransley (1944) 79 CLR 101

39. C.P.O. vs. Abdulla AIR 1971 SC 792

40. Carter v. Cater Coal Co. (1936) 298 US 238

41. Carter v. Egg Marketing Board (1942) 66 CLR 557

42. Case v. Bowles (1946) 327 US 92

43. Central Bank of India vs. State of Kerala (2009) 4 SCC 94

44. City of Burbank v. Lockheed (1973) 411 US 624

45. City of Cleveland v. U.S., (1944) 323 US 329

46. Co-operative Committee on Japanese Canadians vs. A. G. for Canada (1947) AC 87

47. Collector v. Day (1871) 11 Wall 113

48. Colorado Symes (1932) 286 US 510

49. Commonwealth v. Australian Shipping Bd. (1926) 39 CLR 1

50. Commonwealth v. Bogle (1953) 89 CLR 229

51. Commonwealth v. Colonial Combing Co. (1922) 31 CLR 421

52. Commonwealth vs. N.S.W. (1923) 32 CLR 200

53. Coyle vs. Smith (1911) 221 US 559

54. Crown Grain Co. vs. Day (1908) SC 504

55. D.C.G.M. vs. Union of India AIR 1983 SC 937

56. Dakota Central Tel. Co. v. South Dakota (1919) 250 U.S. 135

57. Dawson v. Commonwealth (1946) 73 CLR 174

58. Debs, In Re 158 U.S. 564

59. Deep Chand vs. State of U.P. AIR 1959 SC 648

60. Downes vs. Bidwell (1901) 182 US 194

61. E.E.O.C. v. Wyoming (1983) 460 US 226

62. Elect. Development Co. vs. A.G. Ontario (1919) AC 687

63. F.E.R.C. v. Mississippi (1982) 456 US 742

64. Farey v. Burvett (1916) 21 CLR 433

65. Fed. Saw Mill vs. James Moore, (1908) 8 CLR 465 (530)

66. Ferinandez v. Weimer (1945) 326 US 340

67. First Fed. Savings Assocn. V. Loomis (1939) 305 US 666

68. Fort Frances Pulp Co. v. Manitoba Free Press (1923) SC 695

69. Fullilove v. Klutznick, (1980) 448 US 448

70. G. for Canada v. A. G. for Ontario AIR 1937 PC 89

71. G. for Ontario v. Canada Temperance Federation (1946) AC 193

72. G. of Canada v. A. G. of British Columbia (1930) AC 111

73. G.T.R. vs. A.G. Canada (1907) AC 65

74. G.W. Saddlery Co. v. The King (1921) AC 91 (116)

75. Gajapati vs. State of Orissa AIR 1953 SC 375

76. Ganga Corp. vs. State of A.P. (1980) 1 SCC 223

77. Gibbons v. Ogden (1824) 9 Wh (195)

78. Golak Nath vs. State of Punjab (1967) 2 SCR 762 (834)

79. Grant vs. St. Lawrence Authority (1960) 23 DLR (2d)

80. Gratwick v. Johnson (1945) 70 CLR 1

81. Gulf R. Co. v. Hoffiey (1895) 158 US 89

82. H. H. Maharajadhiraja Madhav Rao vs. Union of India 1971 AIR 530: 1971 SCR (3) 9

83. Hamilton v. Kentucky Districts (1919) 251 US 146

84. Hari vs. Union of India AIR 1966 SC 619

85. Hawke vs. Smith (1920) 253 US 221; C.C.L.

86. Heart of Atlanta v. U.S. (1964) 379 US 241

87. Helvering v. Davis (1936) 301 US 619

88. Hirobayashi v. U.S. (1942) 320 U.S. 81

89. Hodel v. Virginia Assocn. (1981) 452 US 264

90. Hoechst vs. State of Bihar AIR 1983 SC 1020

91. Holmes v. Jennison (1840) 14 Pet 540

92. Horwitz vs. Connor (1908) 6 CLR 38

93. I.T.C. v. State of Karnataka (1985) Supp SCC 476

94. In re Aeronautics (1932) AC 54

95. In re Bd. of Commerce Act, 1919, (1922) 1 AC 191

96. J. R. G. Association vs. Union of India AIR 1970 SC 1589

97. Jalan Trading Co. vs. Mill Mazdoor Sabha AIR 1967 SC 691

98. James v. Commonwealth (1936) AC 578

99. Johannesson vs. West St. Paul (1952) 1 SCR 292

100. Jones vs. U.S., (1890) 137 US 202

101. Joshi vs. Ajit Mills AIR 1974 SC 2278

102. K.S.E. Bd. V. Indian Aluminum AIR 1976 SC 1031

103. K.S.E. vs. Indian Aluminium Co. AIR 1976 SC 1031

104. Kesavananda Bharti vs. State of Kerala (1973) 4 SCC 225; AIR 1973 SC 1461

105. Khaitan Sugar Mills vs. State of U.P. AIR 1980 SC 1955

106. King v. Smith (1968) 392 US 309 (324)

107. L.T.C. vs. State of Karnataka (1985) Supp SCC 476

108. Lace vs. Nichols (1974) 414 US 563 (568)

109. Lamshed v. Lake (1957) 99 CLR 132

110. Lane County v. Oregon (1869) 7 Wall 71

111. Linder v. U.S. (1926) 268 US 15

112. Liquidators of Maritime Bank vs. Receiver General of New Brunswick (1892) AC 437 (441-443)

113. Ludecke v. Watkins (1948) 335 US 160

114. Luther v. Borden 7 How. 1

115. Maganbhai v. Union of India AIR 1969 SC 785

116. Masthan Sahib vs. Chief Commissioner AIR 1963 SC 533

117. McCulloch v. Maryland (1819) 4 Wh 316

118. Melbourne Corporation v. Commonwealth (1974) 74 CLR 31

119. Minerva Mills v. Union of India AIR 1980 SC 1840

120. Mittal v. Union of India AIR 1983 SC 1

121. Monogram Mills vs. State of Gujarat AIR 1976 SC 2177

122. Moore & Tierney v. Rexford Knitting Co. (1918) 250 Fed. 276

123. N. Pacific Ry. Co. v. North Dakota (1919) 250 U.S. 135

124. Naga People's Movement of Human Rights vs. Union of India AIR 1998 SC 431: (1998) 2 SCC 109

125. National League of Cities v. Usery (1976) 426 US 833

126. National League of Cities v. Usery (1976) 426 US 833

127. New York vs. United States (1946) 326 US 572

128. O'Sullivan v. Noarlunga Meat Ltd. (1956) 3 All ER 177 (183) PC

129. Oklahoma v. U.S. (1947) 330 US 127

130. P.E.I. Potato Marketing Rd. vs. Willis (1952) 2 SCR 392 (Can.)

131. Pape vs. Commissioner of Taxation (2009) 238 CLR 1

132. Parker v. Brown (1943) 317 US 341

133. Paterson vs. O'Brien (1978) 138 CLR 276 (280-281)

134. Pennhurst State School v. Halderman (1980) 451 US 1 (16)

135. Peterswald v. Bartley (1904) 1 CLR 497

136. Pollard vs. Hagan (1845) 3 How 212 (223)

137. Prem vs. Chhabra (1984) 2 SCC 302

138. Premnath vs. State of J&K AIR 1959 SC 749

139. Prigg v. Pennsylvania (1824) 16 Pet 536 (618)

140. Proprietary Articles Association vs. A. G. Canada (1931) AC 310 (327) (PC)

141. R v. Foster (1949) 79 CLR 43

142. R vs. Burgess, (1936) 55 CLR 608 (641, 686)

143. R. v. Credit Tribunal (1977) 137 CLR 545

144. R. v. Sharkey (1949) 79 CLR 121

145. R. v. University of Sydney (1943) 67 CLR 95

146. R.M.D.C. vs. State of Mysore AIR 1962 SC 594

147. Rahrer, In re, (1891) 140 US 545

148. Re, Berubari Union, AIR 1960 SC 845

149. Re. Disallowance and Reservation Powers (1938) SCR 71 (Can)

150. Ref. re Regulation of Chemicals (1943) SCR 1

151. Ref. re Wartime Leasehold Regulations (1950) SCR 124

152. Ref. under Art. 143, AIR 1965 SC 745

153. Reference Re Secession of Quebec, [1998] 2 SCR 217 at para 150

154. Russel v. Queen (1882) 7 AC 829

155. S. Australia v. The Commonwealth (1942) 65 CLR 373

156. S. Australia vs. Commonwealth (1942) 65 CLR 373

157. S. Carolina Highway Dept. v. Barnwell (1938) 303 US 177

158. S.R. Bommai vs Union of India (1994) 3 SCC 1

159. Schechter Poultry Corp. v. United States 295 US 495

160. Sodhi Transport vs. State of U.P. AIR 1986 SC 1099

161. Sonapur Tea co. v. Dy. Commr. AIR 1962 SC 137

162. Southern Pharmaceuticals vs. State of Kerala AIR 1981 SC 1865

163. Spratt v. Hermes (1965) 114 CLR 226

164. State of Bihar vs. Kameshwar AIR 1952 SC 252

165. State of Karnataka v. Union of India AIR 1978 SC 68

166. State of Karnataka vs. Union of India AIR 1978 SC 68

167. State of Rajasthan vs. Union of India AIR 1977 SC 1382: (1997) 3 SCC 592

168. Stenhouse v. Coleman (1944) 69 CLR 457

169. Steward Machine Co. v. Davis (1936) 301 US 548

170. Subramaniyam v. Muthuswami AIR 1941 FC 47

171. Sudhir v. W.T.O. AIR 1969 SC 59

172. Tara Prasad vs. Union of India AIR 1980 SC 1682

173. Tennant vs. Union Bank (1894) AC 31 (45)

174. Testa v. Katt (1947) 330 US 386

175. Texas v. White (1868) 7 Wall 700 (720)

176. The Lake Monroe, (1919) 250 US 240

177. Toronto Electric Commr. V. Snider (1925) AC 87

178. U.P.E.S. AIR 1970 SC 237

179. U.S. v. Butler (1936) 297 US 1

180. U.S. v. Curtiss-Wright Corp (1936) 299 US 304

181. U.S. v. David (1968) 20 L Ed (2d) 672

182. U.S. vs. S.E. Underwriters' Assocn. (1944) 322 US 533

183. Ukha vs. State of Maharashtra AIR 1963 SC 1531

184. Union Colliery v. Bryden (1899) AC 580

185. Union of India v. Basavaiah AIR 1972 SC 1415

186. Union of India vs. Atic Industries AIR 1954 SC 1495

187. Victoria v. Commonwealth (1942) 66 CLR 488

188. Victoria vs. Commonwealth (1975) 134 CLR 338

189. Victorian Chamber v. Commonwealth (Industrial Lighting Regulations) (1943) 67 CLR 413

190. Virginia v. Tennessee (1893) 148 US 503

191. W. Australia vs. Commonwealth (1975) 134 CLR 201 (257)

192. Western Coalfields v. S.A.D.A. AIR 1982 SC 697

193. Williams v. Bruffy (1878) 96 US 176 (183)

194. Williams vs. A.G., (1913) 16 CLR 404

195. Woods v. Miller (1948) 333 US 138

196. Yakus v. U.S. (1944) 321 US 414;

197. Zaverbhai v. State of Bombay AIR 1954 SC 752

198. 'What is the Role of Parliament', Parliamentary Archives, United Kingdom

199. 2nd Report, Union Powers Committee, 05.07.1947, 1st Ser.

200. Constituent Assembly Debates, India

201. Creating the United States, Formation of Political Parties, Digital Library of Congress, United States of America

202. Defining Moments – Federation, National Museum Australia

203. Rep. of the Joint Committee of Parliament on the Petition of Western Australia, (1935)

204. Royal Commission on the Constitution of the Commonwealth (Australia). & Peden, John Beverley. & Australia. Inter-Imperial Relations Committee. 1929, *Report of the Royal Commission on the Constitution*

205. Sarkaria Commission Report (1987)

206. White Paper on Indian States (1950)/Part IV/Instrument of Accession, Ministry of States, Government of India

Statutes

1. Act of Union, 1840

2. Alberta Act, SC 1905, c 3

3. British North America (No. 2) Act, 1949

4. British North America Act, 1940

5. Commonwealth of Australia Constitution Act 1900

6. Constituent Assembly Debates

7. Constitution Act of Canada, 1867

8. Constitution of America

9. Constitution of Australia

10. Constitution of India, 1950

11. Constitution of Malaysia, 1957

12. Emergencies Act, 1985

13. Financial Emergency Act of 1931

14. Government of India Act, 1935

15. Indian Independence Act, 1947

16. International Emergency Economic Powers Act, 1977

17. Manitoba Act, 1870, SC 1870, c 3

18. Saskatchewan Act, SC 1905, c 42

19. Sherman Anti-Trust Act in 1890

20. State of Nagaland Act, 1962

21. The North Eastern Areas (Reorganisation) Act, 1971

22. The State of Himachal Pradesh Act, 1970

23. The Supreme Court Act, 1875